RAY BARRA

A Life in Ballet

RAY BARRA

A Life in Ballet

VICTOR HUGHES

The Book Guild Ltd

First published in Great Britain in 2020 by
The Book Guild Ltd
9 Priory Business Park
Wistow Road, Kibworth
Leicestershire, LE8 0RX
Freephone: 0800 999 2982
www.bookguild.co.uk
Email: info@bookguild.co.uk
Twitter: @bookguild

Typeset in 12pt Minion Pro

Printed and bound in the UK by TJ International, Padstow, Cornwall

ISBN 978 1913208 073

British Library Cataloguing in Publication Data.
A catalogue record for this book is available from the British Library.

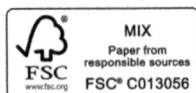

In memory of Maximo

Contents

Acknowledgements

I would never have tackled writing this book – at my age, and indeed having previously only attempted articles on ballet-related themes – without the prompting of Giselle Roberge. Giselle, now a friend, used to be a colleague: we were both dancers and ballet masters with the Hamburg Ballet. When Giselle stopped dancing she served briefly as ballet mistress in the German provinces but had the good fortune of being offered a job by Ray Barra in Spain. At the time Ray was director of the Ballet Nacional de España/Clásico and needed a ballet mistress. From this period, which brought her closer to Ray, arose the feeling that his achievements in the sphere of ballet had not been worthily appraised or documented. She turned to me as someone who had worked with him and was furthermore a friend. Surely I should write his biography before it was too late. Until I started to investigate all the facets of Ray's life, I was hardly aware of the diversity, the richness and length of a career, which spanned the second half of the twentieth century and extended right into the first decade of the new one. Ray seems to have met and/or worked with most of the important figures in ballet history of that period. His association with three choreographers, John Cranko, Kenneth MacMillan and John Neumeier, is particularly in need of a eulogistic airing.

For grammatical and textual surveillance, I am indebted to my dear friend Jacqueline Morley who has examined my manuscript with her sharp and perspicacious intellect. I am deeply grateful for the editorial care she has exercised over the biography and for the hospitality I have enjoyed in her Brighton home. Then for help in tracking down archival material relating to Ray's many activities in various theatres of the globe, I am indebted to Wolfgang Oberender, one-time dramaturge of the Bavarian State Ballet. Wolfgang has been more than a wonderful sleuth in this respect; he has been an enthusiastic and helpful reader of much of the text as it progressed from my laptop. It was indeed a godsend to have someone cognisant of ballet history in general, and of the German scene in particular. In Berlin, Barbara Hering, long time dramaturge of the Deutsche Oper, has been of great help in sorting out Ray's activities during his tenure as ballet director there. My thanks, too, to Judith Reyn, one-time ballerina with the Stuttgart Ballet and someone who knew and still knows many of the main protagonists of this history. She has been especially helpful and greatly partisan in my endeavours to have this biography published.

On the home front I wish to thank my friend and partner, Holger Badekow, for his wholehearted support and enthusiasm for the project. He has been my greatest fan. I am especially grateful for the dramaturgical care he has taken with the photomontage. For her expertise in making the best of old snapshots and damaged pictorial material, I would like to thank Annelies Kroke. A special thank you to John Neumeier for taking the trouble to read this biography with meticulous care and for correcting inevitable inaccuracies and making suggestions. Last, but not least, I would like to thank the Ballettfreunde Hamburg e.V. (Friends of the Hamburg Ballet) for their generous financial support.

Introduction: how I came to write Ray's biography

In the world of ballet it is not unusual for those who have been associated in any way with it to wish to keep *au courant* of the profession's *Who's Who*. Even those who have left the stage to work in a totally different milieu retain an irrepressible curiosity about ex-colleagues. Certainly, in Ray Barra's case, a vast number of dancers know about him, and many cherish the memory of having worked with him. The meeting point had been mainly in the ballet studio where he functioned as ballet master or choreographer. But, in one's mind's eye, the image of him as a ballet master is imprinted on one's memory more strongly than his earlier fame as a principal dancer or his later activities as a ballet director/choreographer. Perhaps few young dancers today know anything of him, still less the achievements of his long career. Since the early 1950s Ray has had direct contact with the crème de la crème of ballet, initially in America where he was born, then in Germany, Denmark, Austria, Greece and Spain. There is hardly a name in the world of dance whom he has not known or worked with, and this stayed the case right into the first decade of the twenty-first century. Inevitably, advancing age has slowed down his pace.

When he relocated himself from America to Stuttgart in Germany in 1958, he made his name as a principal dancer; firstly with Nicholas Beriozoff and then, importantly, with John Cranko, the South African choreographer who succeeded Beriozoff. Luck seems to have been a prominent aspect of his horoscope: he was often in the right place at the right time and this brought him into working relationships with several important choreographers. With Cranko his dancing career peaked. As he so disarmingly declares, 'Cranko made me. Without him I would never have got as far as I did.' Historically, Cranko has been canonised as *the* choreographer that put ballet in Germany on the international map. Adequate tribute has been paid in this direction, yet Ray's participation in the realisation of Cranko's achievement has been somewhat overlooked.

Ray's dancing career was cut short unexpectedly: on his thirty-sixth birthday, while rehearsing, he tore his left Achilles tendon. In retrospect, this crisis also had a positive effect – at this point he was, all things considered, a mature dancer. The injury forced him to consider what to do when his dancing days were over. His career in ballet, though, was not put on ice: he remade himself as an excellent coach and ballet master and his career blossomed. He left Stuttgart to become Kenneth MacMillan's first ballet master in Berlin and when John Neumeier started out as director in Frankfurt, joined him there and followed him to Hamburg. Moving into freelance, he retained his connection to Neumeier and for several years assisted him on commissioned ballets such as *Joseph's Legend*, *Lady of the Camellias* and *A Streetcar Named Desire*.

To those who knew Ray in his dancing prime and as a ballet master, even today he seems relatively unchanged. He has filled out a little but still projects the same lithe, active presence: the familiar physique, trim in jeans and polo shirt, the glasses and his tight curly hair, now grey. He has also retained the engaging open look showing sympathetic interest, ready to break out into a smile. Considering his past activities as ballet master in many corners of the world, more dancers know him than he is able to remember. Incredible as it may seem, I first met Ray Barra over fifty years ago – as dancers often say: the world of ballet is so small! I remember the meeting quite vividly though I don't think he remembers it at all. At the time he had other more serious things to think about. He was on crutches, having recently undergone surgery on his torn Achilles tendon. The operation was casting a shadow on his dancing career. This was in February 1966. How this first meeting came about needs a little explaining and I think, to do so, I should introduce myself and relate the extraordinary coincidences involved in the crossing of our paths.

I was born in South Africa and have been active in ballet since 1961. After high school I had fiddled about with various half-hearted attempts at some sort of profession, had started to study for a BA at the University of Cape Town and then happened upon ballet. Ballet was, at that time, not something young men in sport-orientated South Africa would openly show an interest in, but having attended several performances of the University of Cape Town Ballet Company, a semi-professional group attached to the University's College of Music, my interest was piqued. I decided to investigate ballet at first hand by taking private lessons. Hardly beyond a month's tuition, my teacher, who considered I had some potential, gave me a tip. I should make myself known to the UCT ballet company as this would be a way of having free lessons and, joy of joys, having the chance of participating in their productions.

After my first ballet class with the UCT Ballet, I was approached by David Poole, a South African dancer recently returned to his home country after making a name for himself as a soloist with the Sadler's Wells Theatre Ballet in London. Back home he was appearing as a principal dancer and functioning as ballet master and choreographer. He was also a friend and ex-colleague of John Cranko who, still in the UK, was on the verge of an international career as a choreographer. After Robert Helpmann, Frederick Ashton and Alfred Rodrigues, Cranko was considered the next most important young choreographer in the making. David Poole had participated in most of Cranko's early ballets at Sadler's Wells and, indeed, he had been the main protagonist in Cranko's first choreography, *A Soldier's Tale* back in 1944 for the Cape Town Ballet Club. Charmed and encouraged by David Poole to make a serious attempt at dance as a profession, I decided to give it a go. I will confess that at the time I could hardly do a *tendu* properly. As Ray's tale unfolds in the following chapters, the South African connection with John Cranko as a benevolently nurturing catalyst will become apparent. Both Ray and John Neumeier – my future boss – had worked for Cranko; unfortunately I had not, but as a South African and having had David Poole as my first important teacher, I had some sort of connection to him.

Nowadays, one would definitely be discouraged from attempting a career in ballet at the age of twenty or twenty-one – my age at the time. However, I thought that if it didn't work out, then I would move on to something else. Apart from my efforts to acquire a reasonable ballet technique, there was something else on my mind. I had never undertaken what every culturally interested white South African considered a rite of passage: a visit to the United Kingdom and experiencing, at first hand, the artistic plethora of Europe. I did not have the time or the funds, but by the end of 1965 I had saved enough money to afford a passage on an Italian passenger liner, the MS Europa, from Cape Town to Venice via Africa's east coast.

Most South Africans at the time travelled from Cape Town to Southampton on ships of the Union Castle Line, a journey that took ten days. The Italian ship took longer: twenty-one days, but was doubly attractive because the return journey was cheaper and, en route, one stopped off at exotic places such as Beira, Dar-es-Salaam, Aden, the Suez Canal and bingo, disembarked in Venice. Before I left I made sure I had as many connections, balletic or otherwise, to keep me in Europe for as long as possible or even to help me get a job. John Cranko had by this time moved from the UK to Stuttgart and one heard and read positive reports about what he was accomplishing in Germany. For this reason I asked Gary Burne, a Rhodesian dancer and ex-Stuttgart soloist, about the possibility of auditioning there. Burne had, at one time, been engaged by the Royal Ballet and was doing rather well, but decided to try his luck with Cranko in Stuttgart – probably with the hope of developing into a fully fledged principal. Somehow or other Stuttgart didn't help him realise his ambitions and he upped and left after the long summer break in 1962, without giving notice. Returning to Southern Africa, he was briefly engaged in Johannesburg and then moved to join the Cape Town company where I was employed. Here as star ballerino and partner of Phyllis Spira – also ex Royal Ballet – he enjoyed local fame. Burne told me I should contact Ray Barra when I got to Stuttgart and gave me his telephone number. Now I must confess that I had never heard of Ray Barra, but as he was a principal dancer and said to be Cranko's male muse, I was happy to have his name and number.

When the MS Europa arrived in Venice early one grey winter morning and the towers and domes of the tightly clustered churches slowly emerged through the dissolving mist, I was bowled over. With elated spirit I set about discovering Venice's myriad and labyrinthine alleyways. Ballet and what the future held were of no concern. I saw as much of Italy as I had time and money for. This meant that I explored only Venice and Florence before moving on by train to Vienna. After Vienna I made a short stopover in Munich before arriving in Stuttgart. There I stayed in a Youth Hostel, a rather hardy experience as the establishment brusquely turfed out its guests early in the morning. I called Ray, told him who I was and passed on Gary Burne's good wishes. Ray explained that, because of his injury, he did not have much to do with the Stuttgart Ballet at that moment and that Cranko was not in town. This meant that I couldn't audition. And in any case, I wasn't in a fit state to audition, not having done ballet class for about two months. Ray suggested that I watch a rehearsal and we arranged to meet at the stage door the following morning at 10:30.

Stuttgart seemed a strange place and certainly, after Italy and Vienna, something of a comedown. The theatre, though beautifully located in the park, I thought rather small. When I met Ray I was surprised at encountering someone who, to my eyes, looked rather un-balletic: the possessor of a trim, wiry physique with tight wavy hair and spectacles. He was very friendly though, as he hobbled about on his crutches. He then took me to the smaller of the studios in the theatre, introduced me briefly to the ballet master and left me there. To my disappointment the ballet they were rehearsing wasn't by Cranko; it was Balanchine's *Allegro Brillante*. I remember that Richard Cragun was attempting the male lead for the first time but I have forgotten whom he partnered. I had never seen a Balanchine ballet before so the whole experience in this strange German opera house was quite overwhelming. After the rehearsal I thanked the ballet master and left.

Sobering up after my Stuttgart rehearsal experience, I reconsidered my touristic activities and immediate goals. As my purse was rapidly emptying, I realised that my next port of call would have to be London where I had a friend with whom I could stay. So I took the train and ferry and arrived within a day or two at his flat. London was even more overwhelming than anything I had seen so far and instead of feeling at ease in an English-speaking country and the country of my forefathers, I felt horribly foreign. I embarked on a spate of sightseeing, though my immediate task was to get myself back into shape and see what I could do about a job – otherwise a return journey to South Africa was inevitable.

At that time many dancers gravitated to a dance centre near the Covent Garden Opera House called The Place where open dance classes of all sorts were on offer daily. I chose to take Eileen Ward's classes and after two weeks of her tuition began to feel much fitter. As it happened, I had another South African connection in London, a dancer who was engaged by London Festival Ballet. I had known Terence Etheridge from my UCT days when we had been colleagues. He had settled in the UK and I admired him for having managed to make such a good go of things. He suggested I take class with his company. In the studio I found myself completely in awe of the standard of the excellent Festival Ballet dancers. Nevertheless I did my best, staying in the background and hoping that no one would notice my inadequacies. But it seemed that they were interested as I was asked to audition on the stage before the performance later that day. Actually the ballet masters wanted to see a solo variation, but as I had none prepared they were content to see me do an *enchaînement* or two… I couldn't believe my luck: I was offered a contract.

Yes, I was overjoyed at being employed by a large, professional ballet company, and by having managed, as a foreigner, to get a work permit – no easy feat! But with time, dancing with Festival Ballet soured. I was not ready for the daily drudge of existing on a small salary and touring the English provinces. Festival Ballet was a touring company and, apart from an annual season or two at the Festival Hall London, constantly on the road. We would travel to cities like Birmingham, Bradford or Leeds on a Sunday, do eight performances of a ballet like *Swan Lake* in one week and then move on to the next port of call. There were some tours to the continent, to Spain, Portugal and Italy for example, and that did brighten up one's existence; they were exciting. But, on the whole, it was hard-going. Eventually I decided that I needed a change; I wasn't getting anywhere and I wanted to feel more settled. So I decided to try my luck with the ballet company of the Zürich Opera House, at that time directed by Nicholas Beriozoff.

I arrived in Zürich in August 1968, the year of the Paris student demonstrations and the so-called Prague Spring. In Zürich even the Swiss were on the streets demonstrating against Soviet Russia's crass squashing of the Czechs' bid for reform within the communist system. Switzerland was definitely cosier that the UK and I soon adapted to a more relaxed lifestyle. I made friends with one of the dancers in Zürich's ensemble, Persephone Samaropoulou. She was a very outgoing, wildly anglophile Greek from Alexandria, Egypt. Persephone had also been engaged in Stuttgart under Cranko but, dismayed by an incompetent ballet master there, left for Zürich.

At some point in my second season while we were doing class, she pointed out a dark and extremely attractive young man who sat watching. This was John Neumeier and he had come, I presume, to reassess her as a candidate for the company he was gathering when he took over as ballet director in Frankfurt in 1970. Like Persephone, he had been a dancer in Stuttgart where he had also choreographed and was now at the start of what would turn out to be a most successful career. I had not heard of him nor was I aware that Frankfurt had a ballet company. Through Persephone, he intimated that, if I were interested, he might have a place for me in his company. However, at that time he had a full complement of dancers; the company was not a very large one. I did not give Frankfurt much further thought; anyway I was beginning to enjoy myself in Switzerland.

Toward the end of December 1969, Persephone, all excited, came to tell me that one of the dancers Neumeier had hired wasn't available and if I wished I could have the vacant contract. Well, it was a surprise and something I hadn't anticipated. At first I didn't see the need for a change, I was happy where I was and Germany seemed a bit formidable. Who was this John Neumeier anyway? Then, I allowed myself to be persuaded. Persephone talked me into making a change. She was adamant that I would be missing a remarkable opportunity of being part of a start-up, which, according to her, had every promise of being a creative success. She reasoned that Zürich would be something of a dead end, and she was right. Beriozoff stayed on for one more season and the ballet didn't flourish much until later under other ballet directors. I hastily wrote the letter of resignation that had to be sent before the end of the year and thought: *Well, now let's see what happens.*

Persephone had other good news: 'You know who will be ballet master in Frankfurt? Ray Barra.' Thus it was that in Frankfurt our paths re-crossed and during the three seasons of my engagement there I got to know Ray better. In 1973 on Neumeier's promotion to the directorship of the Hamburg State Opera Ballet – a far more prestigious company – we all moved north: Ray and his friend Maximo, as well as about ten dancers who formed the nucleus of Neumeier's inner and trusted group. In Hamburg after two seasons, I joined the staff as an assistant ballet master and, in this way, became Ray's colleague. I always felt that Ray liked me; he showed it, and I was fortunate to have him as a role model. Ray, though, did not stay longer than 1976 as Neumeier's first ballet master in Hamburg. He moved into freelancing, and later, for a certain time, was director of the Ballet Nacional de España/Clásico and the Berlin Ballet.

We have kept in touch off and on through all these years though it has only been recently, since my retirement, that I have had time to visit him in Marbella. On my first visit there, by chance, I showed him an essay I had written about Antony Tudor as I thought it might interest him. He had worked with Tudor when he was a dancer with American Ballet Theatre and I wanted to hear his reaction. He found the article very interesting and then remarked, 'Maybe you should write my biography.' What did set the ball rolling and ultimately pushed me to write this biography, was the insistent plea from an ex-colleague of mine, Giselle Roberge, that it should be written and soon. Giselle first met Ray when she was a member of American Ballet Theatre and Ray came to set Neumeier's ballet *Baiser de la Fee* on that company. Ray was all too happy to have her as one of the ice maidens in the corps de ballet as she was the only one who could count Stravinsky's music. A few years later she joined the Hamburg Company and after she left, Ray was the one to invite her to join him in Madrid as ballet mistress. Giselle still enthuses vociferously about Ray as a fantastic ballet master and ballet director: 'From whom could one better learn the art of coaching and dealing with dancers in and out of the ballet studio? He was absolutely fair, and while there was always an agreeable atmosphere in his rehearsals he was nevertheless demanding.'

Ray was very pleased about my taking on this task. Just before I agreed to attempt it, he may have been feeling neglected because of several biographies[1] of his ex-Stuttgart colleagues that had recently been published. To clinch the matter, he felt that the various mysterious coincidental encounters that had brought us together would augur well for his story. And above all, he felt he could trust me. I have done my best to be true to the spirit of his recollections and, indeed, he

---

1   Peter Wright's autobiography was published in 2015; the biographies of Egon Madsen and Birgit Keil were published in 2012 and 2014 respectively.

does seem to have wonderful recall. Once or twice I have challenged him on what he thought had happened, but on the whole I have relied on his memory and how he saw things while tidying up on the chronology. It should be remembered that memory is emotionally coloured and protective of the inner self – we all have our own version of the past. I hope I have treated Ray's recounting of his life's story and the frankness of his revelations with the respect they deserve. In hearing his story I have come to admire the all-pervasive enthusiasm he still brings to his profession.

Victor Hughes

1

Californian youth

Anyone meeting Ray Barra for the first time would be in no doubt about his origins: he is an American, and however fluent he is in German and Spanish, one can still detect his mother tongue. But this is beside the point; one immediately is charmed by his engaging and friendly manner, several degrees more open than that of a European. He has, in fact, lived in Europe since 1958, either in Germany or Spain. Proud of being of Spanish descent – both parents came from the Iberian peninsula – it is curious that his command of that language is not perfectly idiomatic. He explained the reason for this: at junior school his English was particularly atrocious and the teachers advised his parents to converse with him only in English. Even if they did so, one might question this tactic; surely their English was equally rudimentary. So Spanish took a back seat until, in fact, he settled in Spain.

Ray's father, Ramon Barallobre, was a merchant seaman from Galicia. By jumping ship in Cuba he was able to enter the United States via Florida and made his way to California. In San Francisco in 1927, he met and married Antonia Ramirez and the couple settled there. Ray was born Raymond Martin Barallobre Ramirez on 3rd January 1930, the second of three siblings. His elder brother, Manuel, and his

1

sister, Josephine, are now deceased. It was only when he joined Ballet Theatre that the short and more convenient form of his name, Ray Barra, was adopted. The ballet company administration argued that his real name was too unwieldy for the posters and programmes and, in the long run, the change certainly proved better for a stage career.

Because of his father's profession, which necessitated him being away from home for long periods, Ray had a much closer relationship with his mother. He says that he hardly knows anything about his father's side of the family. But even with his father absent for long periods, Ray found him a loving parent. He was overjoyed when his father returned from a long trip and was greeted by him rubbing his bearded face against his own baby fluff. His mother, Antonia Ramirez, had accompanied her parents as a four-year-old when they emigrated from Seville to Hawaii. The journey to the Pacific Islands must have been long and uncomfortable for they were accommodated in the ship's hold. Antonia was the second oldest of a family that would steadily grow. Eventually it would total twelve brothers and sisters, though not all survived beyond childhood. Her father, a blacksmith, did not practise his profession in Hawaii but was obliged, as were all able-bodied members of the family, to work on the fruit plantations. After several years in Hawaii the Ramirez family moved to the mainland, to Seattle in the State of Washington. Seattle, a notoriously rainy city, must have come as a shock to them, so they readily accepted a chance to move to California, settling in what is now known as Silicon Valley.

Ray was born in San Francisco and it was in North Beach that he went to his first grammar school. The population of North Beach at that time was made up of immigrants, mostly from Mexico or Italy. There was a widespread attitude of disparagement towards Spanish-speaking citizens, as the presumption was that they were from the lower classes or had entered the country illegally, as indeed Ray's father had done. Ray experienced this at first hand in junior high school. There was some sort of cultural institution in the neighbourhood that taught folk dance to young children and Ray showed an interest in participating. But they refused to accept him as a student. Ray supposes he was not American enough: he was only first generation – a strange reason for the children of immigrants not to learn the dances of immigrants.

One could assume that Ray's mother Antonia would have assimilated the English language quickly, but encapsulated in a sort of Spanish-speaking ghetto, this was not the case. She did not get beyond the sixth grade and her English remained rudimentary. Ray remembers his mother as beautiful and petite and conjectures that the marriage probably presented Antonia with a means of escape from her own family, where she was obliged to mother so many younger siblings. When Ray was young, ballet dancing would have been a somewhat exotic and curious activity, perhaps beyond the interests of the Barallobre family. However, there was an interest in ballroom dancing. Two cousins, Babe and Emilio, twin offspring of his aunt Pearl, were much applauded as a dance couple and were often called upon to perform a show dance à la Fred and Ginger. They competed in ballroom dance competitions and won several prizes.

According to Ray his childhood and adolescence were happy, and judging from an open and endearing disposition he is probably not hiding any Freudian hang-ups. When the family moved to Eureka, a small fishing port that specialised in shark fishing for the fish's oil, he attended the Eureka High School. Here he says he became 'American', moving away from being identified as the son of immigrants even if his looks underlined Latino origins. At school he participated in what most of the youth of that time did: played basketball, took part in track running, sang in the chorus and, significantly, he also took drama lessons. Ray: 'The drama teacher was wonderful in making you understand the technique of projection. For instance he would say, "How can you make me think that you think some object you are looking at is beautiful or ugly? What would you do?"'

Apparently Ray was great at jitterbug dancing, the exuberant dance craze that swept the States during the 1940s. Infected by the music's wild rhythms with its invitation to uninhibited cavorting, he and his partner must have moved like wondrous agitated bugs. The dance floor cleared for all to watch them perform, calling forth enthusiastic applause. He remembers that one of their best 'show dances' – not a jitterbug – was to the slow music of the song *Sentimental Journey* sung by Doris Day. With a chuckle Ray revealed that he had also been a cheerleader. Nowadays, one tends to think of cheerleading as a girls' activity but apparently boys can be involved. His team, chosen by a student committee as having a particular talent for this duty, was made up of himself, a fellow student Keith, and two girls. Keith, who excelled in acrobatics, was the main inventor of their rooting movements. Here one gets an inkling of where Ray's interests lay: choreographed movement.

What did interest him though, and this was the case of many dance-crazed enthusiasts of the time, was the musical film. This was the heyday of Hollywood musicals, with most film studios churning out a plethora of exuberant escapist fare. Of the male dance stars, though Fred Astaire is usually given the palm for suave nonchalance, Ray says he preferred the more masculine Gene Kelly or even the hyper Donald O'Conner. Being a musical fan led to him taking tap-dancing lessons with Betty Merriweather, an ex-Rockette who had settled in Eureka, and of whom he treasures special memories. The Rockettes, an immensely popular American dance ensemble similar to the English Bluebell Girls or the revue dancers of Berlin's *Friedrichstadtpalast*, gave and still give performances on the Radio City Musical Hall stage. They are famous for the perfect synchronisation of their high kicks. At this time Ray was still in high school. To pay for his tap tuition he needed extra money; so just like many other youths, he worked in a drugstore.

Tap offered Ray, a naturally talented musical mover, an ideal dance idiom with its free and easy style. Soon it absorbed his free time and energy, and ambitious as he was, he wished to perfect it. But his tap technique had a weakness: he couldn't turn well. Betty Merriweather, ever encouraging Ray to become a dancer – she had warned him that should he stay on in Eureka, he would get married, have kids and that would be the end of that – told him that if he took ballet lessons he could improve turning by learning how to 'spot'. Spotting is essential in ballet for pirouetting: it prevents one from getting giddy. As the body turns, the dancer keeps his gaze fixed front, until that point can no longer be maintained. Then the head whips around before the body has completed its revolution and fixes on the focal point again. Bettie Merriweather also introduced him to the rudiments of ballet, teaching him several basic exercises: *plié*, *tendu*, *jeté* and little jumps. Through tap he got to know a fellow student, Darlene Becker, well. She was an attractive member of his school class and took a shine to Ray. Musically talented, she played the clarinet in the school's orchestra and was also taking tap lessons with Bettie Merriweather. Often Ray would ask her to show him how to execute steps he found difficult. They became a pair, and for about three years she was his school girlfriend.

2

San Francisco: first ballet lessons

At eighteen, after graduating from high school, Ray moved to San Francisco where he at first stayed with his Mexican godparents. Darlene Becker also moved there to study nursing and probably to continue their relationship. She stayed at a young girls' boarding establishment, according to Ray a somewhat puritanical institution intent on keeping the sexes apart. Freshly out of school with no prospects or plans other than the wish to improve his tap dancing, Ray immediately went to enrol at the tap school Bettie Merriweather had recommended. As for lessons in ballet and 'spotting', the school advised him to try the San Francisco Ballet School. But having enrolled there too, it was obvious that he had to have a job and earn a proper salary; the money he had saved was not enough to pay for tap and ballet tuition on top of his living expenses.

After studying the newspaper ads he applied for a job as a clerk with the Southern Pacific Railways. The advertisement stipulated typewriting skills, generally a feminine activity, but he was chosen. His work involved typing forms (the same one, day in, day out) and documents concerning the logistics of returning troops and supplies at the end of the Second World War. This proficiency at the typewriter – which he had perfected at high school – would, as we shall see, stand him in good stead a few years later, and in fact probably saved his life.

He did not remain at the typewriter long for ballet now became the centre of his interests. Though much more demanding and essentially requiring a long period of intensive training, it proved such fun that it ousted tap. In no time, having made rapid progress, the San Francisco Ballet School offered him a scholarship. This meant that, if he did envisage a future for himself in dance, he could now devote himself full-time to ballet. However, he still needed money to live on. A solution was reached in which he earned pocket money jobbing as the school's janitor – cleaning toilets, washing or hoovering the floors and generally clearing up.

Being a late starter he took as many lessons as he could fit in. At that time the San Francisco Ballet and its affiliated school were run by Harold and William Christensen, two of the three famous Christensen brothers, early dance stars on the vaudeville circuit who had also made their names in classical ballet in America. William founded the San Francisco Ballet and Harold was in charge of the school. The youngest of the three, Lew Christensen, later took over the company; he probably had the more prominent career. Rated as one of America's first classical male stars, he became a soloist with Ballet Caravan and was the first American Apollo in Balanchine's ballet of that name. Lew also choreographed prolifically, especially ballets on American themes: *Pocahontas* (m. Elliott Carter, 1936) and *Filling Station* (m. Virgil Thomson, 1938). All of the Christensen brothers, either as teachers or choreographers, were very much in evidence as Ray pursued his studies, while Harold could be considered his first ballet teacher.

At the San Francisco Ballet School, Ray made friends with Jimmy Hicks, later known as Scott Douglas, and Leo (Dixie) Duggan who, as demobbed servicemen, were going back to ballet school. They were taking advantage of the GI Bill of Rights that provided free education for those who had had their studies interrupted by war service. Jimmy Hicks, later a principal with Ballet Theatre, had served in the navy and Leo Duggan in the army. They, together with Joan Vickers – also a student at the school – would become members of Ballet Theatre and later provide Ray with a link to that company. After only nine months' tuition at the school, Ray was accepted into the San Francisco Ballet. His talents were in immediate demand as there was a general dearth of classically trained male dancers. By this time he had given up tap – there was no time for it – and ballet had taken over completely. Dancing in William Christensen's ballet *Nothing Doing Bar* (m. Darius Milhaud, 1950), Ray had his first chance to dance a solo. He remembers that his role, called the Sleazer, had an interesting variation depicting the characteristics of such a type – disreputable and seedy. Unfortunately the ballet company gave irregular performances and to make do financially the dancers appeared in opera productions of the San Francisco Opera Company. When needed, they danced in the interludes or divertissement of *Carmen, Don Giovanni, Ballo in Maschera* and *Samson and Delilah*, etc. but, more often, they functioned as supernumeraries. As an extra, Ray remembers being a spear-holder in Wagner's *Tristan und Isolde* when the famous Norwegian soprano Kirsten Flagstad appeared in San Francisco. Before the war, Flagstad had been *the* Wagnerian soprano, acclaimed for her interpretations of Isolde and Brünnhilde, and she, together with Lauritz Melchior, were particular favourites at the Met. When war broke out, Flagstad returned to her native Norway, which had been occupied by German Nazi forces. The war over, she was reappearing in her celebrated roles at the opera houses of her previous triumphs, but the press and some opera lovers treated her as *persona non grata*. The accusation of collaboration by supposedly singing before a Nazi audience either in Germany or elsewhere hung over her. In San Francisco the police were out in great force as there were demonstrations against her appearing in this performance. Nonetheless, the show went ahead. Ray relates an amusing incident which happened during this performance: in the Second Act when King Mark, accompanied by a group of boisterous soldiers (the men of the ballet company acting as extras), disturbs the love tryst of Isolde and Tristan, one of the soldiers – the tallest, and positioned at the back – lost his helmet. It slowly rolled between the extras and singers right down to the footlights. With the music surging on, everyone's attention was riveted on this helmet. The dancers could hardly contain themselves as they stood to attention, repressing fits of giggles.

Ray was also hired to dance in the biblical blockbuster *Samson and Delilah,* filmed in Hollywood and directed by Cecil B. de Mille in 1949. Filming, then as now, is an excruciating business of hanging around and waiting for the technical set-up to be completed. When 'Action' is announced the dancers generally have not warmed up and they just have to go on cold. Asked if he could be seen in any of the footage of *Samson,* Ray said that there was a properly choreographed dance but that they were always in the background or very distant from the dramatic action. So, unfortunately, there is no recognisably visual evidence of him on film from this stage of his career.

3

Military Interruption: the Korean War

The Korean War (1950–53) interrupted all this. In 1951 Ray was drafted into the army and after a short period of training in Texas was sent to Yokohama, Japan. There, in an enormous hangar at a muster of newly arrived soldiers, the recruits were instructed to write their last wills. For some soldiers this seemed a curious request; they had nothing much to bequeath, but the real, all too saddening reason for it, underscored by lists of daily casualties, soon became apparent. A day later they were each given a rifle and one bullet. Urged to zero in on a target and fire at it as if this would be the shot that would save their lives, Ray did as he was told but missed by a mile. This did not bode well for military combat. At another muster the recruits were asked if anyone knew how to type and Ray involuntarily stuck up his hand. The soldiers he had recently befriended muttered their disapproval, but the act of volunteering for administrative work probably saved his life. It kept him out of the war arena. He would not see active service in Korea itself but would remain solely in Japan.

Camp Haugen in the village of Mutsu-Ichikawa near Sendai in the North was where he was stationed and where he performed his duties as a supply clerk. But before starting work proper, he was sent to a military base near Hiroshima for a four-week study period to learn bookkeeping and other skills particular to his work. Returning to Camp Haugen he stopped over in Tokyo, and while sightseeing noticed photographs outside a theatre that seemed to indicate ballet performances. He could hardly believe that in post-war Japan, in the early 1950s, there were ballet performances given by Japanese dancers. He persuaded a buddy to accompany him to the performance, and as they took their seats inside the theatre, they noticed that they were the only Caucasians present. The ballet was called *The Dying Swan* but was nothing like the five-minute Fokine solo that came to be identified with Pavlova. The dancer portraying the swan was a Russian-Japanese ballerina of not inconsiderable talent. Her death scene was somewhat hilarious because of the time she took to die with an arrow through her breast.

During the interval a young Japanese woman approached them and in perfect English wanted to know how they came to be attending a ballet performance in Japan. Ray explained that he was, in fact, a ballet dancer himself and was curious to see what the Japanese were doing in the way of ballet. Intrigued by this information, the young lady then introduced him to her mother and brother, also present at the performance. All spoke perfect English. The two servicemen were invited to tea the next day and brought, as a reciprocating gesture, a 'care package' for their hosts. This was a little embarrassing as the family was visibly quite well-off – the father was a banker – and certainly not in need of any food parcel. The mother thanked Ray and his friend saying that that did not really need the kind gift and they would see that a more needy family received it. English tea was served.

With time Ray rose to the rank of corporal and though later recommended for the rank of sergeant, he was not promoted. A freeze was in place: there were too many sergeants at that time. While far away from his beloved dance studio, Ray was much concerned about keeping himself in shape and was constrained to do so in the camp's gym – in shorts and barefoot. This obviously led to teasing and innuendo-like comment. Engaging in such sissy stuff as ballet made him an easy target for macho ribaldry. Determinedly cool, though riled, he confronted his tormentors by challenging them to execute a double *tour en l'air* to the right and to the left, which with easy aplomb he proceeded to demonstrate. He had become an expert at this step and it was a very useful one when a bit of bravura was required or when he needed to impress at an audition. This feat earned him a certain kudos which allowed him to continue training without being ragged too much. Whatever the soldiers said or did, he did not care; stoically he continued the ballet exercises.

Word got to the US Army's entertainment department or Special Services of Camp Haugen that there was a dancer in their midst. Naturally they were interested in having Ray participate in the entertainments organised for servicemen. Entertaining the troops had top priority and was considered essential for keeping up the morale and for steering the mood of servicemen away from the realities of war. During World War II, the Special Services roped in celebrities such as film stars, singers, comedians of the calibre of Marlene Dietrich, Bob Hope, etc. for this purpose, but Camp Haugen made do with the talent that was on hand. Thus Ray joined a group of entertainers, under a non-servicewoman called Jinx Whitlow, and his appearances were mainly solo dances of his own choreography. Looking through Ray's papers relating to his time in the army, we found documents giving exact dates of his induction into the army, the length of his service and his discharge. Among them was a paper that recorded something Ray had completely forgotten. He had given dance workshops. This must have been the earliest occasion on which he acted as dance instructor or ballet master and not solely as a dancer.

4

Finding himself

In the interviews I have conducted with Ray as a guest in his Marbella home he has been very frank about his personal life. Indeed he seems to feel a need to speak openly. He stands by his homosexuality and, as I interpret it, feels that, having lived through a time when being gay was considered either a perversion or sickness as well as contrary to moral and secular law, one should speak openly about it. There was never any doubt in his mind that he was attracted to men. He says that he was born that way. While in high school, though increasingly aware of his predilection, he was far from making a conscious choice about coming out or even aware of gay rituals. And this certain naïvety, together with his swarthy Hispanic good looks, probably made him even more attractive, and would attract friends or lovers who often became mentors. Choosing a profession like ballet dancing, where being gay was, and even today can be, the suspected sexual orientation, saved him from pretending to be otherwise.

In the theatre world being gay does not generally provoke condemnation. Quite disarmingly Ray confessed to having been naïve about many things. For example when the Kinsey Report, *Sexual Behaviour in the Human Male*[2], was published in the USA in 1948, it

---

2   Alfred C. Kinsey, *Sexual Behaviour in the Human Male*, Philadelphia, 1948

provoked considerable controversy and even alarm at the realisation that homosexuality was more prevalent than had been imagined. In the ballet studio, while Ray's friends Jimmy Hicks, Dixie Duggan and other discharged GIs were talking over the report, Ray asked ingenuously, 'What does it mean, homosexuality?' The presence of these ex GIs must have alarmed Harold Christensen, who as Ray's teacher-mentor was particularly concerned that his most promising student not be drawn into the gay ambience, which seemed to have reared an ugly head in his studios. What Harold Christensen did not realise was that there was a bet on to see who would seduce Ray first!

Until very recently homosexuality was something that was not tolerated in the US army; if one was that way inclined, one concealed the truth. Sometimes, declaring oneself gay (whether true or not) was used as an excuse to get out of being drafted. In Ray's case this was never an option. When he served as a soldier in Japan the fact that he intended to become a ballet dancer was all too revealing and he needed some sort of alibi to escape condemnation or ostracism. He had a girlfriend back home, but here on foreign soil, amidst soldierly camaraderie, a local girl could solve the problem. His closest buddies urged him to befriend a beautiful Japanese girl called Yoko who, since the transfer of her erstwhile soldier lover, was available. She was not disinclined and, as Ray related, greatly preferred him to her former lover. Ray has only praise for her and the way she responded to him. She also taught him some Japanese and was happy to show him her country. In return he paid the rent of the apartment and brought her gifts.

Demobbed, at the end of the war, he returned to California and was soon at the ballet *barre*. San Francisco Ballet was all too happy to re-engage him and it was there that his appearance as the Male Creature in *The Creatures of Prometheus* (m. Beethoven), choreographed by Lew Christensen, brought him to the notice of Ballet Theatre. Sam Lurie, one of Ballet Theatre's administrative staff, had seen the performance and reported back to Lucia Chase, the director, that there was a talented young man dancing there. Ballet

Theatre, founded in 1940, was at that time the premier American ballet company – Balanchine's New York City Ballet had not yet been established. Many dancers from San Francisco Ballet had transferred to Ballet Theatre and it was natural that any talented dancer should gravitate towards that company. Thus Ray, too, set his sights on Ballet Theatre. Urged by Jimmy Hicks, Dixie Duggan and Joan Vickers, his San Franciscan friends, all members of Ballet Theatre, Ray took class with the company during the San Francisco season. He was told he should attend the official audition of the company, which was to be held in New York a little later.

Ray's decision to try his luck in New York was very upsetting for his girlfriend Darlene Becker. She sensed that this might be the parting of their ways. She asked him, 'If you go to New York, does this mean that we will never see each other again?' Ray answered, 'I don't know, Darlene, I really don't know. This is my profession and I have to go.' They did not see each other again, although through friends he had news of her.

5

Ballet Theatre (1953-1958)

Ray, ever fearful about not having enough money to live on or to realise his dancing ambitions, had saved where and when he could. The little he earned at the ballet school as a janitor, as well as the wages from his appearances in the operas, had been parsimoniously managed – his family had not been exactly poor, but there was always the feeling money was tight. Thus financially in a position to afford the trip to New York for the Ballet Theatre audition, he packed most of his possessions in one suitcase and in October 1953 flew there. Through the encouragement of his friends Scott Douglas, Leo Duggan and Joan Vickers, he seemed confident that the outcome of the audition would be positive and therefore had no forebodings about having to return to San Francisco.

The audition, held in Ballet Theatre's studios at 316 West 57th Street, was packed. Anatole Vilzak a one-time Russian dancer with Diaghilev's *Ballets Russes*, who had settled in the States, gave the class. Toward the end of it, by being able to execute the *mazurka-double tour enchaînement* to both sides with suitable aplomb, Ray impressed. Not many of the boys taking the audition could manage it to the left as well as to the right. As his Ballet Theatre friends expected, and probably to his relief and joy, Ray was accepted and offered a contract as a corps de ballet dancer. He immediately moved out of his hotel and into the YMCA, an inexpensive hostel for young men. In the Y's canteen he and Dixie Duggan sat considering a stage name for himself. This was necessary as the company's director, Lucia Chase, announced that they could never print Raymond Martin Barallobre in their programmes; it was too long and unwieldy. She suggested he call himself Ray Martin. But Ray didn't like this suggestion, although it did seem logical to retain his first name in the shortened form – everyone called him Ray. But what about the rest? The double L in Barallobre was the problem; so he cut the family name in half and taking the first part just doubled the R. Since then he has been known as Ray Barra. Satisfied with his abbreviated new name, Ray was all set to go. Now began a rehearsal period of serious work during which most of the ballets scheduled for the forthcoming tour were either taught anew or rehearsed.

As luck would have it he was immediately cast in a ballet that was being prepared for television. Eugene Loring, the choreographer of this ballet, *The Capital of the World*, had based it on a short story by Ernest Hemingway. Set in Spain, it is about a youth who dreams of becoming a matador. Ray was cast as a picador. This must have been the easiest of his new duties as the role was being created specifically for him. Otherwise, as a newcomer to the company, he had a big workload: he had to learn innumerable corps de ballet parts of the entire touring repertory. The ballets included: *Theme and Variations* (Balanchine), *The Combat* (William Dollar), *Mademoiselle Angot* (Léonide Massine), *Pillar of Fire* (Antony Tudor), *Lilac Garden* (Antony Tudor), *Fall River Legend* (Agnes de Mille), *Rodeo* (Agnes de Mille), etc. Ray's reaction: 'I had never learned so many f*****g steps in such a short time.'

Ray said that on entering the world of Ballet Theatre and starting out as a small cog in its activities, he felt as if he were going to university. The experience, even if it was essentially work, felt like an education – and an agreeable one at that. For the first time in his dancing career, he came in contact with a spectrum of quality ballets, many of them already considered modern classics, or on the way to attaining that status. It was an exciting, visceral experience to be dancing in them. Additionally, this brought about a broadening of his artistic horizons, for he was automatically exposed to ballet's collaborative arts, music and design. To crown it all, he became associated with superb and celebrated dancers such as Alicia Markova, Alicia Alonso, Nora Kaye, Lupe Serrano, Igor Youskevitch, Erik Bruhn and John Kriza – stars of Ballet Theatre. He trod the same boards they did; he was up close and able to observe what made them special. Settling in to the company, Ray soon came to experience the bonding comradeship that easily arises from a group of dancers who spend considerable time together 'on the road'.

During a performance, just before curtain-up on *Aurora's Wedding* – the divertissement final act of Petipa's *The Sleeping Beauty* – Ray, as was his habit, was waiting on stage, dutifully early and preparing for the performance. Alicia Alonso, the Cuban ballerina who was to dance Aurora that evening, was warming up and wanted someone to help her practise the attitude promenades that are a feature of *The Rose Adage*. Instead of the *grand pas de deux*, this version of *Aurora's Wedding* included *The Rose Adage*, which involves the ballerina and four cavaliers. As there were no cavaliers present on stage, Alonso called Ray over, 'Hey you, come here. Give me your hand. Now promenade me. No, no, hold it straight. Don't move backwards and forwards. And not up and down either.' She had hardly appraised him as new to the company or that he lacked experience in *pas de deux* work, but seemed content to have a novice help her. Ray, moreover, was tickled pink to have had an impromptu partnering lesson from the famous ballerina.

The irony, implicit in this little anecdote, is that Ray did become a very good partner; in fact, with time, all the girls wanted to dance with him. When Jiliana left New York City Ballet for Ballet Theatre, she was given Ray as her partner. Though tall and a little chubby, and as a Balanchine dancer inexperienced in other styles, he managed her rather well and he enjoyed her delightful sense of humour. Later in

Stuttgart, dancing Romeo in the Cranko's version of *Romeo and Juliet*, he partnered not only Marcia Haydée, but also Carla Fracci, Lynn Seymour and Violette Verdy – ballerinas invited to guest in the Juliet role. Ray got on well with Nora Kaye, Ballet Theatre's dramatic ballerina, who was equally good in the classics though perhaps physically less appealing in such roles. A vital, wisecracking personality, great fun to be around, she enjoyed the company of men and could hold her own amidst butch raillery. As the company's celebrated dramatic ballerina, she had considerable influence and Ray thinks she was responsible for advocating him for special roles. She might have thought that, like her, Ray was Jewish and he too felt he had that sort of physiognomy. Once, in Chicago, in an elevator, he was addressed in Hebrew. Ray: 'At a New York party, Nora Kaye even tried to fix me up with Jerome Robbins [Jewish]. Nothing came of her efforts but I was fascinated on that occasion by the stories Robbins regaled to an awed group. He spoke of all the many Russian dance teachers he had studied with and the influence they had had on him, especially that of folk dance. When one thinks of this particular element in one of his most loved ballets, *Dances at a Gathering*, the influence is obvious.'

In the 1950s, Ballet Theatre's roster of choreographers included Antony Tudor, Jerome Robbins, Agnes de Mille, Eugene Loring, William Dollar, Herbert Ross, John Taras and later Kenneth MacMillan. These choreographers were there, on hand, creating and rehearsing their ballets. Ray couldn't believe his luck. Here he was being paid to do what he enjoyed best in an ambience of excellence and creativity. Asked which ballets he liked or preferred to dance in, he replied, 'Oh, I just loved dancing in all of them.' Doubtless with time his preferences became more refined, and with it the knowledge of which roles would suit him best. Ray does not claim to have possessed a bravura dance technique; indeed he is quite modest about his abilities. 'You know, I could do maybe three pirouettes, if I managed four, well, hallelujah that was something to write home about! My best step was *double tour en l'air* to both sides and my *entre-chat six* was not bad.' There was enough self-knowledge to know his limits, but he certainly wanted to get ahead. Nor did he hanker after roles that in ballet terminology are reserved for the *danseur noble*. In fact his trump card was a natural and appealing masculinity, without it being overbearingly macho – unless the role demanded it. What he brought to the stage was a focused concentration; it gave a dramatic edge to his interpretations. This certainly appealed to choreographers interested in exploiting a stage persona that could portray a human being and not a dancing machine. Nicolas Beriozoff, John Cranko and Kenneth MacMillan were to exploit this talent.

The founding policy of Ballet Theatre in 1940 had been the will to create and foster an American classical ballet company that could offer the best: the best dancers and choreographies available at that present time. Unlike the New York City Ballet, which essentially served a single choreographer, George Balanchine, Ballet Theatre offered a diversity of choreographers, styles and genres. The great divide could be formulated in this way: while George Balanchine concentrated on the abstract, or, as he termed it, the plotless ballet, Ballet Theatre offered a more catholic choice, incorporating the talents of leading choreographers worldwide. There was also an emphasis on the narrative; and this was the genre more suited to Ray's talents. Later, dancing in Stuttgart, he would be able to develop his dramatic skills.

Ray had the good fortune of being a member of Ballet Theatre when many of the company's choreographic creators, those responsible for shaping the company's image and artistic direction, were still around. For instance, he danced in several of the English choreographer Antony Tudor's ballets and was coached by him. Tudor had the reputation of having, at least in the rehearsal studio, a sadist streak. Asked if he had been the object of the choreographer's abuse, Ray said, 'Oh, not really; he treated me like a dancer, though he did not correct me very much. But he could be quite horrible in rehearsals. In the studio he used to sit on a chair leaning against the *barre* with his arms extended to each side. That, and his bald head, made him look just like a vulture. He visibly enjoyed the power he had to humiliate. Once, we were rehearsing *Lilac Garden* and he made one of the dancers repeat her entrance again and again; he rehearsed her to death. All she had to do was enter the scene and discreetly put her finger to her lips. In fact, it was not a dance step. Tudor was not satisfied, he made her do it again: 'No Audrey, once more. No, again.' And so it went on for about fifteen minutes. She was in tears. The awful thing about the situation was that Tudor never explained what he wanted or told her what was wrong. Tudor also liked to set up dancers against each other. Slyly, he would make small insinuating remarks that could tip their emotions, and would sit there enjoying the results.' This sort of situation was tolerated probably because Tudor was considered something of a creative genius. Apart from his two English ballets, *Dark Elegies* and *Lilac Garden*, which entered Ballet Theatre's repertory in the inaugural season of 1940, he choreographed several remarkable ballets that established the sort of fare that Ballet Theatre would cultivate. His masterpiece, *Pillar of Fire* of 1942, has been acclaimed as one of the most poignant and gripping of his 'psychological' studies in dance.

Another 'choreographer-beast' Ray encountered in rehearsal was Jerome Robbins – albeit briefly, as Robbins had left to join NYCB in 1949 and had little time for Ballet Theatre due to his Broadway successes. Robbins' *Fancy Free* of 1944 for Ballet Theatre and later the musical *West Side Story* were feted as an authentic twentieth-century American voice in neoclassical and jazz-inspired dance, while he dominated the Broadway musical for several decades. Robbins was a notorious taskmaster. At a rehearsal of *Fancy Free*, he was so dissatisfied with the way the dancers were executing their steps that he hardly got past the entry of the sailors on shore leave as they enter the bar. Ray: 'He [Robbins] demanded tremendous energy and superhuman enthusiasm for the high *rond de jambes*, as if the sailors were stepping over the buildings of New York.' When Ray danced in the ballet, he started out as the bartender who does not have any choreography but who reacts to the situations and serves drinks. Later he was promoted to the sailor who does the first variation. Ray: 'This variation, which starts on the bar counter, was technically very difficult; there were lots of pirouettes, turns in second. Thank goodness Robbins didn't see my first performance; I probably didn't have enough rehearsals. He was known to watch performances and if he didn't like what he saw, he would take you out of his ballets.' Robbins was obsessive about detail and he wanted the dancers to dance full out at every rehearsal regardless of whether there was a performance that night or not. Ray: 'He was only interested in the steps, he didn't want anything shilly-shally, he wanted you to be exactly as he saw the figure and the steps.' In spite of what might be called a demanding tyranny, Robbins was a choreographer of the first order, and Ray did appreciate working with him.

On the other hand Agnes de Mille was fun to work with. Ray danced in two of her ballets, *Fall River Legend* and *Rodeo*. In *Rodeo* he gradually worked his way up to being cast as Champion Roper – the second male lead. John Kriza, who had created this role, was his coach and Ray couldn't believe his luck. In another cowboy ballet, Eugene Loring's *Billy the Kid*, Ray got to dance Pat Garrett. Then William Dollar's ballet *The Combat,* based on the Clorinda–Tancredi episode from Tasso's *Gerusalemme liberata*, provided Ray with one of his early successes. He advanced from a small part, the first knight to be killed, to the intricately syncopated duo (which he danced with Leo Duggan) representing a twin-like rendition of two knights on horseback. Their accuracy in synchronised repartee used to bring the house down. They became veritable stars of that ballet.

Ray must have made some impression on the Scottish choreographer Kenneth MacMillan when he came to choreograph his first ballet for Ballet Theatre. He was given a small solo part in *Winter's Eve*, which MacMillan completed in Monte Carlo before it premiered in Lisbon in January 1957. It probably never dawned on either the choreographer or Ray that this collaboration would be continued in a foreign country (Germany) and would gain in intensity. *Winter's Eve*, set to music by Benjamin Britten, was loosely based on the Carson McCullers story, *The Heart is a Lonely Hunter*, about a deaf mute. Depicting this affliction, even if it were choreographically feasible, is not something that an audience can easily comprehend. It was for this reason that its protagonist became blind. MacMillan, then at the beginning of his career, was steadily making a name for himself at the Royal Ballet. He was a protégé of de Valois and considered, after John Cranko, to be the most promising of the young bloods. MacMillan was all too keen to establish himself internationally and the commission from Ballet Theatre was very enticing. He had seen that company's London season in 1956 and was quite bowled over by Nora Kaye's great dramatic and expressive gifts, and was eager to have her dance in a ballet of his own. Ballet Theatre, in any case, was in need of a creation; the last original one had been six years previously in 1950. Nora Kaye was also MacMillan's choice for *Journey*, his second ballet, based on the German poem *Death and the Maiden* and inspired by paintings by Edvard Munch. Ray was one of a corps of twelve men who, during a certain sequence, sit on chairs and pass the three female soloists aloft. He and Leo Duggan were chosen as rehearsal ballet masters for the corps de ballet sections of *Journey*. It was the practice in Ballet Theatre to elect dancers from these ballets (where possible, sanctioned by the choreographer) to take care of them in rehearsal, especially for revivals or when someone new had to be initiated into the proceedings. MacMillan's ballets did not enjoy much success though he was highly praised as a choreographer to be watched. His inventiveness with an unusual and distinct dance language was singled out.

When Ballet Theatre toured it was usual for the dancers to find their own accommodation. As the basic wage for dancers was not, and has never been, very substantial, there was an effort to avoid spending all the touring allowance on hotel room accommodation. This gave rise to what was called 'ghosting'. A hotel room would be reserved, supposedly for the use of one person, while up to three non-paying guests would surreptitiously cram themselves in. Ray has an amusing anecdote of an occasion when this ruse was uncovered: 'The room was in the name of Enrique Martinez, a soloist with the company. He had been invited to a reception that evening and had given some clothes to the valet service for ironing. When the bellboy knocked on the door, wanting to return the freshly ironed clothes, all the ghosting dancers hid where they could; in the bathroom, under the bed, in the toilet, while Enrique (unnecessarily) hid in the cupboard. Told he could enter, the bellboy went straight to the cupboard in order to hang up the clothes. On opening the door he found a sheepish Enrique who mumbled, "I thought this was the bathroom."'

On one of Ray's first tours with Ballet Theatre, during a stopover in Denver, he met a young aspirant dancer with whom he fell head over heels in love. Ray: 'It must have been about 1954 when I met this young man, who had been married, had a daughter but who discovered he was, in fact, gay. His name was Johnny Ray. Yes, incredible as it may seem that was his name! At the time there was another Johnny Ray, a popular singer with the same name who had a Hollywood film career (*There's No Business Like Show Business*). It was rumoured he was gay too. I met my Denver Johnny Ray after a performance when he came backstage with a group of ballet fans. Although he was into his twenties he had only just started taking ballet lessons. Going out for drinks, we eyed each other with some interest, but it was the following day that things got serious. We had lunch together and as there was a performance that night I said that I really had to go and have a rest before it. He made the suggestion that I didn't need to go to my hotel, just stay on in his house. Well, I didn't get any rest that afternoon and was a bit pooped for the performance. Next day and each following day of the company's season in that city – we were there over a week – we met and our affair started. I was mad for the guy. On Ballet Theatre's next lay-off, I flew to Denver to meet him again. We had a great time. Then when Ballet Theatre announced the next series of rehearsals and performances we decided that he would join me in New York. In New York we found a small flat and he auditioned for the company. Unfortunately he didn't get in, but he did manage to get a job in a musical. That suited his talent fine and that's where he started a great career in musicals. First of all he became an accomplished switch dancer; ready to take on any dancing role when someone was sick. After that he was promoted to being a dance captain, a sort of ballet master for musicals. He went on to make quite a career for himself with the Shubert Organization. But our affair did not last that long; coming back from a tour I had to tell him that things between us were over. I had become involved with someone who really bowled me over – Erik Bruhn.'

6

Erik Bruhn

However poignant Ray's affair with Johnny Ray had been, his intimate relationship with Erik Bruhn is one he particularly treasures to this very day. He considers it, on an emotional and intellectual level, one of the most important of his early career. When Ray first met Bruhn, he was on the verge of being hailed the greatest male dancer of his generation. A matinee at the Metropolitan Opera on 1st May 1955, when he danced Albrecht partnering the celebrated Alicia Markova in *Giselle*, put the seal on stardom. Bruhn was replacing Igor Youskevitch who, according to Ray, was not prepared to dance that role at a matinee. The critic John Martin wrote: 'Alicia Markova made her second appearance [that season] in *Giselle* and Erik Bruhn appeared opposite her in his very first Albrecht. It may well be a date to write down in history books, for it was as if the greatest Giselle of today were handing over a sacred trust to what is probably the greatest Albrecht of tomorrow.'[3] Incredibly, Ray does not remember participating in that performance, but he must have been one of the peasants in the first act. His promotion to the rank of soloist happened much later and so there is every good reason to suppose

---

3   *American Ballet Theatre*, Text & Commentary by Charles Payne, Alfred A. Knopf, New York 1978, p. 321

that he danced at that matinee. Bruhn's performance as Albrecht was enthusiastically feted and for some time became the touchstone of this role. Apart from possessing a brilliant classical dance technique, Bruhn was devastatingly handsome in a cool Scandinavian way: blond with light blue eyes and a lithe stature of great elegance. His stage manner allied to unostentatious bravura made of him the epitome of the *danseur noble*.

When Bruhn returned to Ballet Theatre in 1954 after one of his many engagements with the Royal Danish Ballet, Ray was already a member of the company. Ray got to know Bruhn when he brought his ballet slippers for painting. The slippers had to be coloured according to the tights the dancers wore, or cleaned if they were dirty. Ray and Leo Duggan were responsible for doing this task and it brought them a little extra money. Bruhn, who had the reputation for a roving eye in the company, would engage in light banter and flirtation with the two young men and they responded by teasing him. On a certain occasion when the company was touring by train, Bruhn and several of the dancers were enjoying a cigarette in the buffet car, discussing this and that. Slowly the group got smaller and smaller and all of a sudden Ray and Bruhn found themselves alone. Bruhn in his inimitable dry Danish way posed a supposedly rhetorical question laden with innuendo, 'Well, where do we go from here?' Ray was flustered as it seemed to be an invitation of a certain kind, but had the presence of mind for a hasty reply, 'Nowhere, I think,' and immediately got up and left the nonplussed questioner alone. The dismissive gesture probably made him all the more intriguing. Inevitably, they did get together. It happened while the company was performing in San Francisco and from then on, while on tour, they shared a room. It was at Bruhn's insistence, despite his declaration, 'I don't belong to anyone,' that they lived together when they were not on tour. For this reason they rented an apartment in New York as their base.

From the beginning Bruhn took over as the dominant partner in the friendship and though only two years older than Ray, he came to exercise a mentor-like role. According to Ray, 'I didn't mind one bit, after all, he was the star of the company, a wonderful dancer and I was crazy about him. He really changed my approach to ballet. He taught me to take ballet class seriously and made me think about the motivation behind the steps. In all he was inspirational!' Being the intimate friend of such an accomplished dancer naturally led to long and intensive discussions, invariably instigated by Bruhn, about dance technique and interpretation. Like a sponge, Ray avidly soaked up all that Bruhn had to offer. Stimulated by this exchange, he turned to thinking about his own approach to ballet and how he could improve his technique. Though a latecomer to ballet, Ray was fortunate in having a blithe enthusiasm for dance coupled with an optimistic, insouciant life-view. His progress was determined by sheer observation, application, and determination. Bruhn, on the other hand, by virtue of an intensive and lengthy dance education since his tenth year at the Royal Danish Ballet School, clearly had the advantage, apart from an innate dance facility, of having mastered a well-defined discipline: the Bournonville technique. There had been no Bournonville-trained dancer of his calibre for some time, if at all. Though closely associated with the Royal Danish Ballet throughout his career, he was the first Danish dancer in the twentieth century to enjoy an international career.[4] Hardly past his first season as a member of the Copenhagen company, his career took off when fortuitous circumstances brought him to prominence outside Denmark. While on holiday in England, accompanying a Danish colleague engaged by the Metropolitan Ballet, he was offered a contract with that company – an offer for which he obtained a leave of absence. Then in 1949 he was invited to join Ballet Theatre in America .

Ray's friendship with Erik Bruhn naturally introduced him to a different style in classical dance: Bournonville technique – not that he ever properly studied it, but an awareness of its stylistic elements was definitely part of Ray's educational agenda. Ballet Theatre, at that time, did not yet have any Bournonville choreography in its repertory and

---

4   Dame Adeline Genée (1878–1970) could be said to have preceded Bruhn in the international stakes, though her fame did not extend to Eastern Europe or Russia.

thus Ray had probably never seen anything by the nineteenth-century Danish master. He had no inkling of its quaint and delightfully fleeting dynamic. Therefore it must have come as a revelation when he was able to view the real thing: performances at Jacob's Pillar by ten soloists of the Royal Danish Ballet in July 1955. The dancers included all the important names from the 1950s, including Mona Vansgaa, Kirsten Ralov, Inge Sand, Frank Schaufuss, Stanley Williams and Flemming Flindt. A more prominent assemblage would be hard to imagine; this period marked the start of the Royal Danish Ballet's emergence on to the international stage. The Danes had been invited to that venerable location by, of all people, one of the founding fathers of American modern dance, Ted Shawn. Jacob's Pillar, located in Massachusetts, was originally a farm when Ted Shawn bought the property in 1930. It was altered to serve as a base and theatre for his own troupe of male dancers. With time Jacob's Pillar developed into a highly respected venue for dance in most of its forms: modern, ballet and ethnic. Workshops and performances are still given in summer.

Ray: 'I couldn't believe how wonderful it all was. It really seemed as if I was allowed to see something from the far past but still vibrantly alive. Going to Jacob's Pillar was such an experience; that, and meeting Ted Shawn.' Ted Shawn seems to have been a big fan of Bruhn's; if not, according to Ray, quite in love with him. In Bruhn's (official) biography, a letter of Shawn's is quoted. It begins, 'Dearly beloved Erik.' Written in November 1971, Shawn writes of seeing Bruhn's memorable performance in *Giselle* on 1st May 1955: 'when you did your first Albrecht with Alicia [Markova], and I cooked for you and fed you after that matinee; the next morning when sleepy-eyed you and Ray came in with leftover eggs and butter, etc.'[5] As Bruhn's breakthrough Albrecht debut had just been two months prior to the scheduled appearances of the Danish soloists at Jacob's Pillar, he was invited to dance excerpts from *Giselle* partnering Alicia Markova as well as appearing alongside his colleagues in the final act divertissements from *Napoli*. And Ray was there lapping it all up.

---

5   John Gruen, *Erik Bruhn, Danseur Noble*, The Viking Press, New York 1979, p 70

Later, accompanying Bruhn on one of the lay-off periods in Denmark, he got to know the Danes better. Ray: 'They're always ready to party.'

That Bruhn was a thinking dancer can be gleaned from John Gruen's biography *Erik Bruhn, Danseur Noble*[6] and from the interview the same author published in *The Private Worlds of Ballet*.[7] There, it is apparent that Bruhn was not content to rest on his laurels as a *danseur noble* of formidable technique, but was driven to question the whys and wherefores behind the steps. Ray freely admits that the seeds of his later achievements as a principal dancer in Stuttgart, offering in-depth characterisations of the roles he created, came about from his contact with Bruhn. When Ray came to dance Romeo in *Romeo and Juliet* (choreography: Werner Ulbrich) in Stuttgart in 1959 during Nicolas Beriozoff's tenure as ballet director, he had profited enormously from the fact that Bruhn had already discussed with him how he, Bruhn, would portray that role in the Ashton version. Ashton had choreographed *Romeo and Juliet* for the Royal Danish Ballet in 1955, and Bruhn was to dance Romeo with the Danish company at the Edinburgh Festival that year and later in Copenhagen – albeit as a second cast to Henning Kronstam. There had been innumerable discussions about interpretation and these remained vividly imprinted in Ray's memory when he later came to dance Romeo himself in two productions in Stuttgart.

On the subject of dance technique Bruhn also had much to offer. As a co-author with Lillian Moore of *Bournonville and Ballet Technique*,[8] he clearly had an analytical mind and a deep interest in dance pedagogy. Frequently during his dancing career he was requested to teach and this talent would later become more dominant. From his own experience when dancing outside Denmark, it had become clear to Bruhn that the Bournonville technique alone would not be adequate for modern choreography. It emphasises *ballon*, a term used to describe the jumpy or bouncy quality in the steps of

6   John Gruen, *Erik Bruhn, Danseur Noble*, The Viking Press, New York 1979
7   John Gruen, *The Private World of Ballet*, The Viking Press, New York 1975
8   Erik Bruhn and Lillian Moore, *Bournonville and Ballet Technique*, A & C Black Ltd, London 1961

elevation, as if the dancer remains briefly suspended in the air at the height of the jump. This light, fleeting style gives the impression that the dancer never really touches the floor. The strength of the Danish airiness comes from the feet, the ankles and the calves. This is in contrast to the more physical demands of Russian or non-Bournonville choreography which requires the use of a deeper *plié* and a more grounded preparation for the jumps. And it is in this application that the muscles of the thighs come into play. Bruhn gives credit to the Russian teacher Vera Volkova,[9] respected as an authority of the Vaganova system and an influential teacher in Western Europe, for helping him extend his capabilities. 'The fact is,' said Bruhn, 'Volkova was my primary influence – the biggest and the best!'[10] She played a pivotal role in bringing about a reform in Bournonville pedagogy while serving as artistic advisor to the Royal Danish Ballet. Without drastically altering the Bournonville system, she instigated a rethinking, a refining extension of its tenets. Her influence at the Royal Danish Ballet was ultimately considerable and opened the door of a rather insular company to outside influences.[11]

What Volkova has to do with Ray is the fact that, through Bruhn, he probably absorbed a distillation of her teaching and was also able to experience her tuition first hand. In the long lay-off period during 1956 when Ballet Theatre suspended its activities due to a lack of touring engagements, Bruhn invited Ray to accompany him to Copenhagen. As Bruhn was re-engaged to dance with the Royal Danish Ballet, this meant that Ray was free to do classes and watch performances. He often took Volkova's afternoon class for the school or the aspirants, but his contact with her was not as intensive or intimate as Bruhn's

---

9   Vera Volkova (1904–75) was a Russian teacher who had studied at the Russian School
     of Ballet as well as with Agrippina Vaganova, the illustrious pedagogue and architect
     of the Russian Soviet ballet system. From 1943 to 1950 Volkova taught at Sadler's Wells
     and its school and was respected as the leading authority on the Vaganova system –
     albeit modified to her own taste. She became artistic advisor to the Royal Danish Ballet
     in 1951 and remained in Denmark until her death in 1975. John Gruen, *Erik Bruhn,
     Danseur Noble*, The Viking Press, New York 1979, p. 55
10   John Gruen, *Erik Bruhn, Danseur Noble*, The Viking Press, New York 1979, p. 58
11   Alexander Meinertz, *Vera Volkova, A Biography*, Dance Books, United Kingdom 2007

had been. He did, however, have an interesting conversation with her. Once after class they sat in a corner of the ballet studio where she questioned him about how pointe technique for female dancers was taught at Ballet Theatre. She was also curious to hear about Alicia Alonso, the Cuban ballerina and star of Ballet Theatre in the 1950s. Then she told him something that she considered very important. It had to do with posture and the carriage of the body. She indicated a spot at the centre of his chest and revealed that one had to think that a little button was situated there. She admonished him: 'You push it up and forward while pulling your shoulders and back down. Then you will be straight.' In fact, she had offered exactly this advice to Erik Bruhn. It is mentioned in John Gruen's Bruhn biography where Bruhn extols her teaching method.[12] Thus during an interlude of several months while unemployed, Ray was able to concentrate on improving his technique while, at the same time, experience the inner workings of the traditional Royal Danish Ballet. And he had the opportunity of seeing all the Bournonville performances, many danced by Bruhn, that were in the Royal Theatre's repertory. These included *La Sylphide*, *Napoli* and *A Folk's Tale*.

John Gruen's biography of Erik Bruhn does not whitewash that dancer's personality, indeed it is frank about his interpersonal dealings with those closest to him. Bruhn was prone to depressive bouts caused by a feeling of insecurity about whether he could always live up to and maintain the high artistry he had achieved and that was expected of him. Frequently, feeling the demands and affections of his partners as being too intensive, he needed periods of withdrawal into himself. And he could become cruel and calculating.[13] According to Ray, he drank a lot and smoked like a chimney; habits certainly not conducive to maintaining a healthy physical constitution for dance. However, in spite of the negative characteristics of his personality, there must have been something compensatory, a generosity of spirit that made him a loveable person. To all this neurotic tribulation, Ray

---

12   John Gruen, *Erik Bruhn, Danseur Noble*, The Viking Press, New York 1979, p. 57
13   John Gruen, *Erik Bruhn, Danseur Noble*, The Viking Press, New York 1979, p. 93

must have functioned as an antidote. His was a steadfast commitment to the relationship; his down-to-earth dealings with plain living must have given Bruhn the security he needed and, at the same time, the assurance of being cared for.

When John Gruen wrote his Bruhn biography it was not possible to really come out into the open and make clear statements about such things as sexual orientation, especially if the subject of the book was still alive. There is no overt mention of Bruhn's bisexuality, though it is implied, and therefore nothing concrete about an intimate relationship between him and Ray. The relationship with Ray is mentioned obliquely. Nevertheless, in the last chapter of the book, there is evidence that it did mean something special to Bruhn. Gruen quotes Bruhn: 'There is Ray Barra. He was in my life. We became very great friends when I met him at Ballet Theatre many years ago, and I still love and adore that man to this day. He's done incredibly well for himself, first as a dancer, and later as a ballet master and regisseur. Ray was and is a wonderful person.'[14]

---

14   John Gruen, *Erik Bruhn, Danseur Noble*, The Viking Press, New York 1979, p. 224

7

In and out of work: lay-offs

Ballet Theatre, or to use its present name adopted in 1957, American Ballet Theatre, had, while Ray was a member, one considerable drawback: it was a touring ballet company – its very existence was nomadic and gipsy-like. Travelling from venue to venue, changing city and accommodation, often after what is called a one-night stand (a single performance in a particular city), the dancers were constrained to live out of a suitcase. Things have changed and American Ballet Theatre no longer embarks on the sort of touring it used to undertake. The company now has an agreement with the Metropolitan Opera House guaranteeing an eight-week spring season, but it is not affiliated to a theatre that it could consider its resident base. Major companies like the Royal Ballet, the Ballet of the Paris Opera, the Bolshoi, etc. are all privileged to be part of a state-sponsored mother or umbrella organisation, housed in an opera house. American Ballet Theatre, without an economic and sustaining backbone of this sort, is thus dependant on engagements and, to an even greater extent, on sponsorship, either philanthropic or from the state, for example from the National Endowment for the Arts. In the past, and certainly during the period when Ray was a member, it frequently had to introduce lay-off periods because of a lack of engagements. During the lay-off, dancers were not paid a salary and were, in fact, on hold until performances could be scheduled. They were thus dependent on unemployment payments. Lay-offs obliged most dancers to seek temporary employment: often as waiters in restaurants or coffee shops, or if they were lucky in Broadway shows. Since American Ballet Theatre's inception in 1940 and until 1980, the management, financial and artistic, was in the hands of Lucia Chase (variously together with Richard Pleasant, Sol Hurok and Oliver Smith as co-directors). From Chase's own considerable inherited fortune, the company was kept financially afloat when necessary, but her resources were not limitless.

Ray too was obliged to find work during the lay-off periods, but never had to work as a waiter in restaurants or coffee shops. Rather, he tried his luck at auditioning for Broadway shows whenever dancers were needed. Inevitably, at these auditions, on hearing that he was a dancer with Ballet Theatre, it was obvious that he would only be available for a limited period and the response was that he should just go and draw his unemployment allowance until BT started up again. He did however get a job dancing in a show called *Aladdin's Lamp* in a theatre at Jones Beach, just outside New York. During another lay-off period he was engaged as replacement dancer in *Can Can*, an immensely successful musical with choreography by Michael Kidd. Though ready to step in at a moment's notice, he never did appear in it. Another offer came from Rod Alexander who was to co-choreograph with Agnes de Mille the film version of the musical *Carousel*. But Ray did not wish to give up Ballet Theatre for one Hollywood film. Usually the lay-offs occurred during summer and so he more or less hung out in New York collecting his unemployment and going to the cinema. Ray: 'New York can be stiflingly humid and uncomfortable during summer, so the best place to escape it is in an air-conditioned cinema. Often I would end up watching two films a day.'

On another lay-off period, at considerable expense, he flew first class with Iberia – it was the only ticket available for the flight – to join Erik Bruhn in Northern Spain. Bruhn and Rosella Hightower were appearing as stars of the Grand Ballet du Marquis de Cuevas and Ray went to join them on this tour. He took class with the company and was able to take in and absorb a more international set-up. When that part of the tour finished Ray and Erik accompanied Rosella Hightower to her home outside of Lyon and a few days later to Paris where he and Erik settled into a small *pension*. Now began a period in which Ray developed an antipathy for the French: he complains that they were arrogant, 'In Paris I had the most horrible time of my life!' The main problem was, essentially, that he did not speak French and felt excluded. In the late 1950s when he was there, and until fairly recently, few Parisians spoke English. Ray felt himself an outsider in an extremely sophisticated city; a feeling exacerbated by inactivity. While Erik was busy performing or away guesting in Copenhagen, Ray was left to see the sights and do class. He took class with several famous and colourful dance personalities such as Olga Preobrajenska, the ex-prima ballerina of the Maryinsky who had escaped Russia in 1921. She taught at the Studio Waker in Clichy. Celebrated dancers such as Irina Baronova, Tamara Toumanova and Igor Youskevitch had been amongst her pupils. Studio Waker in the 1950s and '60s was the French Mecca for ballet dancers; most would gravitate at some time of their dancing careers to that shrine of Terpsichore. Another teacher at Studio Waker was Madame Nora Kiss; according to Ray, a rather sergeant-majorish teacher who was terribly *en vogue*. What took some getting used to in those days was the fact that, at Studio Waker, there were no changing rooms. Most dancers knew this and arrived with their tricots or maillots under their street clothes and just disrobed in the studio. And there were certainly no showers (the bidet was another French invention Ray viewed with suspicion). However, at the Paris Opéra, Ray was terribly impressed by this venerable institution, even if puzzled by the performance he saw. *Coppélia* was given in a two-act version with Lycette Darsonval as Swanhilda and Paulette Dynalix as Franz, danced *en travestie* – as, indeed, it had originally been performed. What Ray perhaps did not realise was that, however unappealing he considered the French to be, he was privileged to experience at first hand, in Paris, the classical ballet tradition in all its singularity. Seen more positively, Paris could be regarded as an extension and furtherance of his education.

8

Germany: dancing for Papa Beriozoff (1958-1960)

The German city Stuttgart in the State of Baden-Württemberg, might seem a curious place for the twenty-eight-year-old Ray to have set his sights on. American Ballet Theatre's[15] European tour of 1958 was Ray's first visit to that city. However, it was immediately obvious that there was a ballet company there and, from the look of it, not a bad one. ABT had let it be known that after this tour and a three-week season at the Metropolitan Opera, there would be a long lay-off period with an indefinite date of reassembly. The dancers' contracts were about to run out and had not been renegotiated. Indeed, after the Met season the company closed down – for the second time in its existence.[16] While on tour and unsure of his future, Ray was checking out companies where he might get a job. Perhaps he had heard of Stuttgart as the home of the Porsche and Mercedes-Benz automobile companies, but probably not that Jean-Georges Noverre had been able to put his theories about the *ballet d'action* (a dramatically shaped narrative or story ballet) to the

---

15   During the 1956–7 European tour Ballet Theatre became American Ballet Theatre
16   Alex C. Ewing, *Bravura! Lucia Chase and the American Ballet Theatre*, The University Press of Florida, Gainesville, FL 2009, p. 195

test in this very city in 1760. It would be this genre of ballet, the story or narrative ballet, that 200 years later would become the South African choreographer John Cranko's legacy to ballet.

The Stuttgart company offered certain attractions and advantages: it seemed to have an interesting repertoire, more classically orientated than what he was used to at Ballet Theatre, but importantly, the contracts offered employment throughout the season (a whole year), including a paid six-week holiday period. It was Erik Bruhn who had suggested Ray should try his luck in Europe, and for that matter in Stuttgart where the tour was heading. From a geographical point of view, it offered an important advantage: Stuttgart was not too far from Copenhagen. And that was where Erik would return to dance with his original company, the Royal Danish Ballet, after the Met season. Ray was keen to keep the relationship alive.

Ray, without much ado, sought out Nicholas 'Papa' Beriozoff, Stuttgart's choreographer/ballet director, and asked if he could take company class. Beriozoff, in turn, was curious to know what Ray had danced the previous evening.[17] The reply encouraged him to allow Ray to take class with his company, which then served as a sort of audition without Ray having expressly requested it. Apparently, executing *double tour en l'air* neatly to both sides, his technical trump, again did the trick. Beriozoff offered him a contract as a soloist – there were contracts for three principal male soloists and he would be number three. Beriozoff's choice, according to Ray, had to do with size: Hugo Delavalle was rather short while Donald Barclay was extremely tall and Ray would neatly fit into a middle category. It all happened so fast that Ray, somewhat overawed, could not react one way or the other. He had to think about it. The decision would mean severing himself from the company he had grown to love, and a cold plunge, an immersion, into a foreign culture and language. He did not speak a word of German.

American Ballet Theatre's tour continued into France and it was while the dancers were in Cannes that disaster struck. The twelve-ton

---

17   The American Ballet Theatre performances in Stuttgart took place on 21st and 22nd June 1958.

truck carrying all of the company's equipment for that current tour, on its way from Cannes to Geneva, went up in flames. 'Everything had been lost – the scenery, costumes, and props of twelve full productions; the orchestra music for four ballets, along with several musical instruments, thousands of ballet and pointe shoes, and the personal trunks of the dancers, with all their clothes and possessions. Total disaster.'[18] Help, however, readily came from various European Ballet companies: the Royal Ballet, the Royal Danish Ballet and the Paris Opera all sent costumes, pointe shoes, tutus, etc. The tour was able to continue and the important opening of the US Pavilion at the World Fair in Brussels was met. On that leg of this very tour, a time of great confusion, material loss, and uncertainty about the future, Ray had to come to a decision about Stuttgart. He had the contract in his pocket; it only had to be signed, but it was in German. Fortunately, one of Ballet Theatre's music conductors, Kenneth Schermerhorn, of German descent, could speak German and he translated the terms of the contract for Ray. He said, 'This contract is for a whole year. There are no lay-offs! And you have a paid six-week vacation. If you don't sign it, then you're being pretty stupid.' Ray signed.

Ray's farewell to American Ballet Theatre at that Met season must have proved a bittersweet experience. By this time he enjoyed the rank of a soloist and was seen in several roles that singled him out. Indeed, New York's foremost critic John Martin had, in a review, written, 'Ray Barra is a dancer to be watched.' The irony of it all was: when and where? Ray was on the verge of leaving the company and America. From the repertory of ballets performed at the Met that September, one of Ray's last new roles was in Birgit Cullberg's *Miss Julie*. Ray: 'I was cast as Anders, a peasant, but had practically no steps. I was under the table in the kitchen scene prior to Miss Julie's seduction by the valet, Jean. Birgit Cullberg said that I was something like a dog! Even if my contribution to the ballet was somewhat minor, it was a most exciting evening with Erik debuting in a role completely foreign to his *danseur noble* stature.' Birgit Cullberg had initially objected to Erik Bruhn in

---

18   Alex C. Ewing, *Bravura! Lucia Chase and the American Ballet Theatre*, The University Press of Florida, Gainscille FL 2009, p. 192

this role and thought him totally miscast. She maintained that Jean is no aristocrat – something that Bruhn's stage aura automatically suggested. Jean belongs to the lower social order, an uneducated servant; Erik could never suggest anything as servile as this. However Cullberg was lured into giving in to this casting as she was keen on having a ballet of hers performed in the States (*Miss Julie* would be her first ballet seen there). The other sensation of the production was Violette Verdy as Miss Julie. Nora Kaye had been originally cast in this role, but for some reason had qualms about it. She pulled out of the ballet, upon which Violette Verdy, quite new to the company, made her mark on the American dance scene. Balanchine saw her dance it, and soon enticed her away from Ballet Theatre into his own company.[19]

In Stuttgart the theatre season had already started when Ray arrived. He had been delayed because of his commitment to dance at the Met after the European tour of 1958. He flew to Stuttgart via Frankfurt and arrived there with the address of the theatre, Württembergisches Staatstheater, Oberer Schloßgarten, written on a piece of paper. Ray, of course, spoke not a word of German and, at that time in Germany, not many Germans spoke English. In the State of Baden-Württemberg most spoke German coloured by the Swabian dialect. Thus, even if one did understand a little German, there was always the problem of trying to recognise the Hochdeutsch through it. A taxi brought Ray to the theatre's stage door where the big *Schicksalsbrunnen* sculpture (Fountain of Destiny), as if it were an omen, loomed large in front of the entrance. It no longer occupies this position, having been relocated to the western side of the building when the street was widened. Eventually the stage door concierge got a message through to the ballet direction that the new dancer had arrived. Papa Beriozoff himself came to welcome him. He told him that the company was in rehearsal and asked if he would like to sit in on it; afterwards he would be attended to. Obviously he needed accommodation and was told to apply at a *pension* just up the hill. The good thing about the *pension* was that it was very close to the theatre,

---

19   Gruen, John, *Erik Bruhn, Danseur Noble*, The Viking Press, New York 1979, pp. 73–76

but it must have come as a shock to an American used to a certain standard in living facilities: both the bathroom and toilet were in the corridor.

'Stuttgart, in the late 1950s, was nothing like it is today,' Ray told me. 'For one thing it was still badly war-scarred. In the main shopping street, the *Königstrasse*, amidst derelict buildings, there were still improvised stalls selling their wares.' The main theatre or opera house had not been damaged by the bombings and it had survived more or less intact, though in 1956, two years before Ray's arrival, it had been modernised. A radical refurbishing to restore it to its original state was not undertaken until 1983–84, long after Ray had left. After the war, as this part of Southern Germany was in the American zone, the opera house had immediately been patched up and used by the US Armed Forces as a venue for entertaining their troops. The smaller *Schauspielhaus*, a theatre for spoken drama, was a bombed ruin and would later be completely rebuilt; it would also be used for performances of more intimate ballets.

Germany and Austria (the main German-speaking countries) are perhaps the only countries in the world where one cultural umbrella organisation, in this case the Württembergisches Staatstheater, supports three branches of theatre: an opera, a ballet, and the spoken theatre – not to mention the orchestra. It is called a *Drei-Sparten-Betrieb*, and as it is one organisation there is ready contact between each of the branches. Many members find this proximity most congenial, as if they belong to a large family of great artistic diversity. The opera house is situated in the *Schlossgarten*, the former Palace Park, with its main entrance facing the park so that in the interval spectators can freely wander into a gentle bucolic ambience should they wish. In Ray's eyes, just this park, in front of the theatre, seemed amazingly intact and beautifully well tended. The central pond surrounded by statues of the muses and by many rose beds impressed Ray immensely. Between rehearsals or waiting for the performance, he would often sit on a bench and enjoy the scented freshness of nature right in the middle of the city.

At that time, the Stuttgart Ballet was known as the Ballet of the Württemberg State Theatres and was directed by Nicholas (Papa) Beriozoff. Beriozoff, a lovable figure in the ballet world, was famous for his linguistic mumbo-jumbo. He was incapable of conducting a conversation in one language, mixing up all the ones he had come in contact with into a sort of kaleidoscopic blend. Born in Lithuania, he had danced with René Blum's Ballet de Monte Carlo and the Ballet Russe de Monte Carlo before serving as ballet master for various companies such as the Grand Ballet du Marquis de Cuevas and London's Festival Ballet. He began to specialise in mounting ballets of the nineteenth century (*La Esmeralda*, *Swan Lake* and *The Sleeping Beauty*, etc.) as well as Fokine ballets of the Diaghilev repertory. Later he ventured into more modern territory such as *Romeo and Juliet* (m. Prokofiev) and *Ondine* (m. Henze). As the father of Svetlana Beriosova, a ballerina of great beauty and noble manner engaged by the Royal Ballet Covent Garden, he had contact with that company.[20] What is easily overlooked, especially when the epithet 'the Stuttgart miracle' is applied to Cranko's tenure in that city, is that there was a flourishing ballet culture in Stuttgart under Beriozoff, and it was he who had prepared the ground for Cranko.

When Ray took his first class with the Stuttgart Company all eyes were on him. 'They were like daggers.' As an American and an ex-Ballet Theatre dancer he must have seemed a rather exotic newcomer, for most of the soloists were either European or from Eastern bloc countries with a sprinkling from South America, while most of the *corps de ballet* seems to have been made up of Germans. His first assignment was to dance in the opera *Aida*, for which purpose he and his partner, Gisela Erhardt, were allocated a minute rehearsal room in the depths of the building. 'She taught me the dance, which was rather complicated, with sign language because neither of us could speak the other's language. It was all rather like hieroglyphics.' But probably more intimidating was the performance without a stage rehearsal.

---

20   Horst Koegler, *The Concise Oxford Dictionary of Ballet*, Oxford University Press 2nd Edition, 1982

'During the Triumphant March celebrations we had to dance on a very small area before the amassed chorus who were seated on tiers all around. Everyone looked down on us, but what was unnerving was the way the chorus spoke or whispered privately amongst themselves while we were putting on the show. I was a nervous wreck! One of the chorus members muttered an audible, "*Was für ein hübscher Bursche*" (What a handsome fellow!), which Gisela translated for me in classical dance mime – a circular gesture about the face meaning "beautiful".

The first ballet Ray appeared in was Beriozoff's version of *The Nutcracker* in which he danced in the *Waltz of the Flowers*. But soon he was cast in principal roles, moving on to the *Nutcracker*'s *grand pas de deux*, in the traditional choreography by Ivanov. This was totally new ground for Ray and something that probably would not have been possible had he continued with Ballet Theatre. Ray has very warm memories of his time in Stuttgart and is immensely grateful to Papa Beriozoff for the way he helped to further his career. The German company, with a repertory that included traditional full-length ballets such as *Swan Lake*, *The Sleeping Beauty*, *The Nutcracker* and *Giselle*, presented a completely new dance world to Ray, quite unlike that of Ballet Theatre. Papa Beriozoff gave Ray the opportunity to dance the principal roles in all these ballets except *Giselle*, and sadly, when a possible chance for him to dance Albrecht arose, the guest ballerina, Yvette Chauviré, was given Hugo Delavalle as her partner. She was considered far too petite for Ray. Ray regrets the fact that he missed out on this chance, 'I never ever danced Albrecht; something I would love to have done because of my relationship with Erik.' He still remembers vividly how Erik discussed with him aspects of that role at the time of the latter's breakthrough performance. Thus, in Stuttgart, as the male protagonist in these classical ballets, he graduated to the *danseur noble* category where normally the most important requirement is an appealing appearance and noble manner – with enough technical prowess to do justice to the variation and coda. This he must have accomplished with suitable finesse, though his interpretative talents were not really tested.

Beriozoff's first production for Stuttgart in December 1957 had been the Petipa classic *The Sleeping Beauty*. This ballet generally requires, other than opulent production values, an ensemble schooled in the demanding classicism of the *danse d'école*. In a way it was a clear declaration of intent: a stylistic orientation toward tradition and the classic-academic dance. *Giselle*, *The Nutcracker* and *Swan Lake* followed, along with Fokine's *Ballets Russes* successes: *Les Sylphides*, *The Polovtsian Dances*, *Le Spectre de la Rose* and *Sheherazade*. The last-mentioned ballets seemed to indicate that Stuttgart might become the stronghold of an outmoded Ballet Russe model. However, Beriozoff understood that it would be all these works – but mainly the classics, which he cleverly glamorised with the appearances of foreign ballet stars – that would interest the post-war German audience.[21] His daughter Svetlana Beriosova appeared as a guest, as did the Paris Opera *étoile* Yvette Chauviré. In this way he managed to create an enthusiastic audience for classical dance in Stuttgart.

Apart from the classics, Beriozoff choreographed his own original ballets, but it would seem that he was more of a reproducer than a creator. He certainly had the taste and ability to present a high standard of ballet, but he is not considered an exceptionally gifted choreographer, and it would seem that he knew his own limitations. He did not baulk at inviting other choreographers to work with his company, one of whom, Werner Ulbrich, from Leipzig (then in East Germany, the DDR) created several short ballets and a full-length *Romeo and Juliet* in 1959. Werner Ulbrich's first offering was a programme consisting of three ballets in which Ray danced two: *Symphonie Classique* (m. Prokoviev), an exercise in pure classicism and the more exciting *Bolero* (m. Ravel), choreographed with a flamenco idiom. Ulbrich was himself a consummate flamenco dancer and passionate about this dance style. He must have been very good at it, as the DDR had allowed him out of the country in order to further his skills in Seville. Ray said the Stuttgart dancers in *Bolero* were hardly capable of managing rudimentary zapateado, for which reason

---

21   Horst Koegler, *Ballett in Stuttgart*, Chr. Belser Verlag, Stuttgart 1964, pp. 43–4

Ulbrich simplified the footwork and concentrated on the carriage of the body which he embellished with pseudo gipsy-like *port de bras*. Ray danced the lead; as the offspring of Spanish parents he probably felt he had the right temperament and the style in his blood. He enthused enormously about the collaboration with Ulbrich.

As Ray remembers it, Horst Koegler, a respected German critic, had persuaded Beriozoff to invite Ulbrich to do *Romeo and Juliet* in Stuttgart. Koegler had seen the ballet in Leipzig and praised it enormously. In the event, when Koegler saw *Romeo and Juliet* in Stuttgart, he gave it a slating. Nevertheless, Ray found the experience of working with Ulbrich very fulfilling. Ulbrich had virtually recreated the ballet anew, allowing Ray to introduce his own ideas about interpreting Romeo. For this ballet Ray partnered the first ballerina, Zenia Palley, who appeared as Juliet, rousing her usual partner Donald Barclay to a fury at being relegated to the role of Tybalt. Palley was difficult as, apart from her put-on prima ballerina allures, she had a foible for wearing a stole-like wrap or upper garment for rehearsing. This bit of clothing had large crocheted holes in it and hindered partnering. When Ray caught his fingers in it he was provoked to an expletive tantrum, 'If you're going to wear this f****** thing, then I'm leaving the rehearsal!' Ulbrich had to calm him down.

Ray was soon involved in dancing for television; he said he made hundreds of films. Kurt Jacob, the choreographer of these dance films for the Süddeutsche Rundfunk and the Bavaria Film Studios, organised his own little ad hoc group made up of dancers already employed, like Ray, elsewhere. As, at that time, there were not many ballet performances in the opera house, it was an exciting way to extend one's activities and earn additional income. Kurt Jacob had seen Ray in a ballet performance and the very next day, telephoned asking if he would like to join his group. Ray was all too happy to have this opportunity. In what must have been a daring and perhaps racy venture, he appeared as Stanley Kowalski in Jacob's treatment of the Tennessee Williams play *A Streetcar Named Desire*. This would be Ray's second of three encounters with the play as danced drama.

He had participated in Valerie Bettis's version for Ballet Theatre and would later serve as John Neumeier's assistant for his Stuttgart creation in 1983. In Jacob's television version, Maria Fris, who danced the female lead, Blanche, is most impressive at suggesting a neurotic and vulnerable woman whose fine airs provoke her rape. Ray's characterisation of Stanley Kowalski indicates just why choreographers found him interesting. He was unafraid to tackle brutal or unsympathetic characters – belying his real-life sunny-boy persona. This TV production, with its semi-realistic sets and jazz-inspired choreography, could easily head the list of ballet documentary material (pre Cranko) to be unearthed and reassessed.

The American influence can be seen in another of Jacob's films inspired by Gene Kelly musicals in which Ray danced the lead. Here Ray had the opportunity of dancing extended sequences in which there is a transition from mundane reality to choreographed dream. Kurt Jacob's 'dream ballet' consisted of three episodes in which Ray, waiting at a street corner, leaning against the wall, falls into a dream-like state. He awakes three times to encounter three disparate girl-types with whom he dances. The first episode has him dancing with a modern-day girl; in the second, with choreography reminiscent of a romantic ballet, the object of his interest is a sylph, while in the final sequence he and his partner dance a jazz ballet along the lines of *Frankie and Johnny*. The ballet was filmed at the Bavaria Studios in Munich.

Munich, again, was the scene of another of Ray's guest appearances: he was invited by the Bavarian State Opera Ballet to partner Dulce Anaya, a soloist he had regularly partnered in Stuttgart. Anaya had left Stuttgart to take up an engagement in Munich and needed a partner for the *Nutcracker pas de deux* and, as they had already danced it together in Stuttgart, Ray was duly invited.[22] But other than having Ray come as a guest, Anaya's husband was especially keen that Ray join the Munich company and partner his wife. He said, 'Look how he manages Gisela Erhardt; she's a big girl and he throws her about as

---

22   Danced at a gala in the Prinzregententheater June 1960

if she were a feather. And he's butch!' Munich's ballet director Heinz Rosen made Ray an offer that was indeed enticing: a solo contract and a monthly salary of 1,000 *Deutsche Mark* – in Stuttgart he earned only 800! There were other considerations: the reopening of Munich's National Theatre was not far away. It would boast a much bigger and more attractive stage than Stuttgart's, and it was considered a more prestigious house. The city, too, had a more worldly metropolitan flair. The long and short of it was that on his return to Stuttgart, Ray told Professor Schäfer about the offer. Schäfer, the Intendant, without blinking matched it and so Ray stayed on Stuttgart – to both Stuttgart's and Ray's benefit. As would later become clear it was a fortunate decision to remain in Stuttgart: John Cranko's advent was just around the corner; it would bring the last stage of Ray's dancing career to a glorious culmination.

9

Stuttgart: Introducing John Cranko

Ray's decision to settle in Stuttgart was amazingly serendipitous: he was in the right place at the right time. By chance he had alighted upon a city that, in the immediate post-war years, was doing itself proud. Under the guidance of Professor Walter Erich Schäfer, an exceptionally enlightened intendant (an artistic director-cum-manager), the Württembergisches Staatstheater had the reputation of being one of the best in Germany in all its branches: theatre, ballet, and especially opera. During Professor Schäfer's tenure of twenty-three years he engaged opera director greats such as Wieland Wagner and Günther Rennert, as well as the *crème de la crème* of opera singers. This list includes most of the major stars of that era: Martha Mödl, Wolfgang Windgassen, Fritz Wunderlich, Anja Silja, as well as the conductors Vaclav Neuman and Carlos Kleiber. By inviting the South African-born John Cranko to become ballet director, Professor Schäfer was inadvertently responsible for making Stuttgart the top ballet address in the 1960s and 70s. So convinced was he of Cranko's suitability for the post, both as a creative force and renewer, that he courted Cranko almost immediately after the latter's first creation was seen in Germany. And he persuaded Beriozoff to quit the field. This decision was both prescient and far-reaching.

Beriozoff himself had, in fact, set the ball in motion when, according to Professor Schäfer, he asked to be relieved of the task of choreographing a third ballet programme that season, in November 1960.[23] Perhaps Beriozoff was artistically drained or did not feel like doing another major work so soon after his *Swan Lake* in April 1960. He suggested that a choreographer from the Royal Ballet could replace him; after all, he had very good connections to the English company and he would consult his daughter Svetlana. Svetlana Beriosova had, indeed, a recommendation: John Cranko. She had danced the leading role of Belle Rose in his *The Prince of the Pagodas*, which premiered at Covent Garden in 1957, and she said he was free. *The Prince of the Pagodas* had been Cranko's first attempt at a full-length ballet, which, in combination with a commissioned ballet score from Britain's major composer Benjamin Britten, was a prestigious event. As is often the case, the reception did not level with the hype. At its London premiere there was disappointment and criticism. The ballet was not deemed a success and did not remain in the Royal Ballet's repertory for very long; in the UK it was not performed after 1960. *The Prince of the Pagodas* had its defenders, among them Dame Ninette de Valois, who praised it highly and felt that with some revision it could have succeeded. She considered its loss one of the major tragedies of the English ballet scene.[24] The premiere of *The Prince of the Pagodas* in Stuttgart in November 1960, on the other hand, was a success. The German public proved more open in its appreciation of contemporary music, stage design and inventive dance movement than its English counterpart. This success opened the door on to a new era of dance in Stuttgart, perhaps in the whole of Germany. And on this momentous occasion Ray was involved in the production: he was cast as the male lead.

John Cranko's takeover as Stuttgart's ballet director was not without some soul-searching and embarrassment. According to John Percival in his biography of Cranko, the Stuttgart direction had been discreetly

---

23 Walter Erich Schäfer, *Bühne eines Lebens*, Deutsche Verlags-Anstalt GmbH, Stuttgart 1975, pp. 250–5

24 John Percival, *Theatre in my Blood, A Biography of John Cranko*, The Herbert Press, London 1983, p. 117

put in the picture that, indeed, Cranko might not be disinclined to accept a post in Germany.[25] If they knew about the gay scandal that had recently clouded his reputation in England or the fact that he was having a disappointing time artistically, it did not prevent Professor Schäfer from making an offer. Cranko was in some disgrace, widely reported and circulated in the English press, having been arrested and fined for 'importuning men for an immoral purpose.' He had been caught in a set-up situation in a public toilet. The virulent publicity was presumably a backlash against the Wolfenden report of 1957 which recommended changes in the law relating to homosexuality and prostitution, and the report's recommendation that homosexual behaviour between consenting adults in private should no longer be a criminal offence.[26] The much-publicised arrest and fine had not really affected the dance projects Cranko had with the Royal Ballet, but the failure of his second review, *New Cranks*, and the disaccord which arose between him and Benjamin Britten over his direction of the composer's opera *A Midsummer Night's Dream* at Aldeburgh, exacerbated his feeling of despondency.

Ray said that Professor Schäfer was 'mad about Cranko' and was adamant about having him for Stuttgart. When Professor Schäfer approached Cranko to make his offer, the latter was somewhat taken aback, for he was being offered the position of the person who had generously invited him to mount his ballet in Stuttgart in the first place. In addition Beriozoff was the father of his favourite ballerina, Svetlana Beriosova, who had recently danced the title role of his ballet *Antigone* as well as La Capricciosa in *The Lady and the Fool*. By this time Cranko and Ray were on friendly terms and Cranko sought him out to speak about the dilemma he was in. He bemoaned his difficult position, 'How can I do this to Papa Beriozoff? I do not wish to take away his job. And Svetlana is my favourite dancer.' Meanwhile Professor Schäfer had spoken to Papa Beriozoff who, showing great dignity, then decided to leave, feeling that 'there was no point in his

---

25   *Ibid.*, pp. 131–2
26   *Ibid.*, pp. 124–5

staying if he no longer had the confidence of the director.'[27] To Cranko, he said, 'Don't worry, I can always go to the Marquis de Cuevas.' On his return to London Cranko immediately went to Dame Ninette de Valois to discuss the situation. She was at first angry at the prospect of him leaving the Royal Ballet, but on reflection told him to accept the offer, 'then he would have two companies, because he would always be welcome back to the Royal Ballet.'[28] In mid-season, in January 1961, a little over ten weeks after the German premiere of *The Prince of the Pagodas*, John Cranko replaced Beriozoff as ballet director of the Württemberg State Theatres.

27   *Ibid.*, p. 131
28   *Ibid.*, p. 132

10

Stuttgart: Dancing for John Cranko (1961-1966)

John Cranko's ballet *The Prince of the Pagodas* introduced Ray to yet another major choreographer, and one who would soon peak creatively, simultaneously leading a provincial ballet company to international prominence. *The Prince of the Pagodas,* Cranko's first ballet in Stuttgart, had a libretto which he himself had devised: a 'mythological fairy tale,' made up of a patchwork of themes taken from well-known tales. Its two main sources were *King Lear* and *Beauty and the Beast* to which he added other familiar fairy-tale elements. Intent on having a commissioned score or at least contemporary music for his ballet, Cranko had asked Benjamin Britten if he knew of any composer suitable for the work. Britten himself showed enthusiasm for it and in this way became involved in the commission. (Cranko had met the composer when he choreographed the dances for Britten's 'Coronation' opera *Gloriana*). With Britten on board, *The Prince of the Pagodas* was upgraded to a major musical and theatrical event. It would seem that if Cranko had been able to revise the ballet by tightening the storyline as well as shortening it, it might have become a viable repertory work. This was not to be: Covent Garden's schedule allowed no time for revision and Britten, especially after his falling-out with Cranko over *A Midsummer Night's Dream* in Aldeburgh, would not permit any changes to be made to the score. Though successful at its German premiere, *The Prince of the Pagodas* fared no better in Germany than in the UK. It did not survive long in the repertory, though it did provide Ray with his first Cranko-choreographed principal role – he was the Prince of the ballet's title.

Ray said that Cranko made no adjustment to the choreography of *The Prince of the Pagodas* in consideration of the new dancers and their technical standards: 'None at all, he wanted it to be done exactly as at Covent Garden. The third act *pas de deux* was easy; it was a piece of cake. But I had a hard time with the variation which had been made for David Blair who could pirouette well. The many *double tours* were fine, that was my best step, but the solo was full of Blair's tricks. Cranko suggested I do two classes a day in order to improve my technique, but I said that wouldn't help at all, "John, I'm already thirty." But I did enjoy the first part of the ballet where I am a salamander. I had a spectacular entrance from the pagoda down a slide. And my salamander costume, instead of having the tail attached centrally to my butt, was attached to my left leg. I had to drag it about. This affected the choreography of the first two acts, which was great fun; it was a combination of contemporary and Cranko-ish comic movement. I had a ball.' The role of Belle Rose, the good sister, who is first repelled by the salamander but gains him as a prince after his transformation, was initially given to Zenia Palley, Stuttgart's then first ballerina. She spoilt her chances of dancing the role when she came to a rehearsal and remarked, 'It's not my style.' She expected Cranko to change the choreography to suit her. To which he retorted, 'I'm sorry, but it's my style, so perhaps we had better find another dancer for the part.'[29] He cast Micheline Faure, a young untried soloist, in the part. Helga Heinrich, who danced the evil sister Belle Épine, in Ray's opinion, was great.

For a less adventurous or creative director, taking over a ballet

---

29   *Ibid.*, p. 131

company in mid-season could have proved a disaster. Cranko, though, went at it as if he had nothing much to lose. In the UK, his career, which had got underway so well, was more or less on hold. Cranko was at that time considered the white hope of his generation and probable crown prince to Frederick Ashton. He had chalked up some very impressive successes, notably *Pineapple Poll*, *The Lady and the Fool* and *Antigone*, while his review *Cranks* made him known to a wider public. Princess Margaret's attendance at three performances of *Cranks* had further enhanced his reputation. But feeling artistically becalmed, he had pause to consider the idea of trying his luck in Germany. 'I'd lost confidence in myself. I atrophied from disuse... I went to Stuttgart in the end not out of artistic need, but to exist.'[30]

The German offer practically landed in his lap. The main task that lay before him was establishing a repertory of his own creations; otherwise, he had the unenviable task of busying himself with the running of a company. Having worked for one of the best ballet companies in Europe, the Sadler's Wells Ballet, or the Royal Ballet as it was renamed in 1956, he felt it imperative that the standard of dance in Stuttgart be raised. For this reason some dancers of the German company had been given notice and those who had been fired saw to it that there was an atmosphere of bad blood. According to a German trade union ruling of that time, notice had to be given within the first three months of the season and only to dancers who had not been engaged beyond a period of three years. Cranko also had to acclimatise himself to the theatre's ingrained administrative customs while coping with the setbacks or hindrances that are prevalent in any foreign country, even when one masters the language. Cranko rapidly learned German and learnt to speak it rather well. In this he was helped by his knowledge of Afrikaans, the language of the Boers, the Dutch-descended settlers in South Africa. It is related to Dutch and is of Indo-Germanic origins. According to Peter Wright, who served Cranko as ballet master for several seasons from July 1961, Ray was a boon-like help – 'the backbone of the company'. Ray, having

---

30   *Ibid.*, p. 132

already danced in Stuttgart for over two years before Cranko's arrival, had a good command of German. Optimistically outgoing, someone who would rather solve problems than cause them, he got on well with most in the house: the dancers, the singers, the technical staff and the administration. He was able to smooth the way in numerous awkward situations. On learning that Cranko disliked living in hotel accommodation, Ray generously offered his flat to him, moving out himself and staying with an actor friend. Fortunately, Cranko soon found something suitable: he moved into rooms in Herta Zippel's house in the Botnangerstrasse, acquiring the hospitality of a sort of ersatz family.

In March of 1961, as a first step in establishing his own repertory, Cranko arranged a makeshift ballet programme for performances in the *Liederhalle*. This concert hall, not ideally suitable for dance, was an alternative venue. Ray danced in three of the four ballets presented on that occasion: *Divertimento*, originally called *Pastorale*, a ballet from Cranko's Sadler's Wells days now revived in a more abstract way, and *Family Album*, a medley of danced sketches to the music Ashton had used for his ballet *Façade* (m. Walton) – each number representing a snapshot from a photo album. Ray's contribution was a tap dance. To fill out the programme Cranko had asked Kenneth MacMillan for one of his ballets and was given *Solitaire*. *Intermezzo* brought the programme to a close; it harked back to Cranko's George Shearing jazz-inspired ballet *Dancing*, choreographed in 1952. This time, the dancers, listening to the LP recording 'Latin American' by George Shearing and Peggy Lee, are inspired by the music to dance.

One of the most important concerns Cranko had to attend to was finding a ballerina. Right from the start, through working with Ray on *The Prince of the Pagodas*, Cranko had found within the company ranks a male principal with whom he felt comfortable; all he needed was a female counterpart. Zenia Palley was not at all to Cranko's taste, nor had she made any attempt to ingratiate herself in his favour in order to retain her position as first ballerina in the company. It was soon decided that she should leave at the end of the season and a search for a replacement began. For a creative choreographer such as Cranko it was imperative to find a sympathetic dancer endowed with adequate technique, able to do justice to the classics, the possessor of an appealing charisma but, essentially, someone who would inspire him. In a way, after his experience in choreographing for the ballerina Svetlana Beriosova, whom he adored, he needed a muse. Many a journey was made throughout Germany, even as far as Amsterdam, to find the right dancer. Ray, as his leading male principal, accompanied him, for Cranko needed his choice to be validated by seeing the would-be ballerina together with her future partner. The Brazilian-born Marcia Haydée, who would, as things turned out, become this ballerina and rise to the echelons of the immortal gild, had been engaged by the Grand Ballet du Marquis de Cuevas when Cranko came to choreograph *Cat's Cradle* for that company in 1958. She was a corps de ballet member and though she was not cast in the ballet, had watched rehearsals and was much taken by Cranko's warmth and friendly manner. When she heard he had become ballet director in Stuttgart, she telephoned and asked if there was any possibility of her joining the company. Cranko did not remember her, but told her to come quickly to audition. Haydée arrived, did class with the company and was offered a contract in the corps de ballet. Hardly settled into her new company, she was told to learn the third act *pas de deux* from *The Sleeping Beauty* with Ray, who was to partner her. The choice of *Sleeping Beauty* was presumably to test how Haydée could manage the pure classicism of Petipa and to see what she made of it. Ray and Marcia rehearsed for two days and were then requested to present the *pas de deux* on the main stage of the opera house. Seated in the auditorium, Cranko and Professor Schäfer watched. After Marcia and Ray had finished dancing, they were told to wait. They waited in the dressing room for an hour and a half. It had taken that long for Cranko to convince Professor Schäfer that this was his new ballerina. According to John Percival he threatened to leave Stuttgart if his wish was not complied with. Marcia thus became Cranko and Stuttgart's ballerina. She went on to have a rich and fulfilling career even in the years after Cranko's death.

In Cranko's first full season, 1961–2, he finally presented a completely new creation written for the Stuttgart ensemble. This was *Katalyse* or *The Catalyst* to Schostakovitch's *Concerto for Piano, Trumpet and String Orchestra*, a ballet with two groups of dancers representing two contrasting movement idioms. The group costumed in black, led by Ray and Myrtha Morena, dance in a modern style, while the white group, led by Hugo Delavalle and his partner Micheline Faure, represent classical dance. Gary Burne, ex-Royal Ballet and a newcomer to the company, costumed in a red tricot as the catalyst, brings about a transformation of the two groups. Having covered all the dancers under a big blue cloth, he whisks it away to reveal all costumed in the same colour: blue.

This ballet certainly pleased the German audience much more than *The Lady and the Fool* or *Antigone*, which were on the same programme. The former had already been revised when it transferred from Sadler's Wells to Covent Garden where it had notched up a respectable success. But in Germany, Charles Mackerras's potpourri of music from Verdi's lesser-known operas came in for criticism and the ballet was found trivial. Ray danced the role of one of the clowns, Moondog, originally created for Kenneth MacMillan, who wins the love of La Capricciosa. As Cranko couldn't make up his mind how to end the ballet – it had already gone through a number of changes and revisions with each revival, mainly at Dame Ninette's behest – the choice was left to Ray, Marcia Haydée and Graeme Anderson, who danced the other clown, Bootface. When Dame Ninette interfered with the ending as performed when the ballet transferred to Covent Garden, it was, in Ray's opinion, because she wished to avoid any implication of a sexual connotation in the friendship between the two clowns. In the discussions, Graeme Anderson was adamant that he should be part of the picture at the end, irrespective of just what the bond between the two clowns was, and felt that it should end with them all together. They decided that Moondog and La Capricciosa would snuggle up to each other on a park bench while Bootface curled up under it. It was a poetic conclusion, underlying the ballerina's renunciation of transitory glamour and the developing love between them all.

Antigone, the third ballet of that programme, was much stronger meat. It was one of Cranko's last creations for the Royal Ballet in 1959 to a commissioned score by Mikis Theodorakis. Ray was given the role of Haemon, Antigone's lover, Hugo Delavalle that of Antigone's brother Polynices, while Gary Burne reassumed his original role, the other brother, Eteocles. Marcia's debut as principal in Stuttgart was twofold in this programme: she danced La Capricciosa in *The Lady and the Fool* and the title role in *Antigone* – the latter originally created by Svetlana Beriosova, a non-pointe, soft-shoe role.

When Cranko moved to more satisfactory accommodation at 73B Neue Weinsteige in Stuttgart, on the hill on the other side of town, the house was soon dubbed Cranko's Castle. But it became better known as Crystal Palace. Naming Cranko's home Crystal Palace was, of course, an insider joke and a gay one at that. During the 1960s a sort of code language based on women's names had wide currency in male gay circles. Its propagation and popularity with members of the Stuttgart company seems to have been due to Gary Burne who introduced it there. A female name such as 'Hilda' is thus used to describe a person or situation as ugly, unappealing or unpleasant, based on the alliterative aspect of Hilda = hideous = horrible. Monica = monthly, referred to women's menstrual period, but could equally be attached to Hilda, as well as Riva = revolting, to express a heightened abhorrence or calamity as in Hilda–Monica–Riva.[31] All men, gay or not, belonging to a certain group of gay-orientated friends or colleagues, in this case a ballet company, had female names. Crystal Palace was derived from Cranko's queer or gay name, Crystal, and alluded to the Victorian construction of iron and glass, originally built in Hyde Park for the great Exhibition of 1851. Re-erected at Sydenham, near London,

---

31 Jann Perry, *Different Drummer, The Life of Kenneth MacMillan*, Faber & Faber Ltd, London 2009, p. 271

it burnt down in 1936. The alliteration Crystal–Cranko is obvious, though the wittier aspect of calling Cranko 'Crystal' comes from its connotation with a gay cult movie, *The Women*. In this Hollywood film of 1939, directed by George Cukor and based on the play by Clare Booth Luce, the conceit is that only women take part in the story. It deals with the tribulations of society women regarding marriage and infidelity. Crystal Allen, played by Joan Crawford, is the arch-bitch who is having an affair with the lead, Norma Shearer's husband Stephen Haines – who, needless to say, never makes an appearance in the film.

Ray was also given a film star's name: he was known as Theda. In fact he was already called Theda while in America dancing for Ballet Theatre. Apparent to all movie lovers, the connection here is the similarity of his stage name to that of the famous silent film star Theda Bara. Theda Bara (supposedly an anagram of Arab death), born Theodosia Goodman in Cincinnati, was the original vamp – a term derived from her role in a film based on Kipling's *The Vampire*. Shortened, this became the label for all female movie characters of a seductive and destructive inclination. Ray was certainly no vamp, but an outwardly friendly, perhaps initially naïve American guy. Peter Wright's name was Renee (again alliteration) while Kenneth MacMillan was called Zelda, derived from the title of a pulp fiction novel called *Zelda, Goddess of Love, Wanted by Ten Men, Dead* (not really that witty). Marcia Haydée was honoured with the butch name of Hank.

Cranko's production of *Coppélia* in June 1962 proved a rather unimaginative choice for a prolific young choreographer and was duly berated by the German press. Based on Petipa's version, the only interesting change made in the ballet was the introduction of a new character, Swanhilda's mother, who gets paired off with Dr Coppelius at the end. Horst Koegler, in his book *Ballett in Stuttgart*, marvelled that Cranko managed to pull himself out of that nadir. [32] Unless one is going to radically change *Coppélia*'s libretto and dance aesthetic, as

---

32 Horst Koegler, *Ballett in Stuttgart*, Chr. Belser Verlag, Stuttgart 1964, p. 45

Maguy Marin did with her production in France in 1993, then this ballet remains a dusty, outmoded piece of theatre. It is all too redolent of Sadler's Wells in the 1950s or the two-act version that the Paris Opera used to perform.

Ray does not seem to share Horst Koegler's opinion of just how bad *Coppélia* was, perhaps because he was involved in the Stuttgart production in an unusual way. He appeared as Dr Coppelius. Ray was initially shocked at this casting – after all, his appeal was virile and youthful, and now he was asked to do a character role of an eccentric old inventor. But when Cranko told him, 'You are the only one who could possibly do this role convincingly,' he let himself be persuaded. As rehearsals got under way, Ray needed to have some sort of inspirational source that would help him. He asked Cranko, 'What did Helpmann do?' Robert Helpmann was one of Sadler's Wells's early male stars and had a reputation for overly exaggerated interpretations. He had been an acclaimed Dr Coppelius. So compelling was he as a dramatic performer, that whatever imperfections he had of physique and dance technique went unnoticed. He also made a very successful career for himself on the stage and in the movies (*Chitty Chitty Bang Bang*). With Helpmann as a guiding model, Ray felt free to go to town, 'Boy, did I carry on!'

After Ray and Erik Bruhn parted company in August 1958, the two friends kept in contact. Bruhn continued dancing both in the States and Europe, mainly in Copenhagen, from where it was easy for him, whenever he was free, to visit Ray. He did so with some regularity. However, with time, there was a natural easing in the intensity of their relationship and, in fact, Ray had fallen in love with an actor engaged in Stuttgart. With some remorse he confessed this to Bruhn. Bruhn, much more sophisticated and experienced in amatory matters, told Ray that he should just go ahead and indulge in his passion, after all, he himself had had many an adventure since their parting. Then he proceeded to list people he had been intimate with. The list included many of Ray's best friends from Ballet Theatre and brought about the amazed, incredulous reaction, 'How could you?' This was greatly naïve of Ray.

Of much greater import, an event which brought an end to their long-distance relationship, was Bruhn's encounter with Rudolf Nureyev. Ever since Nureyev's dramatic defection from the Russian Kirov Opera Ballet Company at Le Bourget airport, Paris, in June 1961, the amount of publicity he attracted was quite overwhelming. Not since Nijinsky had a male ballet dancer become the object of such insatiable fascination. The public and the press couldn't get enough of Rudi with his photogenic Tartar looks, the soaring panther-like dancing and his erotically charged androgyny. On and off the stage, his every move was news. Bruhn met Nureyev in Copenhagen through Maria Tallchief whom he was scheduled to partner in *Miss Julie* and *Don Quixote* with the Royal Danish Ballet. She had brought the exiled dancer with her. Nureyev had not yet seen Bruhn perform but he had heard of the great *dancer noble*. His teacher in Leningrad, Alexander Pushkin, had indicated that he could learn much from Bruhn. Unable to attend performances of the American Ballet Theatre on their Russian tour of 1961 – Nureyev had been sent to dance in East Berlin – he had arranged for a friend to film Bruhn, the male star of the company, in action from the wings. He pored over this film and photos, developing an obsession to make Bruhn's acquaintance. In Copenhagen he achieved his goal. There was no holding back; the two men were wildly attracted to one another. It was the beginning of a passionate though turbulent relationship.

Cranko ended the 1961–62 season in a celebratory manner with a Ballet Week Festival in which the full repertory of his creations seen in Stuttgart to date, together with Beriozoff's *Sleeping Beauty* (since amended), were performed. To glamorise the event he invited prominent guests and organised a gala at its conclusion. The Ballet Week opened with a triple bill of which Cranko had choreographed two ballets: *The Four Seasons* (m. Glazunov) and *Daphnis and Chloe* (m. Ravel).[33] On this occasion he permitted himself the luxury of casting the leads of *Daphnis and Chloe* with prominent guests. His original idea was to have Erik Bruhn as Daphnis and Carla Fracci as

---

33   The other ballet on that programme was Peter Wright's *The Great Peacock*.

Chloe. Unfortunately Fracci, La Scala's up-and-coming ballerina, was unavailable due to conflicting dates and Georgina Parkinson from the Royal Ballet appeared in her stead. *Daphnis* was well received and recouped the critical dressing-down *Coppélia* had provoked. It was also held to be an expressive vehicle for Erik Bruhn, sometimes considered a cold and impassive performer. Bruhn himself said that of all the ballets specifically created for him, *Daphnis and Chloe* was one of his favourites. He explained that Cranko sensed what technical capabilities – the tricks – he, Bruhn, possessed and was able to draw on that potential: 'he loosened me up and gave me a freedom that scared me. The fact was that, even I had difficulty in duplicating myself.'[34]

But Bruhn was disturbed by the fact that, at the very moment he had notched up this prestigious success and needing calm and concentration for the performances, the limelight he was enjoying had shifted. Rudolf Nureyev had arrived in Stuttgart. He was curious to see Cranko's new creation for Bruhn, a dancer whom he idolised and whose cultivated technique he emulated. In Stuttgart, the publicity hype was such that one couldn't get enough of it; here were the two most prominent and famous ballet dancers of that period together for the festival, and the rumour was that Bruhn and Nureyev were intimate friends. The brouhaha surrounding their taking class together, being seen together and what Bruhn sensed as a bad atmosphere of sniggering intrigue, got to him. He took to his bed, declaring that he was too sick to dance the third *Daphnis and Chloe* performance. As it was generally mooted that Bruhn was not really sick, Cranko prevailed upon Ray to go and see him in his sickroom and to try to persuade him to dance: 'After all, you were his lover.'[35] MacMillan, who had come to Stuttgart for the Ballet Week, as he was considering doing a ballet for the company, accompanied Ray. Ray's initial plea, 'Please don't do this to us!' was ignored, but it was MacMillan's tut–tutting, 'Now don't be a naughty boy!' that made Bruhn even more resistant to being cajoled into appearing in the ballet again. As soon as MacMillan and Ray had

---

34   John Gruen, *Erik Bruhn, Danseur Noble*, The Viking Press, New York 1979, p. 126
35   This is not the version as reported in John Percival's Cranko biography.

left, he got out of bed, into his car and left Germany. On being asked by Cranko if he would dance Daphnis, Ray replied despairingly, 'How long do you think it will take me to learn the role? And it's all tailored to Erik's qualities.' As no second cast had been prepared, the *Daphnis and Chloe* performance was therefore out of the question. Instead, an extra performance of *The Sleeping Beauty* – with three different Auroras, one for each act, presumably to upgrade the change – was substituted. *Daphnis and Chloe* was revived the next season for the tour to the Edinburgh Festival with another Dane dancing Daphnis: Henning Kronstam. At the end-of-season gala, as if to make up for Bruhn's absence, but profiting from Nureyev's presence, the new star was introduced. Nureyev made his – unplanned – Stuttgart debut. He had quickly learned Gsovky's *Grand Pas Classique* and appeared partnering Yvette Chauviré, who was to have danced it with Bruhn.

Ray was indeed in the picture about how things stood between Bruhn and Nureyev at this stage of their affair. Bruhn had confessed his difficulties to Ray and the fact that he was immensely upset that, whenever Nureyev turned up, he stole the limelight. It was a conflict of opposites, of two egos in the same profession. Bruhn, essentially a private, veiled and controlling personality, had met his opposite in Nureyev whose spontaneous, impetuous, volatile character was becoming a burdening challenge. Deep down, though, Bruhn must have felt and been aware of what was happening: he was being eclipsed by Nureyev. Ten years older, but, in fact, in his prime, Bruhn's 'date of expiry' seemed to loom large. How much time was left for him to sustain his title as the leading male dancer of his generation?

At the same gala, when Nureyev replaced Bruhn dancing the *Grand Pas Classique*, Ray was also part of the show. He danced the *Grand pas de deux* from *The Sleeping Beauty*, partnering Marcia Haydée. 'This was the beginning of my antipathy for Nureyev. We were sharing a dressing room and I had just finished my contribution to the gala. Certainly this role [the prince] did not show me off in any particularly advantageous way and my variation was quite simple, but there you are. Nureyev approached me and in his crude and tactless way said, 'How can *you* go out there and dance that shit? I saw you in Peter Wright's ballet and that suited you, but you shouldn't do this sort of thing.' Maybe he was right, but his manner was highly offensive. When he came to dance his variation in the gala, he ran out of space after a series of *coupé jetés en manège*, finishing too early near the wings. He put his hand against the proscenium arch to support himself while waiting for the music to end and gestured, 'Oh dear, the stage is much too small.'

Ray as Romeo in John Cranko's *Romeo and Juliet* (1962)

Ray's Father, Mother
Ramon Barallobre, Antonia Ramirez
Ray, Sister Josephine, Mother, Father, Darlene Becker

Darlene Becker, Ray,
Cheer-leaders, Ray left
Graduation – Darlene Becker, Ray

Bettie Merriweather, Ray's first dance teacher
Ray in his first solo role, The Sleazer, in *Nothing Doing Bar*
(San Francisco Ballet)

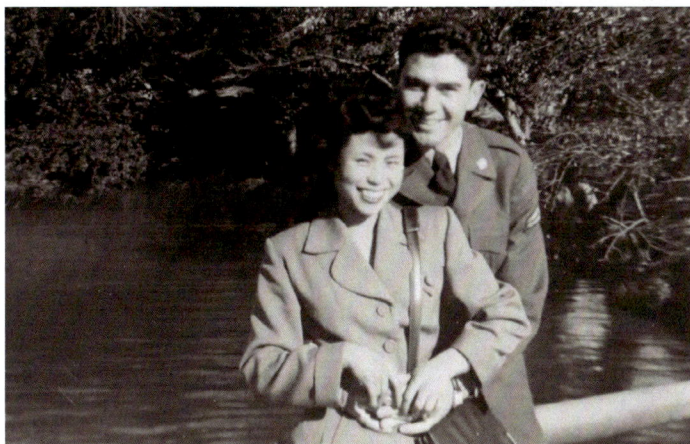

Ray in uniform
Ray, wartime Buddies
Ray, Japanese girlfriend Yoko

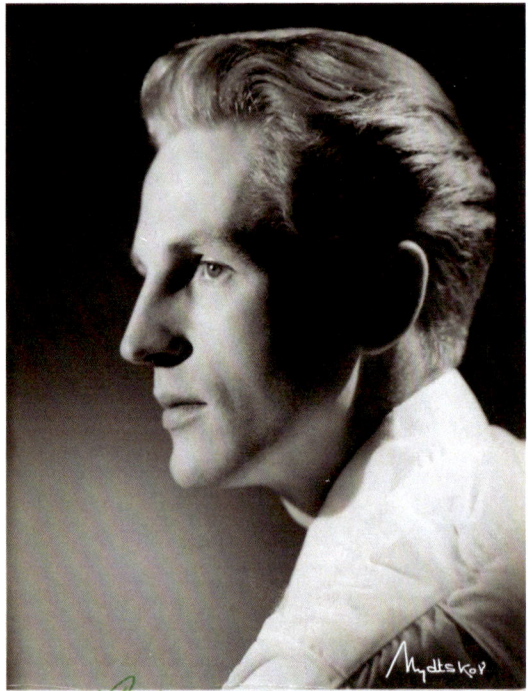

Ballet Theatre: *Fall River Legend, Graduation Ball* (Ray fainting)
Helen of Troy (Ray standing in Greek costume)
Ray and Johnny Ray
Erik Bruhn

Ray, Georgette Tsinguirides in *Catulli Carmina*
Ray, Helga Heinrich in *Shéhèrazade*
Ray, Micheline Faure in *Prince of the Pagodas*
Ray as Frantz in *Coppélia*
Ray, danseur noble

A Streetcar Named Desire (TV production)
Maria Fris as Blanche Du Bois, Ray as Stanley Kowalski
Reinhold Weise, Hugo Delavalle, Ray, Helmut Petick

Family Album: ensemble (Ray and John Cranko in the middle, right)

Ray and John Cranko at Anja Silja's birthday party
after a *Romeo and Juliet* rehearsal

John Cranko

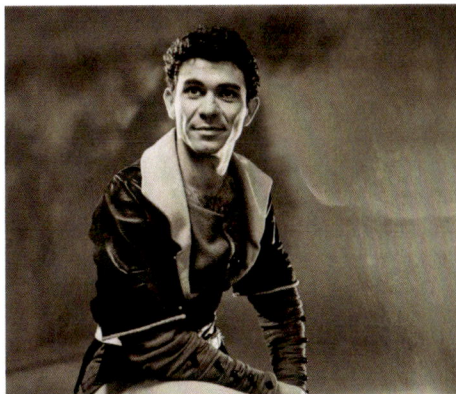

Romeo and Juliet: Ray as Romeo
Romeo and Juliet: Ray, Marcia Haydée
Romeo and Juliet: Ray, Lynn Seymour (right)
Swan Lake: Ray, Marcia Haydée
The Sleeping Beauty: Ray, Marcia Haydée rehearsing
Scènes de Ballet: Ray, Birgit Keil

© Serge Lido

© Hannes Kilian

Onegin: Ray as Eugene Onegin
Onegin: Ray, Marcia Haydée
Onegin: Ray, Marcia Haydée

Onegin: Duel scene: Egon Madsen, Ana Cardus, Marcia Haydée, Ray
Oldies reunion at Stuttgart Ballet's 50th anniversary 2011
Ray, Marcia Haydée, Ana Cardus, Egon Madsen

Ray, Kenneth Macmillan during stage rehearsal of *Las Hermanas*
John Cranko, Marcia Haydée, Peter Wright, Ray, Kenneth MacMillan
watching the youngest sister's suicide try-out in *Las Hermanas*

Las Hermanas: Ray, three of the five sisters, the mother
Las Hermanas: Ray as The Man
Las Hermanas: Ray, Marcia Haydée

Ray, Marcia Haydée, Kenneth MacMillan during creation of *Las Hermanas*

11

Cranko's breakthrough and iconic roles

The breakthrough that established Cranko's German reputation, bringing critical esteem and launching the Stuttgart Ballet as one of the most interesting and creatively vibrant companies in Germany, was his production of *Romeo and Juliet* in December 1962. Several years before his move to Germany, Cranko had already choreographed *Romeo and Juliet*; a joint venture of Milan's Teatro alla Scala and the Teatro La Fenice, Venice. That premiere took place in an open-air amphitheatre on one of the lagoon islands, S. Giorgio, with dancers from La Scala's ballet company. The Juliet of the production was the then twenty-one-year-old Carla Fracci. A few months later *Romeo and Juliet* was mounted at La Scala but did not survive long in the Italian repertory. This, then, was basically the ballet Cranko reproduced in Stuttgart. However, working with Ray as Romeo and Marcia Haydée as Juliet and able to work with his own dancers, attuned to his own style and dramatic flair, he radically revised it. Another contributing factor to *Romeo and Juliet*'s success was Cranko's discovery of Jürgen Rose as a stage designer. Rose was as yet untried in designing for ballet – *Romeo and Juliet* was his first ballet project. He would go on to become one of Germany's leading stage and costume designers, collaborating with Cranko on *Swan Lake*, *Firebird*, *Poème d'extase* and his masterpiece, *Onegin*.

The production, however, which set the *Romeo and Juliet* carousel in motion in the West, had been that of Leonid Lavrovsky – originally choreographed for the Kirov Ballet, Leningrad, in 1940 – and subsequently mounted for the Bolshoi, Moscow. It was among the ballets presented by the Bolshoi Ballet in London in 1956, on the occasion of the first tour undertaken by a Russian ballet company outside the Iron Curtain. Cranko had witnessed this historically important event and had been enormously impressed. The Bolshoi Ballet stunned Western audiences. In *Romeo and Juliet*, employing a weighty soviet realism, the Russians had presented a ballet of great dramatic intensity and passionate sweep. The full-blooded assumption of roles, which were individualised and danced with total commitment, was something quite new to English audiences. Galina Ulanova – despite being forty-six years old – aroused rapturous acclaim for her incandescent Juliet. *Romeo and Juliet* was not only a revelation to English audiences, but also to dancers and choreographers. Cranko certainly took note of its dramatic elements, many of which he later incorporated in his own version, such as giving more weight to the figure of Lady Capulet. Similarly, as in the Russian version, Cranko characterises her as a remote, unapproachable mother. But, at the end of Act II, giving vent to a hysterical and crazed lamentation over Tybalt's dead body – many versions raise the question of an illicit relationship between them – she brings the act to a cathartic conclusion.

Cranko cast Ruth Papendick, a tall, statuesque senior member of the company, as Lady Capulet and Hella Heim as Juliet's nurse. This was a felicitous decision to bring in mature dancers for character parts. Apart from being interesting personalities, their maturity and world experience enriched the productions. Hella Heim was already in her sixties when Cranko coaxed her out of retirement. He had seen her in the canteen where she often came to have lunch and meet with former colleagues. As Cranko's unofficial office was the canteen – he hardly, if ever, used the rooms he had been allocated, preferring the informality of a place where he could be easily approached – his curiosity was naturally aroused when he discovered she had been a dancer. Her CV went back to the war years: she had been engaged as a dancer by the Königliches Hoftheater – predecessor of the Württembergisches Staatstheater. Heim and Papendick became involved for some two decades in Cranko's ballets. Ray remembers Hella Heim wishing him *toi, toi, toi* (good luck) in the wings before he entered for the balcony *pas de deux*. 'She would pat me on my butt or, even more cheekily, on my private parts, to send me off. She was a wonderful woman and I adored her. She really made the nurse an important and rounded character. In the scene in the second act, after her floundering attempts to get Juliet's letter to me and I read it, I picked her up and whirled her around. This was my own invention.'

A much-admired feature of the Russian choreography, first seen on the Bolshoi's tour, was the use in the *pas de deux* of high lifts. This was an element that soon became a feature of ballets by Ashton, Cranko and MacMillan. Although criticised as being acrobatic, these lifts could extend, in choreographic terms, the dimension of the dramatic situation. For example, in *Romeo and Juliet*, the height and daring of the lifts matches the wonderment and exaltation of first love. In Cranko's *oeuvre* the *pas de deux* became the expressive high point. He was probably the choreographer most influenced by the Russians at that time. In his creative hands the *pas de deux* was refined to an expressive medium at the service of the narrative. Ray enthused over the *Romeo* rehearsals and the fact that he had a chance to be part of the process: 'It was the first time I'd worked with a choreographer who allowed his dancers to have such a collaborative say in the choreography. Cranko would tell us in a rather vague way what he imagined, "Lift her… and put her down here. The lift must have three levels: shoulder, back and then on the floor… perhaps starting with a *présage*." Then, while John continued working with other dancers, Marcia and I would go to a corner and try out various things until we arrived at something we thought he wanted.'[36] In the process of choreographing *pas de deux* it is usual for the choreographer to say in words or indicate with gesture what he envisages. It is seldom the case that he will get up and do the lifts himself. Often the experimental process will indicate the way, while many a mistake turns out to be totally apposite. Ray was an excellent partner and thus able to enter fully into the spirit of creation. One could say that his expertise and willingness to help were a decisive factor in the way the *pas de deux* turned out. But Ray does not wish to hog all the praise: 'Actually Marcia was fabulous in working out the lifts. We did them together. She could sense where the placing of her weight would be most beneficial, where a helping hand was necessary or what impetus or thrust she needed to give. She was wonderful!' For the 1964 annual gala, Cranko celebrated the high Russian lift with a *pas de deux* called *Hommage à Bolshoi*. To music by Glazunov, Ray and Marcia rapturously surged about the stage in a series of spectacular lifts. At Fonteyn's invitation they repeated this *pas de deux* at her annual gala in aid of the Royal Academy of Dancing in London.

The creation of *Romeo and Juliet* happened fast and with great spontaneity. Ray: 'We all helped in the creation. I won't go as far as saying that we made up the steps, he [Cranko] did that, but we were involved in the creative process. For example, Romeo's last entrance: there was a technical rehearsal and as I didn't have anything to do at that moment, I decided to look in and see how things were going. They were lighting the scene in the tomb. Cranko immediately came on stage to show me where I should enter from. He explained how I discover Juliet lying in the crypt, "You run in over this bridge, see her and then go down the steps to behind the wings and enter." But I suggested just clambering down from the bridge without leaving the stage. I then showed him how I would do it. He was pleased, "Who do you think you are, Errol Flynn?" This was kept in the ballet. Yes,

36 Interview in *John Cranko, Der Choreograph und seine Arbeit in München*, Bayerisches Staatsballett 2008, p. 30–2 (my translation).

that was my interpretation of the role, youthful and dashing.'[37] Asked if there had been any unpleasant or critical situations during the rehearsals, Ray answered: 'The whole rehearsal time was wonderful, right up to the general rehearsal. Afterwards, Cranko came to me and in a rather brutal way told me it was just terrible, appallingly bad. "You have to read Shakespeare again, tonight!" It was such a shock; I haven't forgotten it to this very day. I felt just God-awful or as they say in German *beschissen*... I was empty. And then in desperation I thought of Erik Bruhn. He had just danced Ashton's *Romeo* in Copenhagen, while I was studying with the famous pedagogue Vera Volkova. We had spoken a lot about Romeo. Erik maintained that Romeo is not a dreamer; he is virile and wild; he is on the lookout for one thing: sex! And then I pored over the play.'[38]

The success of Cranko's *Romeo and Juliet* derived from a providential constellation of contributory elements: apart from the choreography, the shaping of the dramatic structure of the ballet, the decor and costumes by Jürgen Rose, there were the dancers and their strong identification with their roles. Horst Koegler wrote: 'On this evening [the premiere], Stuttgart discovered its prima ballerina: Marcia Haydée, who has been seen variously in different roles, but who here, partnered by Ray Barra, a passionate, virile Romeo, reveals a refined and cultivated art of dance.'[39] The Stuttgart public had already seen Ray as Romeo in Werner Ulbrich's version, but Marcia Haydée was definitely the revelation of the production. She would develop into one of the great dramatic ballerinas of the time.

The next full-length ballet Cranko produced was *Swan Lake* where he retained Lev Ivanov's traditional second act but reworked the rest in a style reminiscent of Petipa. The big change he introduced was the ending of the fourth act, which he treated tragically, maintaining that Tchaikovsky had intended it this way. Here Siegfried, vainly trying to reach Odette, drowns in a great flood conjured up by von Rothbart

---

37 *Ibid.*, p. 30–2
38 *Ibid.*, p. 30–2
39 Horst Koegler, *Ballett in Stuttgart*, Chr. Belser Verlag, Stuttgart 1964, p. 47 (my translation)

while Odette is once more transformed into a swan. Jürgen Rose, again the designer, used bands of blue silk stretched across the stage, waved turbulently to suggest the flooding of the waters.[40] Though not cast in the premiere, Ray and Marcia Haydée danced the leading roles in the second performance. Cranko had divided up the creation of his *Swan Lake* between two casts: he set the choreography for the first scene and the two white swan scenes on Marcia Haydée and Ray while Anita Cardus and Egon Madsen were given the Black Swan *pas de deux*. Possibly the more interesting choreography was in the final act as it was completely new. Ray was not that enthusiastic about Cranko's *Swan Lake*; the role of Prince Siegfried offered no more than a return to being a *danseur noble*.

As Cranko's reputation grew, so did invitations for his works from other companies. Gert Reinholm, former German star dancer and director of the Ballet of the Deutsche Oper, West Berlin, requested a new ballet. Cranko decided on Stravinsky's *Firebird* with the proviso that he choreograph it with his Stuttgart soloists. Reinholm had probably wished to dance the leading male role, Ivan Tsarevich, himself – a role originally created by Fokine that has hardly any dancing. When it became clear that some other dancer would create the part, Reinholm desisted. Ray was thus cast as Prince Ivan who captures the Firebird, but releases it in return for a promise to return should he need help. Ray: 'Cranko told me I should behave quite normally, not really like a prince, more like a cowboy. My entrance into the enchanted garden was by climbing over the wall, and when the Tsarevna loses her golden apple, I retrieve it off stage and enter throwing it up and catching it in a nonchalant way.' Cranko adhered to Fokine's libretto and many of the dance sequences, but made the *pas de deux* between the Bird and Ivan more complex. 'Marcia Haydée danced the Firebird and we had great fun together.' The *pas de deux* at the beginning of the ballet was thus first prepared in Stuttgart, after which the whole ballet was completed with dancers from the Deutsche Oper ballet in Berlin.

---

40 Nureyev employed a similar ending for his production of *Swan Lake* for the Vienna State Opera (1964).

When it was mounted in Stuttgart, Birgit Keil, at the beginning of her career, danced the Tsarevna.

What did it feel like living in Germany? Ray: 'Well, I just loved it. Here I was, settled – not living out of a suitcase – earning a good salary, working with a wonderful choreographer and enjoying fame as the principal male soloist. Stuttgart is not a large city, so when I went shopping, people recognised me and it really bucked me up.' And in Ray's opinion, 'The whole theatre was like a family, at least in the early years, I think because of the way the three departments of the theatre had easy contact with each other. We knew who was who: the singers, the actors, the dancers. We were aware of what the others were doing. I have never experienced anything like that in my life.' John Percival wrote in his Cranko biography that 'John Cranko always wanted to make friends of his collaborators and collaborators of his friends.'[41] This seems to have been his credo in Stuttgart, too, though on a much larger scale than in England. There can be no denying the fact that the art of making ballets is a highly collaborative one. In the act of choreographic creation a choreographer cannot do without the physical presence of the dancer: at its best it is a highly symbiotic collaboration. A good choreographer will lead a dancer to open himself to a realm beyond what he imagines to be his own limitations.

In Stuttgart, as many of the company's dancers were foreign, the small-town feel of the town, coloured by the local Swabian work ethic of diligent citizenship, naturally led to a bonding outside the working hours. For this reason, dancers were all too ready to join Cranko's circle. Any and everyone was welcome, especially people connected with the arts. It was an informal assemblage of people eager for the convivial give and take of ideas and just having fun. Cranko didn't like the fact that after rehearsals everyone would disappear, in fact, he didn't really want a separation of work and the private sphere. Thus going out to eat and drink together after work – as a family – was something to be celebrated. One of Cranko's favourite restaurants was

41 John Percival, *Theatre in my Blood, A Biography of John Cranko*, The Herbert Press, London 1983, p. 133

Kaliergos, run by Nico who came from Paros – Cranko had happy memories of holidaying in Greece and loved the shifting bar measures of Greek music. On weekends there was live Greek music and it was practically impossible for the dancers not to join in dancing to its tricky, infectious rhythms. Another place for after-work gatherings, a favourite watering hole catering to theatre folk and the gay scene, was a bar called Die Bassgeige. Right next door was a studio for ballroom dancing and with Cranko leading the way the place was taken over by the dancers. Ray: 'There was Cranko carrying on no end with the cha-cha-cha, the mumbo and the latest dance crazes of that time. It was loads of fun. Later this sort of place would be called a discothèque and we would dance the twist. Cranko was rather good at these dances; nicely making up for his being a terrible classical ballet dancer.'

Cranko delighted in being the centre of all of this. However, there was a negative aspect to all this rollicking familiarity and one had to be careful not to end up in his company when he had gone beyond the point of no return in alcohol consumption. Cranko was basically lonely. He had no partner; he indulged increasingly in too much drink and indiscriminate sexual encounters. It is surprising that in spite of these excesses he was able to function in the ballet studio, but so he did. According to Ray, 'During working hours, Cranko was often "high" – not completely under the influence of too much alcohol, but in a sort of haze.' Ray certainly participated and enjoyed being part of all this carousing, but being an older, more mature person than most dancers – after all he had served in the American Army in Japan and danced with Ballet Theatre – he was apt to draw the line at going too far. Cranko, once, probably having had a glass too many, accused him of being boringly bourgeois. On the other hand, however much Cranko's private excesses were to be deplored, most of those involved with the Stuttgart Ballet while Cranko was still alive are effusive in paying tribute to what he did for their careers and for his inspirational leadership.

Peter Wright, almost the same age as Cranko and one of his early ballet masters, credits him for giving him the chance to further his ambitions as a choreographer.[42] Wright's productions of *Giselle* and *The Sleeping Beauty* are still performed worldwide and when the Birmingham Royal Ballet was set up in 1990, he was appointed artistic director. He said his career would not have taken the road it did without Cranko's lead. Marcia Haydée, too, profited greatly from her collaboration with Cranko. As his muse and for her creation of the principal leads in several of his perennial ballet successes, she achieved international ballerina status. Later, she herself took over the direction of the company. Ray was equally affirmative when he said, 'Cranko made me! Without him I would never have gone that far with my dancing career; he really pushed me. My technique, if you were to compare it with what most dancers can do nowadays, was not that great. I had my special steps. But I was a great partner and that was what, in a way, was compensatory, and for Cranko's dramatic ballets, an essential element. The drama really happens in his *pas de deux*. And then he encouraged me to choreograph. I did about three ballets for the Noverre Society,[43] and would you believe it, Cranko had the cheek to steal one of my lifts? For my fourth ballet, John Neumeier was going to do the costumes, but that one never happened due to my injury.'

It perhaps needs to be explained why, in spite of what Ray claims to have been his technical limitations, he was the first choice as the leading protagonist of many of Cranko's and the MacMillan ballets created in Stuttgart. Horst Koegler, Germany's one-time foremost dance critic, wrote: 'In his narrative ballets, Cranko redefined the male hero by making him the centre of the drama in his *Swan Lake*, *Romeo and Juliet* and *Firebird*. It was a revolutionary act made possible by the presence and commitment of Ray Barra. His example shows most clearly how Cranko did not create roles in his ballets for a fictitious ideal cast, but precisely for the dancers who were at his disposal. Barra

---

42   Wright, Peter with Paul Arrowsmith, *Wrights & Wrongs, My Life in Dance*, Oberon Books Ltd., London 2016

43   Noverre Gesellschaft: A society founded in 1958 to promote the Stuttgart Ballet. Many aspiring young choreographers made their early ballets for this society. A list includes John Neumeier, Jiri Kilian, Bill Forsythe, Uwe Scholtz etc.

is actually no *danseur noble*, but in reality a character dancer – where it must be emphasised the usual nomenclature does not apply. He is the possessor of a somewhat raw talent which, however, in recent years he has certainly polished. He does not fashion abstract figures but creates sharply defined roles, erect and manly characters – individuals of warm human breath. He is the born cavalier, the most obliging and skilful partner a ballerina could wish for.' [44]

Ray is a gregarious person, up to a point. A friendlier, more open and generous person would be hard to find, but as he matured his needs focussed on having a definite private sphere quite separate from the workplace. He is basically a person who enjoys a stable relationship with a single partner and being faithful to that person. Accordingly, when that person turned up, he was all too ready to nurture a private twosome-ness outside the theatre. From the moment he met Maximo Barra, who became his partner for more than fifty years, he became that private person. 'Maximo changed my life; after we got together there was no more of this endless partying.' Ray explained that, in his case, the fact that Maximo was Spanish was conducive to the relationship's longevity, 'I immediately felt at home with him, his temperament, the way we both had Spanish roots.'

---

44 Koegler, Horst, *Ballett in Stuttgart*, Chr. Belser Verlag, Stuttgart 1964, p. 53 (my translation).

12

Maximo Barra: finding a soulmate

Maximo Barra Molina was born in Malilla, Morocco, on 12th October 1941 to Spanish parents. Malilla is one of the two enclaves on the Moroccan coast that belong to Spain, but when Maximo was young this area had not been demarcated nor was there the problem of refugees and immigrants wanting to enter the EU. And in spite of being situated in North Africa, Malilla had a most cosmopolitan atmosphere. Maximo was an athletic youth, an excellent swimmer and diver – the winner of many prizes. Apart from his sporting skills and growing up in a North African country, nothing could indicate that dance, and specifically ballet, would become his passion and métier. By chance he came into possession of a book on ballet by Serge Lifar, called *Traité de la Danse Académique*, which explained the principles of ballet and had sketches of the various basic positions. This book fascinated him, presenting a glimpse of a marvellous theatrical world of which he had had no experience. He began to imitate the balletic poses of the illustrations and to develop an obsession that maybe he, too, could become a ballet dancer. The path to actually joining that profession presented itself without much effort.

Maximo was blessed with amazing serendipity. In a chance encounter he met an American couple from Seattle, May and Frank

Williams, who were visiting Malilla. They had come to Morocco to meet up with Don, one of their seven sons, who was working on a cruise liner as an entertainer. May and Frank were much taken by Maximo whom they met in a bar. As he spoke English he proved very helpful to them as a translator and guide. Maximo had been taking English lessons with a former French legionnaire who must have mastered the language sufficiently well to teach it. And it was he who had bought the Serge Lifar book on ballet in France and given it to Maximo as a gift. When Maximo spoke of his dream of learning ballet the couple pricked up their ears as in their home town, Seattle, there was a prestigious school of ballet: the Cornish School. It was considered one of the most distinguished in the American Northwest and the founder, Mary Ann Wells, was a highly respected teacher – Robert Joffrey and Gerald Arpino were two of her pupils. Without much ado, the American couple made arrangements for Maximo to come to Seattle to study at the Cornish School. He could stay with them and they would vouch for him – at the time he was still a minor. And so it happened; Maximo stayed two years studying ballet in Seattle, all the while making rapid progress. During the vacations he was able to gain further experience by performing in summer stock (semi-professional entertainment during the summer vacation). He danced in many musicals, but probably the most interesting and demanding was *The King and I* with original choreography by Jerome Robbins. He had the male lead in *The Small House of Uncle Thomas,* which is something like a mini ballet. Maximo said, 'It was the most difficult choreography I had ever danced.' A not surprising comment for someone who had only recently taken up ballet lessons! Wanting to experience the big time and having scraped together enough money, Maximo and two young actor student friends set off by car for New York. They camped along the way, avoiding motels or rooms in order to save money. Just outside New York they abandoned the car and took the subway to Manhattan. There Maximo and one of the friends found an inexpensive room to rent. Maximo started on a round of taking open ballet classes and, as most teachers found him very gifted and charming, he was allowed to take them for free. Once, while taking class in Ballet Theatre's studios, he saw a framed portrait of Ray hanging on the wall. This was one of many publicity photographs of the dancers. The name of the handsome man was Ray Barra. *Curious*, he thought, *there is a dancer in Ballet Theatre with my name, I wonder who he is?*

Maximo also got to know a teacher called Bill Griffith who was very popular at that time and who became a sort of guru-like mentor. But Maximo had to earn money and, in continuation of his lucky streak, he was able to do so legally. By chance he had acquired a social security card in Seattle, probably through working in the summer stock productions. He got work as a dancer in a nightclub in Philadelphia called The Latin Casino, a chic venue offering entertainment by established big names such as Marlene Dietrich, Harry Belafonte, and Sammy Davis Jr. But, of course, work went on into the wee hours of the morning and he was obliged to sleep most of the day. Even though this show was due to transfer to Las Vegas where he would have earned big money, he had had enough of an enervating nocturnal existence. He was keen to return to the ballet studio; in fact his goal was to work in Europe where he could have the chance of dancing with a proper ballet company. After a month's work he had saved enough money, and he and Bill Griffith, who had more or less adopted him, sailed for Barcelona where his family was now living. Moving on to Paris he took class and, again, through Bill Griffith, met the former Paris Opera *étoile* Claire Motte, and the choreographer Pierre LaCotte. They advised him to audition with Janine Charrat who was about to start a company at the Geneva Opera House. Charrat, ballerina and choreographer, was something of an institution in France, having run several of her own companies, but she had recently suffered severe bodily burns that forced her to relinquish work for almost a year. Maximo auditioned successfully for Charrat and started his engagement in Geneva in 1962. Geneva, however, was not to be for long.

Again, in another amazing encounter, Maximo's balletic journey entered yet another incredible stage. In a bar in Geneva he met a Cuban involved in high finance who took a shine to him. He was called Pedro. Pedro was curious about Maximo's real aim in life, his ideals. When Maximo told him that he would really like to dance with the Royal Ballet in England, Pedro, using his connections, acquired a bursary from the Ford Foundation for him to study at the Royal Ballet School. This might provide entry to the company. But while studying at the ballet school Maximo came to realise that, as a foreigner, he was unlikely to get an engagement with the company. In any case his enthusiasm for the Royal Ballet had evaporated. But there was no time for despondency as four possible dance contracts presented themselves: (1) with a company Peter Wright was starting in Scotland, (2) with an Irish Ballet company, (3) with the Munich Opera house under the direction of Heinz Rosen and (4) with the Stuttgart Ballet. Consulting GBL Wilson, member of Royal Academy of Dance, contributor to the *Dancing Times* and various other publications and author of *Dictionary of Ballet*, who seemed to know everyone in the ballet world, he was told, 'Go to Cranko in Stuttgart, young man.'

Maximo started work in Stuttgart at the beginning of the 1964–65 season. As there was already one Barra in the Stuttgart company, and a principal at that, Maximo was not allowed to use his own name. So he took his mother's name and was listed as Maximo Molina. His Spanish lover, Luis, also a dancer whom he had met in Paris, joined him. Ray said, 'I liked Maximo immediately, he was exactly the type of person I was attracted to. He was so handsome, I couldn't help myself.' The fact that Maximo was in a relationship did not daunt Ray one bit; he found him irresistible and started a play of blatant flirtation to attract him. Maximo, however, was not to be prised out of his friendship. Not yet. All of a sudden the situation took on a Feydeauesque turn when an English ballet teacher called BD turned up. While in London, Maximo had attended her ballet school. He had taken classes and impressed her so much that she mounted her own version of *Apollo* especially for him. Not only was his persona and dancing impressive, but she too found him adorable. Unaware of his attachment to Luis, she had followed him to Stuttgart and was prepared to pounce. To thwart her advances, David Sutherland, who later became a close friend, loaned out his girlfriend to act as an alibi, giving the impression that Maximo was already madly involved with someone. B.D. was forced to retreat. And Ray continued plying glances of a come-hither sort.

13

Re-enter Kenneth MacMillan

Cranko was not the only choreographer, during these Stuttgart years, to exploit Ray's talents. Kenneth MacMillan, the Scots-born choreographer of the Royal Ballet, created two ballets on the Stuttgart company while Ray danced there: *Las Hermanas* (1963) and *Das Lied von der Erde* (1965). In both of these he cast Ray in the male lead. These ballets offered roles of outstanding quality that have stood the test of time, while *Das Lied von der Erde* has attained masterpiece status. When Cranko left the UK for Germany, MacMillan automatically assumed the position vacated, becoming, de facto, the next in line to succeed Ashton. Although Stuttgart would never become anything remotely like an annex of the Royal Ballet, Cranko maintained strong ties with the English company. It was natural for him to avail himself of guests from the Royal Ballet for appearances in Germany, or to invite English choreographers to work with his company. MacMillan and Cranko had been close colleagues both at Sadler's Wells and the Royal Opera House; they were almost the same age, only two years apart, and if not exactly the greatest of friends, got on well.

During the summer of 1952 Cranko assembled a group of dancers, among whom were Peter Wright, his future wife Sonya Hana and Kenneth MacMillan, for an improvised season of short ballets at Henley-on-Thames. John Piper, the painter and stage designer who lived nearby, was intent on restoring the semi-derelict Kenton Theatre of the town to its former glory, and in order to raise funds and interest for this purpose had asked Cranko for help. In the most admired ballet of that season, *Dancing*, MacMillan had been given the lead. Cranko, aware of MacMillan's nervousness when performing – a severe case of stage fright that probably would have hindered his career as a dancer – felt that MacMillan might have a talent for choreography. He encouraged him discreetly in this direction. Often, while choreographing, he would start a sequence of steps and ask MacMillan to continue.[45] As MacMillan's career as a choreographer got under way, it was notable that the friendship seemed devoid of crass rivalry. Each had different strengths in ballet making, but on the whole, Cranko was considered to have had a better grasp of stagecraft – most ballets having an intrinsic theatricality – though he was quite envious of MacMillan's ability to create steps (unusual and inventive ones) at the drop of a hat.

Having already acquired two MacMillan ballets for his Stuttgart company, Cranko invited him to create a brand new piece for his company: this was *Las Hermanas* (*The Sisters*) based on Federico García Lorca's play *The House of Bernarda Alba*. The idea of using this play as the basis of a ballet had originally come from Nicholas Georgiadis, the Greek stage and costume designer with whom MacMillan collaborated extensively. As in the play, five sisters suffer under the tyrannical rule of a widowed matriarch; only after the eldest has married can the others engage in their own matrimonial interests. A suitor for the eldest sister is found and introduced into the family, lured into committing himself to marriage by the prospect of a dowry. But his real purpose is to pursue the object of his erotic interests: the youngest sister. MacMillan cast Ruth Papendick as the mother, Marcia Haydée as the eldest sister and Birgit Keil as the youngest. At the time, Keil was an eighteen-year-old student on leave of absence from Stuttgart at the Royal Ballet

---

45   John Percival, *Theatre in my Blood, A Biography of John Cranko*, The Herbert Press, London 1983, p. 92

School. At MacMillan's request, she returned to Stuttgart for this role prior to completing her scholarship studies. When MacMillan arrived in Stuttgart to restage his ballets *Solitaire* and *House of Birds*, he was unaware that Ray had settled in Germany. Bumping into him in the canteen he could hardly hold back a 'What the hell are you doing here?' They had got on very well some years back at Ballet Theatre when Ray had danced in both the ballets MacMillan created for that company and now the friendship deepened. MacMillan loved Ray's frank, naughty humour and the ease with which expletives issued from his lips. There could have been no doubt about Ray's suitability for the part of the suitor in *Las Hermanas*. Apart from his dark Hispanic appearance, he had no qualms about portraying a swaggering cockerel in a hen house: a parody of macho sexuality – which apparently he did very successfully. Jann Parry writes in her MacMillan biography: 'Strong and darkly handsome, he [Ray] had a powerful, virile stage presence. As the male intruder into an all-female household, he conveyed a feral intensity, both compelling and repulsive.'[46] Four years later, MacMillan sent him to mount this ballet in America. American Ballet Theatre presented it in November 1967 with Lucia Chase as the Mother, Lupe Serrano as the Eldest Sister and Royes Ferandez as the Man. 'It was a feather in my cap. Lucia Chase was very impressed that I had become a regisseur and also how I set the ballet on my old company. Working with her as the mother, I was forced to criticise the way she approached her role and explained, "It's not Tudor you know! There is no understatement, or underplaying. The mother is Spanish, a woman of great will and forcefulness." What I did relish, though I was not the one to teach him, was the fact that Erik Bruhn later danced my role! How I would have enjoyed showing him my part. On another occasion, when I was working for John Neumeier and had been sent to mount his version of *Baiser de la Fée* at ABT, Lucia asked me to return to my old company as ballet master. But I preferred to remain in Europe as I had put down too many roots there.' *Las Hermanas* was filmed by BBC television in

---

46 Jann Parry, *Different Drummer, The Life of Kenneth MacMillan*, Faber & Faber, London 2009, p. 260

1965 with a cast made up of dancers from the Royal Ballet and the Stuttgart companies. At MacMillan's insistence, Marcia Haydée, Ruth Papendick and Ray retained their original roles while Monica Mason and Georgina Parkinson were cast as the jealous and the youngest sister respectively. Peter Wright, who was in charge of the production, opened up the ballet to include scenes from outside the sisters' house and also introduced a short prologue to make clear that the man and the youngest sister are on their way to becoming lovers.[47] When Ray was asked by Lady MacMillan to supervise a revival of the ballet at Covent Garden in 2012, he included this scene, though it was never in the original. He explained that MacMillan had been very pleased with it as an expository aid to the rather short ballet. In fact, Ray had had the opportunity several months earlier of adding this short scene to the ballet. He supervised a revival of *Las Hermanas* with the Munich ballet.[48]

MacMillan's working method when creating a ballet was to start with the central *pas de deux* as the nucleus of the piece and then to go on from there. When he started on *Las Hermanas* he called Ray and Marcia Haydée first, letting no one watch the rehearsal. As the *pas de deux* took shape he discovered the marvellous rapport that had developed between the two. Ray described MacMillan's way as being similar to Cranko's: 'He indicated the steps and lifts without really dancing them fully, but he was more controlling during the process of working out the mechanics of the lifts. For example in *Las Hermanas* we once had a complicated lift that we tried a thousand times. She had her legs around my waist and was supposed to do a sort of pirouette in that position, but stay in the air… we managed it once or twice. The next day MacMillan came and told us that the lift was out. We had to start from scratch.'[49] Ray and Marcia were also featured in a short ballet

---

47 Peter Wright with Paul Arrowsmith, *Wrights & Wrongs, My Life in Dance*, Oberon Books Ltd, London 2016, p. 70

48 The ballet was taught by the choreologist Georgette Tsinguirides; Lucia Lacara danced the Eldest Sister, Cyril Pierre, the Man and Trixie Cordua, the Mother.

49 Interview in *John Cranko, Der Choreograph und seine Arbeit in München*, Bayerisches Staatsballet 2008, p. 30 (my translation)

MacMillan created for ABC Television, based in Birmingham, a few months after the premiere of *Las Hermanas*. This was *Dark Descent*, only seen on television, which deals with the Orpheus legend: a man mourning his dead wife imagines his descent to the underworld only to lose her again.

On the wave of critical praise for MacMillan's *Das Lied von der Erde* in Stuttgart, the Royal Opera House Board was forced to reconsider its emphatic 'no' to a ballet using Gustav Mahler's song cycle. They had already rejected MacMillan's proposed ballet twice, on the grounds that great music, addressing elevated subjects, should not be subjected to the imposition of another's permanent visual images.[50] Consequently *Das Lied von der Erde* was created in Stuttgart due to Cranko's generous offer for MacMillan to choreograph it on his company. In Stuttgart, MacMillan was given carte blanche in his casting and a generous amount of rehearsal time. But apparently Cranko had to persuade the administration to allow the orchestra to play this music for a ballet. The singers proved to be less of a problem; Grace Hoffman who sang the contralto part was already a big fan of the Stuttgart ballet. The ballet, though seemingly abstract, does have a narrative thread provided by the six Chinese poems from the T'ang dynasty that Mahler had chosen. He had taken them from an edition freely translated into German by Hans Bethge. In Mahler's composition they form a cycle about the remembrance of the joys of youth and beauty and conclude with a poignant farewell. MacMillan did not try to illustrate the content of the poems; rather he sought to find movement, inspired by the music, which would express an essence. In Mahler's treatment of the last song, in which he combined two poems and himself penned the final lines, there is a promise of renewal. Thus the series becomes a cycle of life, death and rebirth. Some critics detected the influence of Martha Graham in this ballet though MacMillan was quick to deny it; the choreography seems to reflect his own idiomatic response to the music and the themes. In

---

50 Jann Parry, *Different Drummer, The Life of Kenneth MacMillan*, Faber & Faber, London 2009, p. 297

Germany, *Das Lied* initially divided the critics: some considered it a masterpiece while others thought that the music was not suitable for dance and Mahler should be left well alone. Two English critics, Andrew Porter for the *Financial Times* and John Percival for *The Times,* who were present at the premiere in Stuttgart, wrote glowing accounts of it. 'London must acquire it too without delay; for it is a major work and a beautiful one.'[51] Ray was cast as a sort of Everyman who is shadowed by a masked figure of death (*Der Ewige* danced by Egon Madsen) – in MacMillan's view not a demonic or evil spirit – and who is called to the Hereafter just as he is united with the Woman. This role did not present a challenge as far as characterisation was concerned, but required the mastering of an unusual style of choreography. It incorporated a neoclassicism coloured by modern dance elements and, at times, especially in the dances for the women, a hint of chinoiserie. According to MacMillan, 'It was the first ballet I was satisfied with. It had great unity of style, which until then had eluded me.' And it was the one ballet he would like to be remembered by.[52] In the extended last song of the cycle, *Der Abschied*, which is, in turn, a *pas de deux*, a solo and a *pas de trois*, Ray was always moved to tears: 'At the end as the singer, in a diminuendo, repeats "*ewig, ewig…*" tears would well up in my eyes.'

51   *Ibid.*, p. 304
52   *Ibid.*, p. 305

14

Cranko's masterpiece Onegin and estrangement

Cranko's ballet *Onegin* (1965) would seem to be his supreme legacy to balletic posterity: there is hardly a ballet company in the world that has not mounted this ballet. More than most ballets that use world literature as the source for a danced narrative, Cranko's ballet has superb clarity and succinctness. The Pushkin poem is streamlined into three acts and while shedding characters, nuances and poetic connotations, the ballet exists on its own as danced drama. Truth to tell, one does not need to have read Pushkin to understand the ballet. The idea of creating a ballet on this subject went back to a Sadler's Wells production of Tchaikovsky's opera *Eugene Onegin* in 1952, for which Cranko choreographed the dances. It struck him then that the story would make a very good ballet – better than the opera itself, he thought. When Cranko spoke of his plan to make a ballet based on Pushkin's *Onegin*, Ray bought the book and read it. In fact, he needed a couple of readings to grasp it. A dramatic highlight of Tchaikovsky's opera is the scene in which Tatiana pours out her heart in a letter to Onegin, bringing the first act to an impassioned conclusion. The opera, due to the lyric and dramatic possibilities of music, definitely has an expressive advantage over Pushkin's poem. But this scene, in dance terms, provided a choreographic challenge. Here Cranko gives a visualisation, a 'dream *pas de deux*', of Tatiana's emotional state and the purpose of her letter. He has Onegin, or the spirit of what Tatiana imagines Onegin to be, emerge from a mirror. They then dance a rapturous outpouring of love and bliss. Ray says that the key to this *pas de deux* is that Onegin, at that moment, represents a figment of her imagination: a romantic incarnation of her novel reading; what she imagines love to be. He is not real and Ray advocates present dancers undertaking the role to be aware of this. In this *pas de deux* the Bolshoi influence is fulsomely evident: one daring high lift or combination follows another. Again, Ray generously gives credit to Marcia for the way she collaborated with him in the realisation of this exciting *pas de deux*.

The second act, in which Onegin has very little dancing to do, also profited dramatically from a complaint Ray made to Cranko: 'But I can't just stand or sit around all the time, I need to have something to do.' Cranko replied, 'Then why don't you sit down at a table and play solitaire.' In fact this action of studied boredom during the festivities for Tatiana's name day is a felicitous pendant to the main action. Ray: 'John Neumeier, at that time engaged by the Stuttgart Ballet, was cast as one of the elderly guests in this act. He would come up to my table while I was playing cards and we developed a little scene in which he would persistently peer over my shoulder as if he was trying to tell me which cards to play. It was quite a little cameo. Amazing to think that a few years later I would be working for him!' Ray improvised the game of solitaire and all the *mise en scène* leading up to Onegin's flirtation with Olga, Lensky's fiancée, which then culminates in the fatal duel. The emotional heart of the story is, however, the dramatic third act *pas de deux* where Tatiana, in a reversal of roles, rejects Onegin's advances, tearing up his letter in front of him, as he did hers. However steadfast she is in her resolve to send him packing, we realise that her actions are tearing her apart. In this *pas de deux* there is the famous passage in which Onegin, literally walking on his knees, drags himself behind Tatiana, catching her twice as she falls toward him. 'When Cranko choreographed this section he told me, "Now I want you to walk on your knees," to which I replied, "Are you serious?" Walking on one's knees is not something every dancer loves to do and some who have a knee injury just can't do it. Perhaps nowadays it's not such a big deal.' But in the end the dramatic situation, together with the powerful emotional surge of the music, brought Ray to a wholehearted acceptance of it. 'I loved this section.' Years later he effusively declared: 'I would have walked all the way to Madrid on my knees for Cranko.' Ray readily acknowledges that Cranko's ballet *Onegin* provided him with a superb culmination to his dancing career. 'It was my greatest role.'

On his thirty-sixth birthday, the 3rd January 1966, Ray tore his left Achilles tendon while rehearsing *Swan Lake* in Bonn. This fatally brought his dancing career to an end. There had already been warning signs and the tendon was probably partially torn, but never one to miss a performance, he dutifully fulfilled his scheduled performances. Before rehearsing or performing, he was always careful to warm up properly and used a liniment in bandaging the damaged tendon. But his tendons were in any case rather taught – he had a shallow *demi-plié* – and in retrospect a serious trauma seemed inevitable. By the time of MacMillan's *Das Lied von der Erde,* which premiered on 7th November 1965, he sensed that his condition was serious, but he was never going to give that ballet a miss. Sadly he was to dance only the *Das Lied* performances of November and December of that year. The torn tendon was operated on and treated as well as was possible for the time, but medical treatment for such injuries has improved considerably since then. For example, after the operation, the ankle was put in a cast; this treatment is now obsolete. Cranko thoughtfully relieved Maximo Barra from dancing duties in order for him to attend to Ray while he was in hospital.

Ray was faced with a dilemma. What was he going to do now that he couldn't dance? Once able to get about, he returned to the studio to rehearse his roles with dancers who were now going to take them over. This was a heart-wrenching activity, for deep down, he realised that he would never dance his roles again. But his position within the company was vague and it seemed as if Cranko couldn't make up his mind about what to do with him. It was a distressing time; the torn tendon had precipitated a crisis for which he was not prepared and he was depressed. In every dancer's career there comes a time when, due to age or failing technical powers, they will have to face the problem of what to do next. Many decide to remain in the sphere of ballet by becoming coaches, teachers or ballet masters. Others make a total break and enter a completely different profession: ex-dancers have become doctors, architects or lawyers, despite the lengthy time required to study for such professions. Ray wanted to remain in the world of ballet, but had to consider seriously whether becoming a ballet master was his thing. In the spring of 1966 he and Marcia Haydée were sent to the Royal Ballet to teach that company Kenneth MacMillan's *Das Lied von der Erde*. The Royal Ballet premiere was scheduled for May 1966, and MacMillan had insisted that Marcia Haydée dance the role she had created in Stuttgart. She would be a guest with the Royal Ballet after which Lynn Seymour would inherit the role of the Woman. Donald MacLeary would dance Ray's role, the Man, and Anthony Dowell, the Messenger of Death/Der Ewige. Ray: ' I hated teaching Donald MacLeary my role. The creation of the ballet lay only a few months back and I had loved dancing it. To think that Marcia was going to dance with the Royal Ballet and I couldn't participate as well; that really got at me!'

While teaching the ballet, Ray went to see Cranko, who was in London at that time, in order to discuss his future. Ray remembers this meeting very vividly because it was at this point that he came to the decision that severed his ties with Stuttgart. Cranko was lodging with friends in a magnificent house in Mayfair. Marcia was also present. This meeting brought forth no concrete suggestions and became emotionally fraught. At one point Cranko, in exasperation, asked Ray, 'Do you want me to fire her?' He was referring to Anne Woolliams,

Stuttgart's ballet mistress and someone for whom Ray felt a particular antipathy. This thought was not even at the back of Ray's mind. Cranko was insistent that Ray stay with Stuttgart but was, as ever, unclear about the position he would have. Ray then said, 'I'm not going to be the coffee boy, and if this is the situation, then I'm going to Berlin.' He announced that he would accept Kenneth MacMillan's invitation to become ballet master at the Deutsche Oper, Berlin. MacMillan was designated as the next artistic director starting in August 1966. He had told Ray, 'I'll only go if you come.' And, as Ray continued to relate in the interview, 'And I *did* become the coffee boy!' The immediate aftermath of his decision to leave Stuttgart was that both Cranko and Marcia considered him disloyal and behaved accordingly. Ray: 'That I left Stuttgart to become Kenneth MacMillan's ballet master in Berlin – that, Cranko never forgave me for. He was furious when I told him I was leaving for Berlin. He wouldn't speak to me any more.' Marcia, too, at that meeting in London, was beside herself at Ray's so-called betrayal. Here was the most senior member of the Stuttgart Ballet, her special partner and close colleague with whom she had shared critical acclaim in at least two of Cranko's major successes, selfishly severing himself from the communal path they were all on. A more drastic repercussion was that Ray would not have anything to do with the Stuttgart Ballet between his departure at the end of that season in July 1966, and 1978. Even after Cranko's death he remained *persona non grata*. Things finally took a turn for the better when Stuttgart was more or less obliged to have him back: John Neumeier, commissioned to create a full-length ballet for the Stuttgart Ballet starring Marcia Haydèe, had decided on *Lady of the Camellias*. Ray accompanied him as his assistant.

'My last meeting with Cranko was in an elevator in the Frankfurt Opera House. By this time several years had gone by and I was currently working as John Neumeier's ballet master at the Ballet of the Municipal Stages, Frankfurt am Main. This must have been the early 1970s. We were alone in the lift and he looked at me and, with a wisp of nostalgia in his voice, said, "Well, how are you, Theda?" This was the coded gay lingo of the early sixties, to which I replied, "I'm fine, Crystal, and you?" There was much left unspoken in this short conversation. His last words were, "Perhaps you'll come back to us sometime?"

15

Berlin and Kenneth MacMillan: a new start

Ray: 'In retrospect and with hindsight, having to stop because of my injury was the best thing that could have happened to me. I was then, 1966, thirty-six, and would have had to, sooner or later, taken a decision about stopping dancing. But, at the time, being forced to stop so unexpectedly triggered off a most unhappy year. I think it was the unhappiest time of my life – a whole year long. To top it all, Maximo and I were also having a difficult time. Our relationship was being severely tested by my confused, depressed, undecided frame of mind, and it seemed as if it might come to an end. The business about leaving Stuttgart was heart-wrenching, but I had made my decision. Berlin and MacMillan promised a new start and a way out of my dilemma; so I tried to be as optimistic as possible and set about planning the move.'

MacMillan, as circumstances would become clear to Ray, was someone who needed someone to take care of him. Working at Cranko's base in Stuttgart when he created *Las Hermanas* and *Das Lied von der Erde*, MacMillan had enjoyed being a guest and not worrying about much except the creation of his ballets. Cranko smoothed the way for him to operate solely on an artistic level. The atmosphere among the dancers was most friendly and informal. There were no battles to be fought like the ones he had had to confront with the Royal Opera House Board in London. He was respected, the work was fun. Importantly, after work, he was not alone, he was able to socialise with the dancers he was particularly close to, like Ray, with whom he would lodge whenever he came to Stuttgart. Not for him the party-like carousing Cranko indulged in. Cranko was, indeed, rather put out and jealous of the exclusive ties Ray and Maximo had with MacMillan. Ray and Maximo, who were now living together, went out of their way to provide for his every need, mothering him in every way possible. They became a sort of ersatz family; Maximo even cut his hair just as he did for Ray. This was the sort of set-up MacMillan eagerly sought amongst his intimate friends and had enjoyed lately in London with Georgina Parkinson and her husband Roy Round. She had given him all her attention and care, becoming almost indispensible. In Germany, the Stuttgart Ballet had cocooned him in a most agreeable way, but Berlin would be different.

Berlin was not new to Ray; he had worked with the company there when Cranko created his *Firebird* in 1964 and he had danced the male lead. But Berlin and Germany – as a semi-permanent home – were new to MacMillan and he did not take to them well. Ray had the advantage of speaking fluent, if not absolutely grammatically correct, German, having lived and worked in Stuttgart from 1958 until mid-July of 1966. He was used to the German way of life, how a German opera house was run, what the dancers' union regulations were, as well as staying level-headed in his dealing with people and difficult situations. MacMillan never made the effort to learn German and thus was constantly in need of English-speaking colleagues to run the company. The language of the ensemble, also German, placed him at another disadvantage. In an interview he gave after he had left Germany, MacMillan misrepresented the state of ballet in Berlin before his arrival. He maintained that the Germans were bitterly opposed to classical ballet and therefore resistant to what he was offering. Curiously, what had actually happened, due to special circumstances, was that classical ballet had edged out Ausdruckstanz (expressionist dance).[53] This was due mainly to the Russian-born Tatjana Gsovsky who, after the war, as director/choreographer of her own company, the Berliner Ballett (a touring company), and as Ballet Director of the Deutsche Oper, had built up the West German company into a bastion of classical ballet. Her company was, indeed, in many ways, superior to the Soviet-influenced Staatsoper in East Berlin. Gsovsky had applied a modern approach to classical ballet, uniting it with expressionistic elements, and collaborating frequently with contemporary composers, whereas the Staatsoper had remained heavily under Soviet influence. Although already sixty-five, Gsovsky had elected to stay on with the company under MacMillan and function as a teacher and *répétiteur*. Both she and Gert Rheinholm, who had had a highly successful career as a solo dancer with Gsovsky, were in fact unexpectedly supportive of his endeavours. Gsovsky did not stay much longer than two seasons, but Rheinholm, in his function as manager of the company, proved to be worth more than his weight in gold. During the final year of MacMillan's directorship he acted as his deputy and later, from 1972 to 1990, took over the company as full-time ballet director. Ray knew both Gsovsky and Reinholm from his time in Berlin dancing in Cranko's *Firebird*. He got on well with them; Gsovsky nicknamed him 'Raychick'. Reinholm became a very good friend and the friendship deepened when they both had to run the company after MacMillan's heart attack. Ray: 'He [Reinholm] was a wonderful man.'

It was not without some misgivings that Ray left Stuttgart. He had been happy there, indeed, he had been very happy. For a little over five years he had enjoyed the position of first male soloist and had been the creator of several important roles for both Cranko and MacMillan. The outcome of his move to Berlin and his new duties, though

---

53   Parry J., *Different Drummer, The Life of Kenneth MacMillan*, Faber & Faber Ltd, London 2009, pp. 316–7

promising a new beginning, still seemed uncertain. He had not been MacMillan's first choice for ballet master. MacMillan had approached Peter Wright and then an old friend, Gilbert Vernon, both of whom had declined the offer. Then when MacMillan petitioned Ray he was anxious that Maximo accompany him. He told MacMillan, 'If I go to Berlin, Maximo must come too.' MacMillan replied, 'Absolutely, no problem.' However, Maximo, who was still bound by his contract to the Stuttgart Ballet, was not free to make the move with Ray. He thus gave notice to leave at the end of the 1966–67 season, and the plan was for him to join the Berlin company then. In the event, this was not to be. MacMillan reneged on his promise, saying that he could not condone having a ballet master in a relationship with a member of the company. 'I don't want you to have a lover in the company.' But this was not apparent until after Ray had committed himself and the move had happened. MacMillan was bringing only two dancers from the Royal Ballet with him: Lynn Seymour and Vergie Derman. As the Berlin company had recently been reduced from eighty-three to fifty-nine dancers, the union was rigorous about his giving notice to existing members or engaging any others.[54]

In July 1966 Ray set off for Berlin to find an apartment while Maximo went on holiday to Greece with several other Stuttgart dancers. MacMillan suggested, and it seemed a good idea, that Lynn Seymour, who was leaving the Royal Ballet to become his Berlin ballerina, and Ray both move into one large flat with him. Berlin promised to be an exciting new venture for all three of them; Ray was already acclimatised to the German way of life and spoke the language. He would be able to help the two foreign newcomers to find their feet. 'I found what I thought was the solution to all our problems. It was a very large flat consisting of ten rooms at *107 Reichstrasse*, off what had previously been *Adolf Hitler Platz* (now called *Theodor-Heuss Platz*), and not far from the opera house. The apartment was in a semi-derelict state, and I set about having it fixed up. It cost me a fortune!

---

54 Jann Parry, *Different Drummer, The Life of Kenneth MacMillan*, Faber and Faber Ltd, London 2009, p. 316

When I asked Lynn and Kenneth to share the costs, the answer was no; the flat was in my name. They never paid me a penny! I swallowed this but it did not bode well for living together. MacMillan, as Queen Bee of our trio, had chosen two rooms which were on a separate floor but connected by stairs to the main part of the flat. It provided him with a sort of flatlet, all to himself. I settled into two rooms at the back next to the kitchen. However, when Lynn arrived just before the beginning of the season, she wanted the rooms I had already fixed up and was occupying. I gave in to her request because she was now the prima ballerina "absolutely" of the company. She needed to have the sun shine in through her windows and a bathroom close by. Her request seemed reasonable enough.'

Ray: 'On the night I had to move all my things to new rooms, there was a party at Jürgen Rose's. I didn't want to go as I wasn't interested in all the socialising Kenneth and Lynn did. So I set about dismantling the cupboards and shelving that I had so painstakingly assembled. Doing it alone was a foolhardy thing and soon the whole cupboard just collapsed on me. It made me even more miserable. I was on the verge of tears.' However, Ray's new rooms, which faced the street and were bigger, did provide him with privacy, something he was dearly in need of. But he missed Maximo. The main disadvantage to his new quarters was that the telephone was situated in his living room and all calls, incoming or outgoing, took place there. Ray: 'Then there were the phone bills! Astronomical! I, certainly, was not calling Australia or the UK. They both denied having made them. Why should I call the Royal Ballet on tour in Australia?' He had a minute bathroom right next to the entrance. It was not big enough to shower in – for that he used the theatre. It only had cold water but at least he could shave there. Sharing a flat with people who did not exactly share the same concerns about personal property inevitably led to other irritations. In the kitchen Ray had installed the table he had brought with him from Stuttgart. It was teak, a piece of furniture he was proud to own. But it was beginning to show signs of unthinking vandalism. There were burn marks all along the edge caused by smokers leaving lit cigarettes on the bare wood. 'They couldn't think of using an ashtray!' Ray himself smoked but was fastidiously house-proud.

At that meeting with Cranko in London when Ray announced he was going to Berlin, he had indignantly vociferated that he was not going to be Stuttgart Ballet's coffee boy. In Berlin, he discovered that his position with MacMillan, nominally ballet master, embraced that and a lot more. 'Not only was I a coffee boy but I became a slave.' This was more or less what MacMillan wanted and needed, while the ten-room apartment for the three of them rapidly proved to be a trap. Ray: 'As the only one who could speak German, I had to organise everything: I did the shopping, the laundry, found a cleaning lady, generally tidied up. If anything was broken, I had to get it repaired. On Sunday, when I went out for our breakfast rolls, I bought Lynn and Kenneth their newspapers.' The working hours at the opera house played a part in his sense of being bound and trapped in some sort of infernal machine. The ballet company worked two shifts a day, or one if there was a performance. According to German union regulations there had to be a rest period of four hours between the morning rehearsals, which lasted from 10:00 until 13:00, and the afternoon ones which started at 17:00. Work finished at 21:00 and this meant that one did not get home before 21:30.

Outside his intimate circle MacMillan was considered somewhat aloof, vague and reticent, but once surrounded by people he trusted and felt at home with he became quite expansive and wonderfully ribald, delighting in hearing all the back-stage gossip. There was no doubting his pasha-like authority as he held court in the kitchen – his sanctum – drinking and talking into the early hours. Insatiably in need of company as a sounding board for his wit and intellect, as well as an antidote to his deeply ingrained sense of loneliness, he was very reluctant to close shop. He did not seem to need a good night's sleep. 'It was Kenneth's ritual that we all have supper together, and he was the one to prepare it. Smoking and drinking at least a bottle of whisky a night, Kenneth would then, while entertaining us with his plans and gossip, prepare the food. He loved to make fishcakes. For

Christ's sake, fishcakes? And they didn't even taste that good! And then we would finish eating about midnight. I was the one who had to be at the studio bright and early the next morning to give class. This was not my sort of daily rhythm. I used to prepare my classes before breakfast when no one was up and I could concentrate. I found that I loved giving class even if it meant that I would be busy all day long. In Stuttgart, I had started to teach after my injury with my foot still in the cast; first at the school attached to the company run by Anneliese Mörike. For my Berlin classes, I made sure that, during the week, I included different big jumps in each of them. Lynn actually gave me a good tip, "Your class is very good but you must get away from 2/4 and 4/4, try 3/4 sometime; it's better for *fondu*." Ray's new duties as ballet master were something that he found immensely fulfilling and it rapidly took the place of his own dancing.

Ninette de Valois's career as founder of a national company, and one as respected as the Royal Ballet, became a template, admired and copied. MacMillan probably had high hopes of developing the Berlin Ballet into something, perhaps not as grand as the Royal Ballet, but at least as successful as Cranko's achievement in Stuttgart. At the beginning there was therefore talk of establishing a school attached to the company. Cranko had been all too aware of this necessity and his school was rapidly gaining prestige and producing suitable material for his company. This did not happen in Berlin, mainly because of the financial burden it would have put on the Deutsche Oper's budget. In the event, Tatjana Gsovsky, together with Rheinholm, re-established her own private school as the Berlin Dance Academy. MacMillan began his first season at the Deutsche Oper with performances of ballets that were already in the repertory before his arrival: *Giselle* in Antony Tudor's production, and a triple bill programme that included Tatjana Gsovsky's *Labyrinth of Truth* and several Cranko ballets. Ray thought that *Labyrinth of Truth*, based on the Kurosawa film *Rashomon*, was great. 'She [Gsovsky] was very clever and inventive. It was a wonderful and gripping transposition of that film into dance.' MacMillan's first self-choreographed evening was likewise a triple bill: *Valses nobles et sentimentales*, *The Invitation* and *Concerto*. The last named, to Shostakovich's Second Piano Concerto, was a creation for the company, a showpiece designed to test and show off the ensemble's strength. At the same time it proved instrumental in improving the dancers' technique. It received a standing ovation at its premiere. The soloists of the first movement were Didi Carli and Falco Kapuste; the second was an adagio *pas de deux* inspired by MacMillan's observation of Lynn Seymour stretching at the bar – she was partnered by Rudolf Holz. The solo couple of the third movement should have been Silvia Kesselheim and Klaus Beelitz, but Beelitz injured himself just before the premiere and could not be replaced at such short notice. In the premiere Kesselheim improvised the *pas de deux* as a solo, making quite a splash of it, with the result that, from then on, it was performed this way. *Concerto* was immediately much in demand: ABT, the Royal Ballet and the Royal Swedish Ballet all wanted it. It augured well for MacMillan's future in Berlin while establishing his international reputation.

Concerto was Ray's first experience at assisting a choreographer while the ballet was being created. As a quick and accessible memory aid, he devised a system of making notes in words and little stick-figure drawings of how the steps fitted the music. For example where the musical phrase has been counted out, it is then easy for one to write 1. *piq R* with a little arrow giving the direction, to mean piqué on the right foot on the count of 1. Ray developed his own shorthand, such as *pir inside* for a *pirouette en de dans* or *bat* for grand battement. Later, assisting John Neumeier, a prolific choreographer, he had notebooks for each of the ballets that were created during the time he worked for him; sometimes two or three for each ballet, according to their complexity. These notebooks, now part of John Neumeier's archive, are still referred to by succeeding ballet masters mounting or reviving ballets that were created some time ago. They are valuable aids, though not in any way an equivalent of the Benesh or Laban notation systems, which would require trained choreologists to read them.

In the beginning, Ray enjoyed the comradeship the flat provided, a sort of *ménage à trois* without any sexual involvement, and the new circumstances of working in Berlin. But, inevitably, the burden of all the chores he allowed to be imposed on him, the functioning of the flat, the work and taking care of MacMillan, eventually got to him. Ray: 'At first, as Kenneth was a world-famous choreographer and my boss, I thought I didn't mind being exploited. But it soon led to me being drained emotionally and physically. Kenneth was totally inept at living alone, required constant company and wanted to run our lives. I was so lonely, and I missed Maximo tremendously.' Lynn Seymour has even more drastic words to describe the situation: 'He [MacMillan] wanted unconditional love… But his love was conditional: "Be entirely available to me when I need you, otherwise you're betraying me."'[55]

Taking advantage of a brief lull in his working schedule, Ray travelled to Stuttgart to see Maximo. He was lonely despite the workload at the Opera and his even more demanding attendance on MacMillan, 'I have never felt so lonely in my life; I just had to see Maxi.' It was December 1966 and Cranko had just premiered *The Nutcracker*. Ray went to the flat which he and Maximo used to share, as if to collect his mail. Seeing Maximo again he could not help himself; the words issued from his lips of their own volition. 'I literally begged him, "Please come to Berlin." Without giving my plea any sort of deliberation, he replied, "Of course, I will."' Thus, although he did not have a contract with the Berlin Ballet and would have to freelance, Maximo committed himself to Ray. On Ray's return to Berlin, even if the season still had six months to run, he now had a relieving prospective. Soon he would be free from the corseting commitments of the Reichstrasse apartment, and he would be with Maximo again.

De Valois and the Royal Ballet's influence were clearly evident in MacMillan's choice for his next ballet: *The Sleeping Beauty*. Once the glory of the Maryinsky Theatre, St Petersburg, Petipa's ballet had been

---

55 Jann Parry, *Different Drummer, The Life of Kenneth MacMillan*, Faber & Faber, London 2009, p. 322

more or less appropriated by the Sadler's Wells Ballet and had become the signature ballet of the Royal Ballet. Any ballet company capable of mounting this classic asserted that it had the technical proficiency and funds necessary to do it justice. MacMillan's ambition ran in this direction, possibly with the hope of outdoing the Royal Ballet in terms of opulence. But, apart from the cost, *The Sleeping Beauty* was not exactly what the Deutsche Oper expected of MacMillan. The administration would have preferred him to continue creating original works for the house or even mounting his Stuttgart success, *Das Lied von der Erde*. As things turned out, due to lack of adequate time to prepare such a costly and complicated production, *The Sleeping Beauty* premiere was postponed until October 1967 of the next season. This meant that the slot allocated to a ballet premiere that first season would have to be improvised. And it occasioned one of MacMillan's strongest dance dramas of his German directorship, *Anastasia*.

The atmosphere in the *Reichstrasse* flat was slowly getting oppressive. Lynn Seymour, not one to be cowed into any guru-like attendance on MacMillan, had embarked on a love affair. Having left behind a broken marriage in London, she now flaunted a devil-may-care Berlin persona.[56] MacMillan, as he sat in his dressing gown in the kitchen, smoking and sipping whisky diluted with tea, observed her comings and goings. Lynn's rooms were at the back and accessed by the corridor that passed by the kitchen. Anyone sitting there was sure to see her. As MacMillan practically never went to bed until the early hours of the morning, he could keep tabs on her every move. She resented this sort of surveillance and called her passage near the kitchen Checkpoint Charlie. MacMillan muttered to Ray, 'How can she, with him [Falco Kapuste, a dancer in the company]? And she comes home at all hours, when she's meant to be fresh for class in the morning.'[57] According to Lynn, both MacMillan and Ray disapproved of Kapuste because they believed he was using her to further his career.

---

56   Jann Parry, *Different Drummer, A Life of Kenneth MacMillan*, Faber & Faber, London 2009 p 321

57   *Ibid.*, p. 322

Actually Ray considered him a very good dancer and thought, on the contrary, that her behaviour in enticing him into her favours was not very discreet – Kapuste was already involved in a relationship with a dancer in the company. When MacMillan made it clear to Kapuste that he had lost interest in him as a dancer, the affair immediately came to an end.[58]

Meanwhile, Lynn had started to become accident-prone. In her dressing room at the theatre, she had accidently knocked over a coffee pot and scalded her leg. It was mooted that she and Kapuste had been engaged in some sexual dalliance in her dressing room, but Lynn, in her autobiography, energetically denies this. Then she developed a flu, which worsened to such an extent that she flew to London to recover. In London, glandular fever was diagnosed and she was unable to dance for weeks. Later, back in Berlin, during the creation of *Anastasia*, a much more dramatic and life-threatening accident happened. While soaping herself in the bathtub, Lynn suddenly became aware of a dark bruise on her upper right arm. It had been caused during the *Anastasia* rehearsals when she and the dancer portraying her rustic husband repeatedly tried out a lift. She rushed out of the bathroom and went to Ray. He was in fact packing up his belongings as he intended to move out of Reichsstrasse apartment soon. Ray: 'The bruise just got larger and larger in front of our eyes as blood spread in the injured area. I hastily phoned for a doctor.' The doctor, however, did not seem to think it was serious. The next day it was not better and a second doctor diagnosed a thrombosis. Lynn was rushed to hospital and immediately treated with medication to dissolve the blood clot. After some time in the hospital, restless and bored, Lynn got out of bed and went shopping, though she had been warned not to take the arm out of the sling during the treatment. She bought sparkling wine, nuts and crackers from Berlin's famous department store *Kaufhaus des Westens* (KDW); things to sip and nibble. And when visitors came, she was able to entertain them with

---

58 Lynn Seymour with Paul Gardner, *Lynn, The Autobiography of Lynn Seymour*, Granada, London 1984, pp. 209–12

a little party at her hospital bedside. Ridiculously, MacMillan blamed her for putting his new ballet in jeopardy. But it was hardly her fault; injuries are commonplace in the dance studio and she certainly would not have wished to miss out on the chance of creating a role of such dramatic potential.

MacMillan, frantic with worry about *Anastasia*'s premiere, contacted the Royal Ballet to arrange for Georgina Parkinson to come to Berlin and learn Lynn's role. Parkinson duly arrived and settled into the Berlin apartment and for a time calmed MacMillan's emotional turmoil. She set about learning the role. Faith Worth, a Benesh notator at the Royal Ballet, also lodging at the Reichstrasse apartment during this period, was there to teach the two other ballets on the same programme as *Anastasia*: *Diversions* and *Solitaire*. 'She remembers the atmosphere in the apartment as being "absolutely poisonous" before Parkinson arrived: "Kenneth was criticising people behind their backs, taking out his tensions by badmouthing his friends to each other. He was very manipulative."[59] Ray was caught in the middle of this drama as the apartment absorbed more and more visitors.

Anastasia, in spite of being a stopgap ballet with practically no budget, profited from exactly these constraints – MacMillan was creatively challenged. The theme, the plight of the outsider, in this case of Anna Anderson's claim to be the Grand Duchess Anastasia, the sole surviving daughter of Tsar Nicolas II, was greatly to his taste. Stimulated by his reading of the biography *I, Anastasia*, which relates how the protagonist had been rescued from drowning in a Berlin canal in 1920 and admitted to a mental hospital, MacMillan treated the ballet as a series of recalled hallucinatory incidents. The dancer portraying Anna/Anastasia is shown real filmed footage, projected onto screens that are let down from the flies, of the Tsar's family and their entourage. This triggers her memory. Assisted by the stage and costume designer Barry Kay, who had come to Berlin for *The*

---

59   Jann Parry, *Different Drummer, The Life of Kenneth MacMillan*, Faber & Faber, London 2009, p. 330

Sleeping Beauty, Macmillan used the rehearsal time scheduled for the postponed ballet to devise a setting for *Anastasia*. The two improvised a simple setting for the new production: an empty stage with a revolve on it, extending right up to the back wall, to suggest a dark void, as if the action was taking place in Anna/Anastasia's head. Costumes that were more or less suggestive of the period had been scavenged from old opera productions or hired from a television studio. Although Parkinson was ready to take over the role, and in spite of warnings from Lynn's doctor against starting rehearsals before the thrombosis had completely cleared up, she was adamant about dancing it. She was in and out of her hospital bed for classes and rehearsals, and danced the premiere.

After the success of *Anastasia* MacMillan concentrated his attention fully on *The Sleeping Beauty*. Day in, day out, seated in the main living room, and sipping diluted whisky from a tea service in an attempt to hide his increasingly excessive alcohol intake, he listened to the Antal Dorati recording. This recording purportedly contains all the music Tchaikovsky wrote for this ballet. He had to make decisions about which of the so-called traditional Petipa choreographies would be retained, who would teach them, and which parts he would have to choreograph himself. MacMillan's choice of designer, for what he intended to be a lavish production, was Barry Kay. He had been very impressed by the palatial decor the Australian designer had created for Nureyev's *Raymonda Act III* at Covent Garden, and wished for his ballet a matching Russian – not French – grandeur. Together with Kay, they decided that the scenery should be in the style of the court of Alexander III – the Tsar at the time of the ballet's creation. This all-out attempt to trump previous productions of *The Sleeping Beauty* – especially the Royal Ballet's – was, as it turned out, very detrimental. It would seem that scene-change logistics had not been properly investigated, or that MacMillan and his designer simply overruled the objections of the technical administration, or that the task was beyond their capabilities. With three intervals, each lasting at least half an hour, the performance naturally went into overtime.

The production, however sumptuous it might have been, dragged on, becoming a seemingly never-ending entertainment. However, according to Ray, the highlight of MacMillan's ballet was the mazurka of the third act. Ray enthused, 'It was the hit of the ballet, it brought the house down.' This ensemble piece would not normally have been the sort of thing MacMillan would excel in. He was probably at his best choreographing *pas de deux*, where he would develop or explore a dramatic narrative – but seldom a formal national group dance. He was wise to have consulted Tatjana Gsvosky about the mazurka as she had enjoyed, from her Russian schooling, a very grounded knowledge of national dance. She asked, 'Have you ever heard the whole mazurka, it's wonderful complete?' He replied, 'No, I could never do it complete.' She showed him a variety of steps and combinations, which he then arranged as he saw fit, for thirty dancers. The mazurka begins in a stately way and gradually builds up to an exhilarating finish with great panache.

By the summer of 1967 the apartment on the Reichstrasse had been abandoned by its lodgers. Before the season ended Ray had already moved into his own apartment and awaited the arrival of Maximo. And Maximo, true to his word, came to Berlin to join Ray in spite of having no job. He confronted MacMillan; 'I've come here even if you don't want me in the company!' Vergie Derman, who eventually moved into the apartment, had returned to the Royal Ballet where she would later become a soloist. Lynn Seymour, too, unable to face MacMillan alone without having Ray as a buffer, moved out and rented a house in Grunewald, a suburb of Berlin. Later, her lover, Eike Waltz, joined her. MacMillan, not able to face an enormous apartment alone, let alone pay the rent, had moved to a canalside flat on Helgoländerufer. Apparently he did not unpack his trunks and suitcases. According to Lynn, it was not a concerted plan to abandon him, but rather that each had their own lives to lead and the initial pioneering spirit had run its course. In any case, looking after MacMillan was a full-time occupation; his mood had turned morose and he had become more and more dependent on alcohol. It seems that, like Cranko, his alcohol consumption did not make him completely incapable of functioning when choreographing.

Gert Reinholm fortunately stepped into the breach and made it his business to take care of MacMillan when the *Reichstrasse* apartment was vacated. Hugely supportive of MacMillan, he blithely pretended he didn't notice, or, out of loyalty to him, was not willing to acknowledge the full extent of MacMillan's dependence on the bottle. But Ray felt the full brunt, as well as MacMillan's underlying resentment at having been abandoned. In October 1967, shortly before the premiere of *The Sleeping Beauty*, there was a stage rehearsal at which Ray was on tenterhooks, as he knew that the allotted time of three hours was not going to be sufficient. This would be the first important rehearsal for placing the choreography. Ray: 'Kenneth was late; I knew, or sensed, that he was still in bed, or in his dressing gown, sipping away at his whisky. We just had to get on with the placing as the ballet was so long. Even running it without corrections would have been impossible. So I started without him. Eventually he turned up and was furious, "How dare you start without me?" Justification was of no avail. Gert Reinholm told me that MacMillan was incensed that I had started without him. "Who did I think I was? Did I want his job?"'

It was lamentable that the rapport between MacMillan and Lynn Seymour soured in Berlin and later in London. Judging by the roles she created in his ballets, one could designate her as his principal muse and one sorely missed in ballets such as *Isadora*, where she would have been ideal. Starting with her role as the Adolescent Girl in Love in *The Barrow*, and progressing to the Young Girl in *The Invitation*, then Juliet in his Covent Garden production of *Romeo and Juliet*, she crowned her creations in one of MacMillan's best ballets, as Mary Vetsera in *Meyerling*. The slowly widening rift between MacMillan and Lynn Seymour was exacerbated when she became pregnant and not able to dance for some time. MacMillan, also, could hardly tolerate her relationship with Eike Waltz, father of her twin sons. Almost to the detriment of two of his Berlin creations, MacMillan would not speak to her directly during the final rehearsals. For *Anastasia*, he gave his corrections to Georgina Parkinson for her to pass on to Lynn. And when she danced Aurora in *The Sleeping Beauty*, they were given to Ray. Corrections would take the form of 'Why is she doing that?' or 'Tell her to do such and such.'[60]

Ray adored Lynn and got on well with her. She was great fun, a bit of a rebel but a dancer of lyrical and supreme dramatic qualities unlike any of the Royal Ballet ballerinas of her day. Ray had partnered her in Stuttgart when she guested there as Juliet in Cranko's *Romeo and Juliet*. Amazingly, she learnt the role for only one performance. In Berlin, as first ballerina, she had the opportunity of dancing the classics as well as an array of modern neoclassical pieces. She had already danced Aurora in *The Sleeping Beauty* when she was a member of the Royal Ballet's touring company, but in Berlin, under par health-wise, she enjoyed only a qualified success. The role was soon passed on to Didi Carli, the Argentinian soloist in the company. Aurora might not be a role especially suited to Lynn's talents as a dramatic dancer-actress but, according to Ray, she made up for it in other ways. Ray: 'Maximo and I adored her. She was fantastically musical. During an orchestra rehearsal of the Rose Adage she admonished the conductor for slowing down, as if she needed more time for her balances. She said, "Play the music as it is written. I will follow you."' In an interview with John Gruen, she described her approach to ballet as being, firstly, inspired by the music: 'You try to be part of it. The rest has to do with imagination – with what you're trying to translate or realise.' And then she explained that, in her case, the real key lay in concentration, of not losing oneself in emotionalism.[61] But, however much she might have reined herself in, she is revered as a dancer of supreme expressive powers, capable of expressing emotion in situations of great vulnerability. This was a very special time for classical ballet, just before the ballet boom of the 1970s, when both the foremost dancer-actresses of that generation, Marcia Haydée and Lynn Seymour, were employed in Germany.

---

60 Parry, Jann, *Different Drummer, The Life of Kenneth MacMillan*, Faber & Faber, London 2009, p. 334
61 Gruen, John, *The Private World of Ballet*, The Viking Press, New York 1975, p. 134

Maximo – always one to land on his feet – in spite of arriving in Berlin without a job, was soon dancing and earning good money. Through his contact with an ex-Stuttgart dancer called Chesterina Sim Zecha, he started to dance for television and was much in demand. Ray: 'He earned a fortune.' But in 1968, when the Deutsche Oper mounted Peter Darrell's Carl Orf ballets, *Carmina Burana/ Catulli Carmina*, a large cast with many male dancers was needed. Gert Reinholm offered Maximo a contract. Maximo thus, without needing MacMillan's consent, obtained the engagement he and Ray had wished for. He was cast in MacMillan's next production, *Swan Lake*, and danced the tarantella of the third act with Monika Radamm.

When MacMillan was a young member of the Sadler's Wells Ballet at Covent Garden, he had danced in Balanchine's *Ballet Imperial*. He found the experience of dancing in this ballet, outside the usual English repertory, most enjoyable, besides which he was fascinated by the choreography. He felt, however, that the English company had not grasped the essence of the Balanchine style, but that now, in Berlin, it would be a suitable ballet for his company. Unfortunately, the first performance, which most probably had not had adequate coaching, provoked whistling and catcalls from the German audience. More to their taste, on the same programme, was MacMillan's *Cain and Abel* (November 1968) where he created, for the first time, a ballet focussing on a single male protagonist. Without his muse/ballerina Lynn Seymour, who was on maternity leave, MacMillan turned his attention to a new young dancer in the company: Frank Frey, a tall, blond Bavarian dancer with a soaring jump and a strikingly virile stage aura. MacMillan seems to have sublimated his fascination for this dancer – what can only be interpreted as an erotic infatuation – into, according to Ray, one of the best ballets he created in Berlin.

Frey had come to Berlin in order to obtain a visa for Cuba where he wanted to audition for the Cuban National Ballet. Visiting his friend Eike Waltz before the proposed trip, he had met MacMillan at Lynn's Grunewald house. MacMillan, much taken with him, proposed that he audition for his company. Frey, a political idealist and activist, a free spirit and apt to get into trouble with the authorities, auditioned and was hired. Somewhat nonplussed by MacMillan's attentions, he was all too gratified to be at the receiving end of the choreographer's creative efforts, which, needless to say, advanced his career. In a disarmingly naïve way, he accepted MacMillan's all too obvious interest. However, Frey was heterosexual and MacMillan's attentions were not going to lead anywhere. To outsiders it seemed like a simple tease.[62] Ray knew about this as MacMillan had told him, 'You know he showed me his new underpants; did he want me to make a pass?' MacMillan, possibly inspired by Frey's gauche way of moving, experimented more radically in *Cain and Abel* with the non-classical direction he had begun in *Anastasia*. The choreography moved a notch further from *danse d'école*. The ballet took on both archetypal and Freudian aspects rather than biblical: both brothers vie for the love of their mother, Eve. As the insinuating destructive force that goads Cain to fratricide, MacMillan introduced the Serpent, danced by Gerhard Bohner. *Cain and Abel* became a bleak and desperate indictment of the outsider – MacMillan's pet theme. If anything positive came out MacMillan's Berlin tenure, and he was, on the whole, very deprecatory about it, then it could be the influence of German Expressionism experienced directly in a German ambience. This stark vein would be pursued in his darkest work, *Meyerling*: a cul-de-sac of sexual excess, madness and suicide. Ray says, 'It is a great pity *Cain and Abel* is lost, the ballet was so exciting and one of his best. The fight between the brothers just made your hair stand on end.'

Frank Frey was roundly feted for his interpretation. According to Jann Parry, 'Kenneth had spotted qualities that Frank did not even know he had, investing him with an artistry he might not otherwise have developed so fully. Like the young Lynn Seymour, Frey was an instinctive actor, capable of expressing emotions he could not yet have experienced.'[63] The ballet certainly impressed Nureyev who was present at the premiere and, as he thought it a suitable vehicle for

62   Jann Parry, *Distant Drummer, The Life of Kenneth MacMillan*, Faber & Faber, London 2009, pp. 350–1
63   *Ibid.*, p. 350

himself, recommended it to the Royal Ballet. And the Royal Ballet, in view of the fact that MacMillan had been designated Ashton's successor, was interested in acquiring a new MacMillan choreography before his directorship began. Negotiations for *Cain and Abel* came to a halt when MacMillan insisted that Frey be engaged as a guest. He did not want a repeat of the humiliation he endured when Nureyev had usurped Christopher Gable's role of Romeo in *Romeo and Juliet*. Ashton would not accept Frey as a guest, reasoning that Frey was not a soloist. *Cain and Abel* was therefore not seen in London,[64] nor did the ballet survive its Berlin performances.

MacMillan, mulling over how to approach his next ballet for Berlin, *Swan Lake*, decided to take into consideration the taste of the German public as it had reacted to his ballets. A German audience, he thought, would not be content to view this ballet in its usual fairy-tale form. He decided on changing the central predicament of the scenario, the transformation of Odette into a swan and the efforts to break von Rothbart's spell, by making Prince Siegfried the central character. MacMillan kept the traditional Petipa/Ivanov sections of *Swan Lake* with additional choreography of his own and framed the ballet with a prologue and epilogue. In his treatment, Von Rothbart was not only an evil genius, but also took on the features of an *eminence grise* or father figure. *Swan Lake* thus became Siegfried's dream with Freudian overtones. In Ray's eyes, Frey, as Siegfried, was a case of wilful miscasting as he lacked the essential attributes of the *danseur noble* for this role. Lynn Seymour, returning to full-time dancing as Odette/Odile, was in Ray's opinion: '... just wonderful, for me she was the greatest ballerina ever.' Further, Ray commented, 'You didn't know which one to look at, Frank or Lynn – they were both so interesting on stage, it almost didn't matter how they danced technically. You wanted to know more about them as characters, not whether they could bring off the virtuoso stuff – which they couldn't.'[65]

---

64 Instead of *Cain and Abel*, the Royal Ballet acquired MacMillan's *Olympiade*, which proved to be a flop. It was taken out of the repertory after six performances.

65 Jann Parry, *Different Drummer, The Life of Kenneth MacMillan*, Faber & Faber, London 2009, p. 357

MacMillan had been right about the German audience's response to *Swan Lake* and the dramatic framing he had devised for it paid off. The ballet was a success even if the actual dancing was criticised and an *esprit de corps* seemed lacking. The latter could be explained by the announcement of MacMillan's imminent departure, as well as the fact that the production had gone through a difficult period of gestation. *Swan Lake* was so bedevilled by disputes with the administration that MacMillan had threatened to withdraw it completely. In addition, not a month away from the premiere, MacMillan's favourite sister Jean had died in a road accident. Depressed and almost totally incapacitated by the tragic news and alcohol abuse, he was not in a fit state to attend the funeral, nor, at times, to leave his rooms to attend rehearsals. *Swan Lake* proved to be MacMillan's swansong in Berlin, and ironically it became the most frequently danced of all the ballets he had mounted in that city. It remained in the repertory of the Deutsche Oper for the next twenty years.

Shortly after the premiere of *Swan Lake*, MacMillan travelled to Munich to meet Cranko and discuss plans for a new ballet for Stuttgart. By this time Cranko was joint director of both the Stuttgart and Munich ballet companies, and his home company was taking part in the Ballet Week Festival at Munich's National Theatre. Frank Frey also made the journey to Munich where the plan was for him to show the illustrious guests his Bavaria. An excursion to the mountains was planned. But on the morning of the outing MacMillan was discovered semi-conscious in his hotel bathroom. He had suffered a minor stroke, which initially partially paralysed him, but fortunately the symptoms soon went away. Discharged from the Munich hospital two weeks later, the German doctors' diagnosis was confirmed in London and he started a period of convalescence at the home of Georgina Parkinson and her husband Roy Round. Henceforth, MacMillan heeded the doctors' warnings about alcohol and immediately became a teetotaller, but it was impossible for him to renounce smoking. He returned briefly to Berlin to pack up and arrange his departure. Gert Reinholm, who had all along enjoyed MacMillan's trust, was already running the company and now became the official deputy director. He and Ray were in charge of the company until the end of the season.

Almost a year after MacMillan's stroke the Frank Frey saga continued with another dramatic episode. This time it provoked a breach in MacMillan's friendship with Cranko which, sadly, would not be repaired before the latter's untimely death in 1973. MacMillan's ill-fated trip to Munich had been to discuss *Miss Julie* (based on the Strindberg play), the ballet he had proposed to choreograph in Stuttgart. It would star Marcia Haydée in the title role, partnered, according to Cranko's wish, with one of Stuttgart's male soloists as the valet Jean. MacMillan, though, insisted on Frey for the part and in the end got his way. This was the first of several disagreements; and one could question Cranko's resistance to this casting. Had *he* not been particularly sensitive to the qualities of his favoured dancers and the way choreography is influenced by their collaboration? Further disaffection occurred when it seemed that the decor for *Miss Julie* had been shoddily constructed and that Cranko had interfered with both the set and with decisions about the costuming. Barry Kay, the designer, stormed out after the general rehearsal, requesting his name to be removed from the production. MacMillan, too, was not present at the premiere and Cranko cancelled the ballet after four performances. It was never mounted again.[66] Ray heard about all this from afar, and as the ballet was created in Stuttgart and was a Stuttgart production, he had nothing to do with it, nor was he present at the premiere.

The Berlin experience, with Ray functioning for the first time as a full-time ballet master and assisting a world famous choreographer in trying circumstances, had proved not only very challenging but, initially, a despairing period of Ray's life. Not one to be dragged under, he coped with the difficulties in a pragmatic way. Ray emerged from the experience unruffled and able to write it up to life's experience. In a certain way, this was a rite of passage, which later, when he was

---

66 Jann Parry, *Different Drummer, The Life of Kenneth MacMillan*, Faber & Faber, London 2009, pp. 371–2

at the helm, would stand him in good stead. What rescued him from being completely swallowed up in servitude to a difficult master was, ultimately, Maximo's presence and their togetherness. The bond that had brought them together strengthened and it lasted.

Ray, reflecting on his career in ballet and how he had made good in Germany, is grateful to the mentors he was lucky to have had. In particular, he wishes to give credit, firstly, to Papa Beriozoff who, when he first moved to Stuttgart, entrusted him with solo roles for which, in Ray's own words, 'I was perhaps not suited nor did I have the technique.' Secondly Cranko, not unduly concerned with his age and technical proficiency, gave him the most fulfilling roles of his career. He had the opportunity of extending his interpretative skills in a range and depth not usual in dance. And again, it was Cranko who encouraged him to choreograph, a talent he would later develop as he made his way in the world of freelance. As for MacMillan, Ray was thankful to have worked for, and with, this Scottish choreographer who, during the second half of the twentieth century, became one of the most important and inventive of his generation. At the time, neither MacMillan nor Ray saw Berlin as a glorious episode in their careers. But it was in retrospect not without its positive side. MacMillan, to his credit, though being all along *au courant* about being Ashton's successor at the Royal Ballet, had not treated Berlin as a stepping stone. As early as November 1966, after the premiere of his first programme of ballets – which included the much-applauded *Concerto* – he had been told that when Ashton retired in 1970, the post would be his. This was kept a closely guarded secret and MacMillan certainly did not behave as if his term in Berlin would be a short one. Ray, too, had no inkling: 'No, I wasn't aware that he would be leaving us to take over the Royal Ballet. It came as a surprise.' In Berlin, MacMillan made use of the opportunity offered him to explore and extend his dance vocabulary while also able to try his hand at the full-length ballet – a genre which would soon become an important part of his *oeuvre* – and to direct a large company. All told, MacMillan left the Ballet of the Deutsche Oper with an enhanced reputation and a repertory that demanded both classical sovereignty and expressive modernity. Whatever difficulties were experienced along the way, due to his own psychological make-up or collaborative ineptitude, the profile of the German company was raised to international standards.

MacMillan's premature departure from Berlin threw the Deutsche Oper's planning for the next season into complete disarray. As one of the larger ballet companies in Germany, not only was it imperative to organise the repertory for the forthcoming season, but a new director had to be found. A provisional solution was reached with George Balanchine elected artistic advisor to the company. De facto, though, this was something of an honorary title. He would never be in residence in Germany but this arrangement allowed the company to draw on works from his large *oeuvre* while continuing to perform the MacMillan ballets that were already in the repertory. For the time being Gert Reinholm remained responsible for the daily running of the company – as he had more or less been doing since MacMillan's indisposition. This would be the situation until John Taras, choreographer and ballet master of the New York City Ballet, took over from the 1970–71 season. Curiously, the fact that Balanchine entered the picture at this stage filled in a gap in Ray's education. Ray encountered the master of neoclassicism in Berlin and in person. Dancing at ABT, Ray had enjoyed the eclectic nature of that company's repertory, coming into contact with most of the established choreographers of the mid-twentieth century, either by dancing their ballets or, often, being coached by them. But Balanchine had been missing.

John Taras, apart from his own activities as a choreographer, often functioned as Balanchine's deputy, mounting his works all over the world. He had already come to Berlin to teach the company *Ballet Imperial* in 1968. In September/October 1969 during the first post-MacMillan season, he returned to supervise a Balanchine triple bill consisting of *Apollo, Episodes,* and *Symphony in C*. Ray, as first ballet master, was naturally involved in this rehearsal period. He got on well with Taras who found in him a kindred spirit. When Balanchine arrived for the final rehearsal period Ray was thrilled to be part of the preparations and observe the Russian master at work. According to Ray, 'It was a revelation seeing Balanchine rehearsing his own works. For example, in *Apollo*, he explained that the role of Apollo, contrary to expectation, is not at all classical. It shows all those modernistic tendencies he had been exposed to while a young choreographer in Russia.' Taras enthused to Balanchine about Ray's assistance, 'You know, without him [Ray], the ballets would have been in a terrible mess. We're lucky he helped prepare them.' But unexpected and remarkable praise for Maximo came from the master himself. 'He [Balanchine] said, "I'm going to take you with me to New York and have you show the men there how to dance this."' Maximo was cast in the fourth movement of *Symphony in C*, and in *Episodes*, in the section called 'Concerto', he partnered Kay Mazzo. Mazzo and Karin von Aroldingen, from the New York City Ballet, were appearing as guests.[67]

---

67   My main source of most of the detailed information about Kenneth MacMillan's life and work that touches on Ray Barra's story has been Jann Parry's excellent *Different Drummer, The Life of Kenneth MacMillian*, Faber & Faber Ltd, London 2009.

16

Minorca: property owners and plans for the future

Balanchine certainly livened up the working atmosphere in Berlin with his hands-on approach and the enthusiasm he generated in rehearsals. But Balanchine, experienced live, would be a one-off event. Gert Reinholm had told Ray that he was not in a position to guarantee a long-term contract even with Balanchine nominally in charge. Ray, ever one for planning ahead and making sure, after his so-called penurious youth, that he would be financially secure, felt he needed a guaranteed three-year contract. And there was a good reason for a steady source of income: he and Maximo had spent all their savings. They had bought three parcels of land on the island of Minorca. The idea of buying property on Minorca came from a tip Maximo had been given while still dancing in Stuttgart. His dresser there, a Catalan, had urged him to investigate the island of Minorca for acquiring property at a very reasonable price. The market was still totally undeveloped. This was before the holiday property boom flooded over from Majorca to all the other Balearic Islands. Maximo, already thinking of the future, was adamant about not getting old in

Germany and was already considering where he would like to live once he stopped dancing. For both of them, Ray and Maximo, the choice of Spain as their future base was a foregone conclusion; both had Spanish blood and felt a natural bond to the country of their parents. In addition, apart from the hoped-for reasonable property prices, Minorca was, in itself, a major attraction: an island encompassed by the Mediterranean. This took care of Maximo's primary concern that their future home should be close to the sea. Maximo's dream was to have his own sailing boat. As a youth he had excelled in most water sports: he was a graceful diver and had won prizes in swimming competitions; water was his element. Living on the coast and being able to sail the seas would therefore be the realisation of his dream. Ray, on the other hand, was not that comfortable about deep water. 'I had a tremendous fear of water. When I was very young my father threw me into the swimming pool at a public baths. He imagined that this would be a good way of getting me to learn how to swim. But he was wrong. I almost drowned – or so I imagined. Another traumatic experience was when my father took me out in a fishing boat in stormy weather. We were still living in San Francisco, so it must have been a just a short time after the swimming pool incident. Far out at sea – in the Pacific Ocean – I became terrified by the alarming heaving and plunging of the boat as it cut through the swell. I suppose my father thought that I might follow his footsteps by becoming a seaman. For some time afterwards I was absolutely terrified of water, and was very reluctant to get out of my depth. Of course, later, I did learn how to swim, but remained very much an amateur. For Maxi's sake I went along with his sailing dreams – and grew to love it!'

In the summer of 1967 they decided to see what Minorca was like and if it could be the sort of place that would suit them. Ray: 'As we wanted to be mobile on the island, we decided to motor there in our own car. At the time we had a red Volkswagen Beetle; not exactly the sort of car for long distances but that's what one did in those days. Motoring all the way to Spain then was a much more strenuous undertaking than it is today, because, in spite of the distance, the network of highways was less extensive. Our route took us from Berlin through Germany and France and on to Spain. In Barcelona we stopped over to visit Maximo's family who had settled there. Then we took the ferry to Mahón, the main port of Minorca. But our destination was Ciutadella from where we wanted to investigate the northern coast, in particular Cala Morell (*cala* in Spanish means bay or cove). In Ciutadella, by chance, we met a delightful family who had a small *pension* situated on the inlet of the sea to the town. It was most picturesque. The owners more or less adopted us and were very helpful in giving us directions about how to get to Cala Morell. They even provided us with a picnic snack. On hearing that we were thinking about buying property there, they reacted as if Cala Morell were miles away, even though it was only some twelve kilometres distant. In the dialect of the island, an offshoot of Catalan, they said, "Oh, it's in the north and the weather can be quite something. You wait for the first storms." At that time we weren't much interested in such warnings; later, permanently settled there, we knew otherwise. In the mid-sixties Cala Morell was on the verge of development: the land had been parcelled off and there was some attempt at road building. This was the spot recommended by our Catalan friends in Stuttgart. We thought that, should the location take our fancy, it would be good to stake an early claim. Well, we were much taken by Cala Morell. Standing on one side of the bay and taking in the natural beauty of an unspoiled coastline, we marvelled that there was not yet a building or person in sight. Our gaze followed the curving coastline to a part of land that jutted out like a peninsula.' Ray could not restrain himself, 'Wow, wouldn't it be wonderful if we could buy something in that part?' Maximo was equally enthusiastic. All of a sudden a voice from behind them, as if an island spirit was responding to their rhetorical query, said, 'Yes, you can, the land is for sale and I can tell you where to go should you be interested.' Turning around they saw a man who had quietly approached them without their noticing it. He was from the island, was very friendly and told them he knew the property agents. He gave directions as to where they would find the office. But, for the moment, they wanted to investigate the cove and clambered down to the beach.

Heading for that part of land that jutted out like a peninsula, they continued along the water's edge in the soft sand. But soon, in order to progress further, they had to leave the beach. With some difficulty, they clambered up the hillside – an ascent of some forty metres and no paths; it was like mountain climbing. Having reached the top they still had to make their way through the weather-beaten vegetation of thick bramble to get to the peninsula-like point. There they halted in their tracks. It was way beyond their imagined vision of what the island could offer: 'Wonderful, this was it – fantastic!' Here, the land, too, had already been divided up and it looked as if they would need four plots on which to build their dream house. Later, at negotiations, it was explained that, according to the regulations, they were not permitted more than three. The land they had selected for their future property was on the Punta de s'Elefant. There was an obvious reason for this name. At that point nature had carved out a rock formation that resembled an elephant: it had four sturdy legs and a trunk. The next day they went in search of the estate agency's office. Actually it was hardly an office; it was situated in a windmill that had been transformed into a bar. It all seemed too good to be true; was destiny tricking them in some way? But no, there was no hitch to the proposed sale except that, as yet, there was no road access to the land they wanted to build on. It would take another ten years before a road was built. The reason for the delay was the need to construct a bridge over the gulley in the curve of the cove. This gulley became a rivulet when it rained in winter causing erosion; it needed proper sluicing pipes to control the flow of water. For the moment this didn't matter as they couldn't start building yet; the money they had saved was just enough to pay for the land. They arranged to pay outright in order to avoid taking a mortgage, but this meant that henceforth, they would have to be careful about daily expenditure. With future austerity looming, both decided there and then to give up smoking. As a symbolical gesture they handed over their cigarette lighters to the son of the *pension* owners who, somewhat puzzled, took custody of them. He couldn't believe his luck being the new owner of such elegant accessories: Dunhill lighters. Another decision, in order to save money, was not to frequent the barbershop: they would cut each other's hair.

Almost immediately they became the talk of the town. It must have been the red Beetle in which they toured about the island: it signified something both exotic and modern, visible evidence of Germany's 'economic miracle' that showed up a rather underdeveloped Minorca with its donkeys and carts. Whether perceived of as a gay couple or not, the two young men, now known to be dancers, intrigued the local natives and were rapidly and warmly welcomed as future inhabitants of their island. For the remainder of that first summer, taking picnic lunches with them, they went each day to Cala Morell. It was as if they needed to have physical proof of their acquisition while planning their future home on the site. As no one was about they were free to enjoy the cove, swimming and sunning themselves in the nude. It was decided, once again in an endeavour to save money, that next summer they would not go to Minorca for the holidays but stay with Maximo's parents and family in Barcelona. Ray: 'It was a big mistake. We spent more money than we ever would have holidaying on Minorca!' The following year, 1969, when they returned to Cala Morell, they saw that some property development had taken place: a block of holiday apartments had been built on the bay. In fact this offered a practical solution to their problem of having a *pied-à-terre* on the island while their house was being built. They immediately set about purchasing an apartment and each summer, for the next two successive years, they acquired an additional one, ending up with three. Ultimately, of course, the apartments proved a sound investment and were sold off at a profit when they were no longer needed.

17

Ballet Master in Frankfurt (1970-1973): re-enter John Neumeier

The question of what would happen after Berlin solved itself without much to-do by a request from an unexpected source. John Neumeier, whom Ray had known as a colleague in Stuttgart, contacted him. He wanted to know if Ray would be his ballet master when he took over as director of Frankfurt's ballet company. The company there was part of the *Städtische Bühnen* (Municipal Stages), Frankfurt am Main's opera house/theatre complex as it was then known. Ray's connection to John Neumeier went back a few years. They had first met in 1963 when Neumeier was a student of the Royal Ballet School. Ray and Marcia Haydée were in London at that time, invited to appear in Dame Margot Fonteyn's annual gala in aid of the Royal Academy of Dancing. They were scheduled to dance the *Balcony pas de deux* from Cranko's *Romeo and Juliet*. Cranko, ever on the lookout for prospective dancers for his company – especially male – had asked them, while they were in London, to check out possible candidates from the Royal Ballet School. With this in mind, they went to watch classes of the senior students at the Upper School, Baron's Court.

Sitting in on a national dance class given by Maria Fey, they watched student John Neumeier practising the steps with great concentration and enthusiasm. Afterwards, in discussion with the school's teachers who highly recommended Neumeier as a suitable candidate for Cranko's company, Marcia and Ray approached him about seeking an engagement with Stuttgart.

By the mid 1960s, the Royal Ballet School had acquired the reputation of a respected pedagogic institution for classical ballet. It attracted many young dancers who were eager to join the mother company on graduation. However, not every graduate would, or could, have the chance of an engagement with the Royal Ballet. Of the school's most talented graduates, the company was obliged to offer places to those originating from the UK itself or from the Commonwealth, i.e. from Canada, Australia, New Zealand and previously, former colonies such as South Africa and the Rhodesias. This had been the situation former students such as Marcia Haydée and Maximo, as foreigners, had faced (this ruling no longer applies). Neumeier probably had no illusions about gaining a place with the Royal Ballet, even if he might have harboured such a wish. He was attending the Royal Ballet School on a scholarship from his university.

John Neumeier was born in Milwaukee, Wisconson, USA. Like many a dance-crazed youth of the time, he was inspired by the Hollywood musical film to want to become a dancer. He began learning tap dancing before progressing to acrobatics and then to classical ballet. Much later, while a BA undergraduate at the Jesuit Marquette University, he was introduced to Sybil Shearer, an established dancer/choreographer of the American modern dance scene. His mentor at the university, Father John J Walsh SJ, had arranged this influential encounter. Shearer had been a member of the Doris Humphrey-Weidmann company before establishing herself as a solo recitalist of remarkable individuality. At the time she had her own small company at Northbrook near Chicago and Neumeier joined it briefly before leaving for the UK. The not-inconsiderable influence of Sybil Shearer for dance, and that of Father Walsh's intellectual stimulation for literature and theatre, would colour Neumeier's creative path as he made his way in the world of dance. Ray and Marcia's recommendation for Neumeier to join the Stuttgart Ballet was most appealing. It seemed an attractive choice for his first engagement, as by this time the Stuttgart Ballet was emerging as an important address of the ballet scene. Neumeier knew of Cranko; he had seen his ballet *Antigone* when the Royal Ballet toured North America and had been impressed by it. And, curiously, while studying with Vera Volkova in Copenhagen during vacation time, she had introduced him to the South African choreographer. Neumeier arrived in Stuttgart in 1963 at a time when Ray's dancing career was blossoming. Both, in fact, participated in the premieres of Cranko's *Onegin* and of MacMillan's *Das Lied von der Erde*. At this stage of their careers Ray was a principal dancer and Neumeier a member of the corps de ballet. Within a few years this set-up would be inverted with Ray serving the creative talents of an up-and-coming choreographer.

Frankfurt am Main's *Städtische Bühnen*, like Stuttgart, used to be a *Drei-Spaten-Betrieb*, housing under one roof the three main divisions of theatrical presentation: opera, spoken theatre and ballet. Nowadays this combination has gone out of fashion. It would seem that each theatrical unit prefers to have its own separate autonomy and, in any case, the most essential reason for a marriage of opera and ballet has become almost obsolete. Opera productions are now generally given without proper dance interludes, and ballet companies prefer to maintain this exclusion. In the 1970s the ballet company of the Frankfurt opera house was one of many administered by middle-to-large-sized German cities. In the post-war years it was not in the first league. However, there was an interest in classical dance and established choreographers such as Walter Gore, Tatjana Gsovsky and Neumeier's immediate predecessor, Todd Bolender, had served there. Neumeier's engagement from December 1969 had been precipitated by the early departure of Todd Bolender and for half a season he took over the company as it was, presenting his first programme of ballets on 16th March 1970. For that occasion he choreographed two original works: *Brandenburg 3* and *Firebird*, while Cranko's *Opus 1* made up the middle piece of a triple bill. It was the latter ballet that Ray had been asked to mount. Curiously, *Opus 1* had been on the same programme at the premiere of MacMillan's *Das Lied von der Erde* and seemed to have enjoyed a better reception. Ray had not danced in *Opus 1* and was thus obliged to return to Stuttgart in order to study the ballet and make notes. The rather short ballet deals, like *Das Lied*, with a birth-death cycle – though in a much more abbreviated form. As Ray was still employed by the Berlin ballet and would be until the end of that season, he was not in Frankfurt to assist Neumeier with the creation of the two new ballets. Rosa Sicart, a Spanish dancer engaged in Frankfurt when Neumeier arrived to start choreographing, tells of the first rehearsals: 'There was this handsome young man looking somewhat like a flower-power creature with long dark hair almost to his shoulders and an unsettling penetrating gaze showing us the steps. We were all quite gaga about him.' From Stuttgart, Marianne Kruuse, whom one could consider Neumeier's first muse, was the guest soloist in *Brandenburg 3*. Very much in the spirit of the time, this ballet presented alternate versions of the same musical piece: the orchestral version of Bach's music followed by Walter Carlos's arrangement of the same music for synthesiser. Ray, on leave of absence from Berlin, taught *Opus 1*; the original male soloist, Richard Cragun, appeared as a guest partnering Heidrun Schwarz.

In Stuttgart both John Neumeier and Ray had availed themselves of the opportunities offered by the *Noverre Gesellschaft*, a society originally founded to promote the Stuttgart Ballet. Simultaneously, it provided young and aspirant choreographers a chance to have their works tried out in a professional way. Indeed, it was the *Noverre Gesellschaft* that helped establish Neumeier's choreographic reputation. Neumeier not only possessed a talent for making dances, but also showed a gift for costume design and Cranko, ever concerned about furthering the talents of members of his own company, generously gave him the opportunity of designing two of his (Cranko's) own ballets: *Die Befragung* and *Oiseaux Exotiques*. Ray, too, had asked

Neumeier to design the costumes for a ballet he was planning, but unfortunately was forced to abandon due to his torn Achilles tendon. Neumeier's ballet *Haiku*, created in 1968 for the Noverre Gesellschaft, an atmospheric mini dance narrative based on a Japanese poem, confirmed him as one of the emerging choreographers nurtured in Stuttgart. *Haiku*'s success was such that it was filmed for television by the WDR and probably played a part in Neumeier being offered the directorship of Frankfurt. Both Marianne Kruuse and Truman Finney who appeared in it joined Neumeier in Frankfurt from the start of the new season in August 1970. It was at this point that Neumeier was able to take over the company properly, engaging dancers and a ballet master of his choice.

When Neumeier became director in Frankfurt the company was not large; the dancers numbered twenty-eight – and when he left, thirty-two. Amongst the new members Neumeier assembled were the Danish Marianne Kruuse, a Stuttgart dancer who would feature prominently in nearly all of Neumeier's early works, and Truman Finney. Truman and John were already friends from the time they had studied at the Stone-Camryn ballet school in Chicago. Truman went on to the School of American Ballet and then joined the New York City Ballet, while John went to study at the Royal Ballet School in England. Both ended up in Stuttgart at more or less the same time. Truman, however, did not stay there long; he became a soloist in Cologne prior to joining Neumeier. Two other dancers, Max Midinet and Fred Howald, who created important roles in Neumeier's early works, also came from Stuttgart; Ray had taught both of them at the ballet school after his injury. Closing the ranks of the first soloists was Persephone Samaropoulou, a Greek, born in Alexandria, who had danced for Nasser in front of the pyramids of Gizeh. She had also been a dancer at Stuttgart but had left for the Zürich Opera House under the direction of Papa Beriozoff. With this nucleus of former Stuttgart dancers and trusted congenial friends, Neumeier set about creating a repertory of his own works. Gaining expertise with each programme of ballets, he developed his stagecraft skills, particularly in works with a dramatic component. This was the beginning of a phenomenal career.

Ray: 'Moving from Berlin to Frankfurt was something of a comedown. Obviously the set-up was much smaller and the possibilities limited but, on the other hand, there was the promise of a new beginning with a choreographer who seemed to know where he was going. Maxi and I both needed to earn money now that we were property owners and had plans for building a house. The work in Berlin, however exciting it had been under MacMillan, had wound down and the future was unclear. I immediately cleared up the matter of Maximo accompanying me, not wanting a repeat of what happened to us with MacMillan. John was fine about having Maximo; they had been colleagues in Stuttgart. In fact, as dancer colleagues, we were all on very friendly terms. As far as our working relationship in Frankfurt was concerned, I didn't mind the fact that I would be playing a subordinate role to John. He was very ambitious and I just didn't have that in me – where everything revolves around asserting oneself so intensively. In any case, my private life was much more important and I wasn't prepared to sacrifice that. And to be frank, just how talented I was as a choreographer was perhaps something I had thought about. Ever since I started ballet in San Francisco, I have loved and still love it. Even now I have a million ideas for choreography... but at my age? I think John's single-mindedness is a quality he might have acquired from his Jesuit university education or it was just innate: the ability to focus with the full force of his intellectual powers and carry a project through to its end. Besides, he was very talented! But, boy, was I busy.'

Ray: 'Obviously, at this stage of his career, John was new to directing a ballet company and I felt I had to help him. After I stopped dancing I had had about four years' experience as a ballet master and, especially after my time with MacMillan, I certainly knew how to run a company. It's all very well creating ballets, but the day-to-day planning requires a comprehensive overview. After the ballets are cast one has to decide how to divide up the rehearsal time. How long should a rehearsal last? Should one call all the dancers involved, etc.? And we were pretty low on staff: there was only John and me – the pianist was not much help either. We would spend hours counting out the music. Each new ballet had to be prepared in this way. Not every choreographer likes to have the music counted according to the musical phrases, or in a scheme that follows the rhythm of bar measures. Antony Tudor was famous for not counting the music, he wanted the dancers to breathe with the musical phrase. John definitely was a counting choreographer.'

Ray: 'We got an apartment through the theatre where our neighbours were Riccardo Duse and his wife Reka Tobias, both dancers in the company. We got on very well with them. Riccardo soon became a ballet master assistant and was with John when he choreographed the *Bacchanal* in Wagner's *Tannhäuser* at the Bayreuther Festival. In Frankfurt, I had such a workload that most days I didn't get back home until 10:00 at night. I was with John constantly… I had absolutely no private life. Fortunately there was Maximo, and he complained about hardly seeing me. Our dog, Habiba – Arab for sweetheart – suffered too, as we often had to leave her alone in the flat. She was a German shepherd and wouldn't let anyone come anywhere near us. Out walking she had to be muzzled. When she was alone in the apartment she barked and barked; the neighbours complained, so we had to give her back to the original owner – a policeman in Berlin.'

Ray: 'I must confess that I was disappointed with the two ballets, *Brandenburg 3* and *Firebird*, which John had choreographed as his first offering in Frankfurt in 1970 – during the half season before he properly took over. I didn't really have anything to do with them as I was still working in Berlin. These ballets were certainly not helped by the sets and costumes of Dorothea Zippel, a protégée of Cranko. I can remember being on stage during one of the final rehearsals when Dorothea casually told John that he could place various painted bits of scenery she had designed for *Firebird* where he wished. She said, 'I'm going to do Rosa's [Sicart] make-up,' and left. The set had awful borders and plastic wings which just hung down looking like bathroom shower curtains. I think John was much inspired by the Beatles film *The Yellow Submarine*.'

Neither of these ballets remained in the repertory very long. When Neumeier went about his next programme for the *Kammerspiele* (the smallest theatre of the *Städtische Bühnen* complex) in October 1970, there was a marked improvement, indicating care in selecting ballets that could complement each other. He presented three disparate ballets under the title *Unsichtbare Grenzen* (*Invisible Boundaries*) where each, in a certain way, referred to this theme. The programme was made up of *Aria da Capo*, an early Stuttgart ballet, *Frontier*, which he had choreographed for Scottish Theatre Ballet in 1969, and *Rondo* – the latter a new creation. *Rondo* was later filmed for television. '*Rondo* was definitely the best ballet he had choreographed to this date and showed the beginnings of maturity. It was very interesting, a collage ballet and the first time he used Gustav Mahler's music: the Rückert song "*Ich bin der Welt abhanden gekommen*".'

Of crucial importance in establishing Neumeier's reputation was *Romeo and Juliet*, which he choreographed the following season in 1971. This ballet offered abundant proof of Neumeier's gift for treating a dramatic subject on an epic level. It was his first full-length ballet. After a keen reading of Shakespeare's text, he focussed on the youth of nearly all the protagonists, which gave the familiar love story a logical freshness and thrust. Ray: 'When John did his *Romeo* ballet I had certain reservations. I suppose it was difficult for me to accept a new version after having done two in Stuttgart. And Cranko's *Romeo* had definitely been a big experience for me, not to mention it being the door-opener to his reputation. At the beginning I wasn't so taken by John's choreography, but as he worked on it, it became a revelation in dramatic terms. John was full of wonderful ideas for storytelling. For the narrative ballet, he can't be beaten. Filippo Sanjust's set and costumes, I didn't like much; they were rather minimalistic. However, when we mounted the ballet in Copenhagen on the Royal Danish Ballet with Jürgen Rose's set and costumes, now that was magnificent. Nureyev, by the way, stole many of John's ideas for his version. Working with the Danes on that occasion was a wonderful experience, almost like a love affair. I knew most of the dancers from the time I had accompanied Erik [Bruhn] when he danced there. When we were together Erik took me everywhere with him and didn't give a damn about what one thought or knew about the nature of our relationship – something quite daring for the time. The Danes joked about knowing my butt better than my front. Apparently I was continually bent over – with my back to them – peering into my notebook as I taught them the choreography. Most times the book was on the floor or on a chair. I had invitations to go out with them all the time. It was great fun.'

Going from strength to strength, Neumeier's next full-length ballet was one he managed to introduce into the 1971–72 season without incurring substantial production costs. This was his version of *The Nutcracker* for which he used sets and costumes stored in the theatre from a previous production – Todd Bolender's. Neumeier's *The Nutcracker* succeeded wonderfully on many levels beyond those usually associated with this ballet. The traditional second act, *The Kingdom of Sweets*, for instance, is anticlimactic; it often becomes just a banal series of divertissements. In Neumeier's version there is no Christmas celebration and therefore no Christmas tree. Instead it starts out as a birthday party; that of the twelve-year-old Marie who receives two special gifts, the nutcracker and a pair of pointe shoes. This version was immediately acquired by the Royal Winnipeg Ballet, Canada, and Ray was sent to mount it. Then Munich's Bavarian State Opera Ballet also requested it and there it acquired its ultimate form – a celebration of the Petipa era and of ballet itself – in an opulent staging with sets and costumes by Jürgen Rose. This production was also mounted in Hamburg when Neumeier transferred there. Setting John's ballets on foreign companies thus developed into an extensive freelance activity for Ray. After he quit his services as Neumeier's ballet master in Hamburg, this, for some time after, continued to be his connection to him.

The following ballet season in Frankfurt confirmed Neumeier's reputation as an emerging heavyweight on the choreographic scene in Germany. After showing that he could handle the full-length genre with *Romeo and Juliet* and *The Nutcracker,* and a memorable rethinking of *Daphnis and Chloe* that premiered in 1972, he naturally became a contender for the directorship of one of Germany's bigger opera houses. Ray remembers *Daphnis and Chloe* as perhaps his favourite ballet from the Frankfurt seasons. 'What he did with the libretto Fokine had devised was nothing short of genius. The atmosphere of the ballet was magnificent: the beginning with the arrival of the students on the island of Lesbos, the suggestion of heat, the prim governess protecting her brood of adolescents from the erotic playfulness of the sailors, the descent of the three goddesses from the flies on the lighting beam... and their choreography! He gave Maximo a wonderful double role: at first he is the sexy sailor Dorkon who teases Chloe. Later, in Daphnis's dream, he appears as the pirate leader who abducts her. The way John incorporated his own autobiographical experiences of his first visit to Greece was so clever. For instance there is the breathless awe with which Daphnis/John experiences Greek art at first hand. Then there is the incident of a mature woman tourist who, erotically aroused, must have pursued him. This figure became Lykainion who seduces Daphnis, after which he has an attack of sunstroke. Maybe John also suffered from sunstroke on that trip? With these details he personalised a rather naïve story, taking the whole out of the realm of Ancient Greece. I think one must give a word of praise to Jürgen Rose for his costumes and the set. *Daphnis* was his first collaboration with John. Rose developed, more so with John than with Cranko, into a fully fledged creative partner with an endless stream of wonderful ideas on offer. Otherwise I remember admiring the ballet *Dämmern,* which John choreographed to a selection of Scriabin's piano pieces – a very individual and atmospheric piece. And then indelible in my memory remains the Woman in White (a figure of death) portrayed by Phoni (Persephone Samaropoulou) in John's *Don Juan.* This was a very stylish ballet to the Gluck score, not often choreographed. In it, John created a variation to a spoken text taken from the Max Frisch play *Don Juan or The Love of Geometry.* One of the lines was, "He [Don Juan] could have been a dancer... !"'

The ballet that accompanied *Don Juan* at the November 1972 premiere was *Le Sacre*, Neumeier's version of *Le Sacre du Printemps*. This was one of the last ballets he choreographed in Frankfurt and one that has certainly stood the test of time. Frequently performed by foreign companies, it is perhaps one of the strongest versions around. Ray: 'At the end of one of the studio rehearsals, when the ballet was more or less finished, John dismissed the dancers and called Trixie to him, "Trixie could you stay a while and let's work on your solo."' Trixie Cordua was a strongly expressive dancer who had been in the company before John took over. It seemed as if German Expressionism in dance had found an outlet in her classical style. In Neumeier's *Le Sacre* she had been cast in a role equivalent to the original libretto's chosen victim. This meant she was to dance the final solo: a gruelling five-minute piece of auto-destruction. Ray: 'When she came up John said, "Trixie, take your clothes off." Somewhat perplexed, I looked at John and said, "Are you serious?" Trixie was delighted. I think that during all her solo rehearsals she had discreetly been trying to get John round to the idea of a naked dancer in his ballet. With each rehearsal she wore less and less, and sometimes her practice clothes were almost transparent.' At that time, in the early 1970s, there was a pervasive interest in appearing naked on the stage. Permissive sexual attitudes were in the air, generated by the hippie movement and musicals such as *Hair* and *Oh Calcutta* where nudity, in the latter, was the sensation of the production. In the world of dance, too, dancing naked was in an early experimental phase. For the Netherlands Dance Theatre, Glen Tetley and Hans van Manen had collaborated on a piece called *Mutations* where one section was danced naked. Ray: 'Even though we were alone, I hastened to lock the doors of the studio because the cleaning ladies often took a shortcut through after rehearsals. Trixie did her solo two or three times. It was quite shocking and her nakedness, in a way, emphasised the cruel and flagellating movements – a sort of auto-destruction. I kept thinking, *I hope nobody finds us like this, with a naked dancer. They'll think we're perverts!* Right up to the premiere, John was uncertain about her dancing nude, but in the interval after the first ballet, *Don Juan*, which went very well, he said to me. "I think I'm going to let her take her clothes off." We went on stage just before *Le Sacre* was about to begin and when John told Trixie, she screeched with joy: "Oh please, yes, you will make my mother so happy." After the performance, which was a big success, I bumped into Anne Wooliams [Stuttgart's ballet mistress], who had come to see the premiere. I asked her what she thought of the naked dancer. She looked at me quizzically, "What nudity? Was there any?" Trixie's solo is danced on an empty dark stage with a follow spot on her. The contrast between light and dark was thus quite extreme and perhaps that is why Anne Wooliams did not realise that Trixie had taken off her flesh-coloured tricot before entering for the solo. But, I presume, most of the audience was aware that there was a naked dancer. For me, though, I don't see the need for nudity and find the choreography strong enough.'

Someone who did take note of Neumeier's achievements in Frankfurt was August Everding who was due to become Intendant of the Hamburg State Opera from 1973. He invited Neumeier to become the company's ballet director. The Hamburg company was much larger than that of Frankfurt and, in the mid 1960s, had become the most important centre for performances of Balanchine's ballets in Germany.[68] Of course, being invited to direct a bigger company with greater resources and financial backing was most enticing, and Neumeier could hardly refuse. He took with him a small nucleus of dancers, mainly his soloists, and his trusted ballet master, Ray. For Ray, the move was equally desirable: not only was the opera house more prestigious, but the workload would be shared. There would be another ballet master and assistants.

Shortly before the move to Hamburg a tragic event happened: John Cranko died. He died on 26th June 1973 during the Stuttgart Ballet's return flight from a tour to the States. Ray was informed of

---

68   This came about through the warm collegial contact that Rolf Liebermann, composer and the Hamburg State Opera's former Intendant, had cultivated with Igor Stravinsky. It was Stravinsky who brought the works of his fellow Russian George Balanchine, with whom he had often collaborated, to Liebermann's attention.

his death while giving class: 'Class had started and, having finished the *barre* exercises, we were in the centre. The telephone at the back of the studio rang; something that normally shouldn't happen during class as it is disturbing. I was called to the phone, so I thought it might be something important. On the line was the artistic director of the Stuttgart Opera. He asked me if I knew what had happened. "Have you heard the news? Cranko has just died." I was speechless; it was just unbelievable… for several seconds I couldn't bring myself to say anything. The shock was so great. Then I managed to croak out, "Cranko has just died… class is finished." With my back against the wall I slid down to the floor.' The early death of the choreographer who had been instrumental in putting ballet in Germany on the international scene was a traumatic event. Cranko was just forty-five years old and it seemed that Stuttgart's potential for joining the upper echelons of the established ballet companies would be stymied. With Stuttgart deprived of its helmsman, its very existence seemed to hang in the balance. After a desperate what-shall-we-do-now period, a successor was found; in 1974 Glen Tetley was appointed director.

Ray was not in any way directly affected by the dilemma the Stuttgart Ballet faced – the loss of its creative leader – but he was devastated. Even though their distressful break-up had ruptured contact with Cranko for about eight years, his death meant the loss of a former mentor and a friend. There was only a three-year gap in their ages; Cranko, born 1927, was older. Ray: 'Stuttgart and Cranko were the best things that happened to me in my dancing career. I just couldn't believe he was dead. He had been the one to push me as a dancer and encouraged me to choreograph; we were very close.' Ray owed Cranko a lot, but of course it was a two-way deal: their relationship, besides that of Ray's serving a creative artist, was also one of comradeship bonded by the path they had trodden together in the making of the Stuttgart Ballet.

18

Hamburg with John Neumeier (1973-1976)

Hamburg was undoubtedly a step up the ladder in German ballet company ratings, though at the time, not yet a prime address – John Neumeier would soon bring about an upgrade. The Hamburg State Opera Ballet boasted more dancers and performances than Frankfurt; however, as was generally a widespread practice, the company was still obliged to participate in some opera productions. Overall, the ballet in Hamburg was treated as a much more important branch of the house. Nevertheless, John Neumeier's appointment as ballet director was not plain sailing. The press launched a storm of protest when it transpired he was not renewing the contracts of sixteen dancers of the ensemble. The Dancers' Union took the case to court but Neumeier's dismissals were upheld. It seemed like a bad start for the new director and for a while he was *persona non grata*. Unexpectedly, the ice was broken when he appeared for the first time before a Hamburg audience conducting a ballet workshop. This proved to be the turning point. A curious audience was immediately won over by the director's charm and manner of presentation.

Ray: ' I must say that I did like the move to Hamburg even if the workload was considerably more than in Frankfurt. One was drawn into giving one's best as it became clear that John would achieve an important place in the ballet scene. For a short time I was part of it.' Thanks to Neumeier's pedagogic skills as well as his choreographic demands, the Hamburg company rapidly showed signs of technical improvement and commitment in performance. The defining quality prevalent in his large and ever-growing *oeuvre* is the care he devotes to the dramaturgy: the shaping and structuring of his ballets, giving them a logical, dramatic cohesion – in a certain sense a *Gesamtkunstwerk*. Neumeier has developed a mastery of two genres: the narrative or story ballet and the symphonic ballet. The story ballet has remained an important pillar of his work, and though Ray did not remain long in Hamburg as a full-time ballet master – just three seasons – he assisted him often on such projects. Ray: 'John is an amazing storyteller; perhaps he is indebted to the "method" style of acting developed at the New York Actor's Studio during the 1950s and 60s and seen in film and on the stage during his youth. He has a fascinating take on projection in his ballets. I have heard him remark that the audience does not need to know exactly what is going on, be it an action or an emotional state, but it needs to know that the dancer has a firm intent and purpose: a commitment that will induce it to accept the danced text or situation, without necessarily knowing why.'

Ray: 'While I was engaged in Hamburg I assisted him on one of the most important and amazing ballets he created during that period: his version of *Swan Lake*, which he called *Illusions – like Swan Lake* (1976). The title is the only thing I don't like about the ballet; I find it a little clumsy. Why not just *Swan Lake* or *Ludwig*? But John's new title does tell you that what you are going to see will be quite unlike anything you've seen before. I would say that his version is one of the most poetic and moving I know.' The whole conception of the ballet showed great originality, uniting features of *Swan Lake*'s original libretto with an actual historical person: Ludwig II of Bavaria who became the ballet's main protagonist – in the ballet he is called the King. The ballet draws parallels between Ludwig II, Siegfried of the traditional *Swan Lake*, and even Tchaikovsky. Jürgen Rose, who had designed Cranko's *Swan Lake* in 1963, had at that time suggested setting the ballet in the period of Ludwig II, the Wittelsbacher 'fairy-tale king' who was crazy about building castles. The most well known, Neuschwanstein, in pseudo-mediaeval style, could serve as an emblematic setting for the production. A further persuasive connection was Ludwig's fascination with the swan motif – derived from his enthusiasm for Wagner's opera *Lohengrin*. However Cranko was not convinced and demurred about incorporating it. But it was Jürgen Rose who fired Neumeier's imagination for this project, just as they were on the verge of tackling another Tchaikovsky ballet, *The Sleeping Beauty*.[69] *The Sleeping Beauty* was postponed and *Swan Lake* took its place. Ray: 'John asked me to show some of the traditional choreography I had danced in Stuttgart. In fact, except for Ivanov's first swan scene, which was presented as "theatre in the theatre", the only original choreography he used was the Black Swan *pas de deux* and its variations. I can still remember the fun I had with Max Midinet, who danced the King, as we practised managing his coronation cape. We were alone on the stage. This scene happens when the King, sequestered in his own palace in a state of arrest, discovers a painting of himself in coronation robes. His memory is jogged and in a flashback we are presented with that event. Oh what fun we had swishing that beautiful heavy cape about!'

As for the symphonic ballet, it was in his second Hamburg season that John Neumeier boldly embarked on a series of ballets inspired by the music of Gustav Mahler. Symphonic ballet is a term coined during the 1930s and 1940s at a time when Léonide Massine, then considered the foremost choreographer of his age, co-opted symphonies of Tchaikovsky, Brahms, Beethoven and Berlioz for his ballets. He was not the inventor of this genre; there had been numerous choreographers before him who used symphonic music – thus the name – for their works. What distinguishes the 'symphonic ballet' as such, is the fact

---

69   Zehle, Sibylle, *Jürgen Rose*, Verlag für moderne Kunst, Nürnberg 2014, pp. 130–136

that the source of its emotional narrative or themes originates from the music. In contrast to the story ballet, the symphonic ballet's point of departure is the music itself. Should a choreographer wish to create a ballet based on the novel *Lady of the Camellias*, for example, then he or she has to find music on which to structure the narrative and hang the steps. In the symphonic ballet's case, it is the music itself that provokes an emotional response, determining the choreographer's kinetic reaction.

Both John Neumeier and Ray had danced in the premiere of Kenneth MacMillan's *Das Lied von der Erde* in Stuttgart – a ballet that bears all the hallmarks of the symphonic genre. This ballet, to Gustav Mahler's orchestral cycle of six songs based on Chinese poetry, seems to have been a seminal experience for Neumeier. He would, during a long and prolific career, devote himself to choreographing most of Mahler's *oeuvre*. Of the ten symphonies Mahler composed (the last was incomplete), he has choreographed eight; not to mention several of the song cycles. It was in Frankfurt, in his ballet *Rondo*, that he used Mahler's music for the first time: the Rückert song, '*Ich bin der Welt abhanden gekommen*'. Neumeier's commitment to Mahler started in 1974, when, for a commemorative gala in Stuttgart honouring the recently deceased Cranko, he choreographed the fourth movement of Mahler's Third Symphony. Titled *Nacht (Night)*, and dedicated to the Stuttgart Ballet, it featured that company's three main principals, Marcia Haydée, Egon Madsen and Richard Cragun. It proved to be such a compelling experience that he decided to complete the whole symphony with his own company. Ray: 'This work was quite something. Mahler's music had only recently been accepted into the musical canon, due to conductors like Leonard Bernstein who made it central to their repertoire. The symphony's length and the disparateness of the six movements made it a very challenging undertaking.' Incredibly, at the very same time, Maurice Béjart was himself busy with the same symphony, though, in the end, he choreographed the last three movements only. For his *Third Symphony* ballet, Neumeier developed separate themes for each of the movements according to his response to the music. In some cases he took as an inspirational nudge the programmatic titles Mahler had given them. (The Third Symphony is the only symphony where Gustav Mahler gave all the movements titles). In the symphony's final movement Neumeier matched the music's searing ecstasy with a beautifully extended *pas de deux* for Zhandra Rodrigues and François Klaus. Keeping Mahler's title of the movement, '*Was mir die Liebe erzählt*' ('What love tells me'), it attains a metaphysical level in the encounter of an angel with the male protagonist of the piece. Zhandra Rodrigues was exceptional as the androgynous angel on an arcane mission. Ray: 'Other than assisting John when he completed the *Third Symphony* in Hamburg, I was with him when he choreographed two others by Mahler: the *Fourth Symphony* for the Royal Ballet, London in 1977, and the First Symphony combined with the first movement of Mahler's incomplete Tenth Symphony under the title *Lieb' und Leid und Welt und Traum*, for Maurice Béjart's Ballet du XXe Siècle in Brussels.

The *Third Symphony* premiered at the end of the 1974–75 season. It inaugurated the end of the season Ballet Festival that concluded with a gala devoted to Vaslav Nijinsky. This gala was unique in that, unlike most that host a bevy of star guests who perform bravura pieces, it focussed on a single theme: the life and times of Vaslav Nijinsky. Guests included Mikhail Barishnikov, making his German debut, and Lynn Seymour. Alexandra Danilova was also present having been commissioned by Neumeier to mount the *pas de trois* from *Le Pavillon d'Armide* in which Nijinsky had made his Paris debut in 1909. Danilova seems to have been the only person who knew any steps from this forgotten ballet. Barishnikov, in Hamburg, learnt Nijinsky's role. Another first for Barishnikov was *Le Spectre de la Rose*, also one of Nijinsky's iconic roles, which he danced with Lynn Seymour. Ray: 'It was a most exciting gala, unlike any other I'd known. My duty was to film the evening from the central back loge.'

Ray gave notice to quit at the end of his third Hamburg season. The reason for leaving the company so soon is not quite clear and

Ray is not sure exactly what provoked a disagreement with John. As far as he remembers things came to a head when, at the end of a ballet workshop, he felt he was being unfairly criticised. Perhaps if one had allowed a day or two for the incident to simmer down, the matter could have been patched up. However, the snap decision to leave brought to a head what Maximo had been mulling over for some time. By now he had tired of ballet and wanted to stop. He had achieved his goals: dancing with reputable companies and becoming a soloist. Making a break while still young would allow him to devote himself to starting a new life with Ray on Minorca. The properties he and Ray had bought in Minorca beckoned; it was time to set up home in a sunnier clime. Again, as in Frankfurt, Maximo felt that he did not see enough of his partner even if the workload was now shared with other ballet masters. Neumeier's career had taken off with a great burst of creativity and ambition. This brought about new and manifold duties for Ray.

The third Hamburg season 1975–76 finished with a tour to Paris. It was there in *Théâtre de la Ville, Place Châtelet*, that Maximo took his final bow as a dancer and played out his own farewell ritual to the stage. This concerned his hair. Ever since his engagement in Stuttgart, a dismaying thinning of the hair was becoming more and more noticeable. In view of performing etiquette where ballet dancers are generally young and elegant, a toupee was deemed necessary. This hairpiece, which is glued on to the scalp and combed to blend in with existing hair, is fine if it is properly fixed and one is dancing alone. When dancing a *pas de deux* one has to be careful, but it is choreography of a modern and clinging sort that is perilous. Wearing a toupee is perhaps no big deal and, in fact, there are quite a few dancers obliged to do so, but losing it while dancing can be mortifying. This had happened to Maximo on the Frankfurt stage while dancing in Neumeier's *Baiser de la Fée*. The ballet ends with a *pas de trois*, a sort of apotheosis in which the fairy claims the bridegroom (Maximo) for herself and leads him to her kingdom of ice. Maximo, Fred Howald and Persephone Samaropoulou were involved in a series of complicated lifts when something started to go wrong. Persephone, to save herself from falling, groped blindly below her towards Maximo's head. In this way she managed to grip his toupee, which during the ensuing manipulations eventually fell to the floor. Maximo and Fred Howald were cast in a double role: both represented the same person and all of a sudden one of them was partially bald. The ballet came to an end but at the bows Maximo did not appear. The embarrassment of losing his hairpiece on stage was just too much for him.

Several years later, on the verge of retiring from ballet and relieved at being freed of the toupee obligation at every performance, Maximo ceremoniously did away with it. The final Paris performance over, and recovering from the exertion of his last appearance, he sat at his make-up desk in a state of undress. He had just removed the hairpiece and wiped off his make-up. With some deliberation he lit a match. A strange acrid smell of burning hairs mingled with leftover glue and perspiration spread over the dressing room and down the corridor. Dancers from neighbouring rooms, thinking there was possibly a fire, were drawn to the source of the smell. Entering Maximo's dressing room, they were reassured that there was no real danger. He was just busy with a little chore. He sat thoughtfully gazing at the expiring embers of the hairpiece.

19

Freelancing 1: The Neumeier ballets

Ray re-established contact with the Stuttgart Ballet by way of Neumeier's ballet *Hamlet Connotations*, which was commissioned by American Ballet Theatre. The stellar cast Neumeier had chosen for his creation included their superstar Mikhail Barishnikov in the title role, Gelsey Kirkland as Ophelia, Erik Bruhn as Claudius and Marcia Haydée as Gertrude. The Hamlet ballet came about at Barishnikov's insistence that Neumeier create a ballet based on the Shakespeare play for him. Neumeier began working on various solo parts with Barishnikov in Hamburg and then, during the Hamburg Ballet's first tour to Stuttgart, choreographed the anguished *pas de deux* between him and his mother Gertrude there. The rest of the ballet was completed in New York. *Hamlet Connotations* is a short ballet to music by Aaron Copland in which Shakespeare's play is reduced to its main protagonists: Hamlet, Gertrude, Claudius, Ophelia and the Ghost of Hamlet's dead father. Neumeier approached the drama in an abstract way as if it were a criminal investigation. The first part of the ballet is made up of testimonies: each character is introduced by making a statement concerning the death of Hamlet's father – in dance steps. Ray does not remember much about the early rehearsal period but he does remember that Barishnikov, early in his career in the West, was eager to open himself to as many choreographers and directions in dance as he could. Barishnikov was as accommodating and open to the demands the most exigent choreographer could wish for. There was never a 'Do you think I could do it to the other side?' or 'Maybe I could turn instead of jumping?' According to Neumeier, Ray rehearsed *Hamlet Connotations* in New York when he, Neumeier, was unavailable. When revived, at Marcia Haydée's behest in Stuttgart – she had by this time become ballet director – and later in Hamburg, Ray helped mount it. The German title of the ballet became, *Der Fall Hamlet* or *The Hamlet Case/Investigation*.

Although Ray had given notice to leave the Hamburg Ballet at the end of the 1975–76 season, he agreed to stay on for a few months into the new season to bridge the gap before his successor, Peter Appel, could take over. Peter Appel, at that time employed by the Basel Ballet in Switzerland, was not able to begin his duties at the beginning of the season. In a way, doing Neumeier a favour, and being around with no employment in the offing, brought about new and favourable circumstances for Ray. Neumeier asked Ray to assist on ballets he was creating for foreign companies. The first occasion was when the Vienna State Opera Ballet commissioned a ballet. This ballet, *Joseph's Legend* (m. Richard Strauss), was Neumeier's first creation for Vienna and premiered in February 1977. It proved to be a major event on all artistic levels. For a start, the choice of a seldom-performed ballet score by Richard Strauss, a favourite of Vienna's opera and concert-going public, was sure to please. Then, the two guests engaged for the central roles, both possessors of charismatic star quality, certainly upgraded the occasion. In the title role Kevin Haigen, a young dancer from Neumeier's own Hamburg company, interpreted Joseph with youthful, innocent vibrancy (the original Ballets Russes production of 1914 commissioned by Diaghilev had been intended for Vaslav Nijinsky – both in the title role and the choreography). Haigen was paired with an impressive guest from America: Judith Jamison. In fact Ray had seen Jamison in performance during the rehearsal period of *Hamlet* in the States and spoken enthusiastically of her to Neumeier.

Jamison, an exceptional dancer from Alvin Ailey's all-black dance company, wowed the Viennese audience. They had perhaps not seen anything in ballet like it before. Tall, statuesque and dancing barefoot, Jamison gave a searing interpretation as Potiphar's wife. The next important role, the Angel, was danced by Austria's own international star, Karl Musil. However, the production's 'cherry on the top' proved to be the decor and costumes by Ernst Fuchs – celebrated as one of the founding members of the Austrian school of 'fantastic realism'.

Ray: 'The working atmosphere during the creation in Vienna was great fun; I got on well with Judith Jamison. It was interesting to see that Judith, a dancer brought up in a modern American idiom, immediately coloured the movements John improvised or indicated with her own style. She made them her own. In a way we were an American team – Kevin, too, is American – and spent much of our free time together. When we went out to restaurants we tried all the Austrian specialities: *Wiener Schnitzel cordon bleu* – a favourite – the *Kalbsschnitzel* itself and *Tafelspitz*. Inevitably, once or twice, we just had to indulge in *Salzburger Nockerl* – to knock us out at the end of a meal. *Joseph's Legend* was such a success that it was filmed, the same year, with its original cast. I don't think the camera team was that familiar with filming ballet. Judith Jamison complained that she was filmed from too low an angle, emphasising her nostrils. In Kevin's case, there was almost open rebellion when it was discovered that a hair over the lens had ruined one of his solo's takes – and the one in which he had danced especially brilliantly. It just had to be filmed again. This solo lasts about ten minutes, which is really a marathon; there is practically no solo of this length in any of the ballets I know. Well thank goodness we, and he, have this documentation of him dancing this role. He was at the beginning of a great career.'

Of all the many full-length narrative ballets Neumeier created, *Lady of the Camellias*, to music by Frédéric Chopin, is probably one of his most important and successful. More than *Hamlet Connotations*, this ballet reopened the Stuttgart Ballet's door to Ray with a welcoming and amicable working atmosphere. There were several factors that favoured the prodigal's return: several years had passed since Cranko's death, *Lady of the Camellias* involved Marcia Haydée in the title role, and importantly, Ray was Neumeier's choice as his assistant. When Ray left Stuttgart to join MacMillan in Berlin, he had become *persona non grata* not only in Cranko's, but also in Marcia Haydée's eyes. After he left there was hardly any reference to him as the creator of two of the repertory's important roles: Romeo and Onegin. Indeed when the latter was presented in New York on Stuttgart's groundbreaking tour to the States, it was assumed that Heinz Clauss, who danced Onegin, was the creator of the role. Seldom was Ray's name mentioned in connection with these ballets or even with something of less importance like the *Hommage à Bolshoi pas de deux*.

Lady of the Camellias was an exciting project that brought out the best in all involved and provided Ray with an exhilarating fresh start in his old stamping ground. From the beginning, Neumeier communicated an insouciant affinity for the drama and period feel of Alexandre Dumas *fils'* novel. He had structured his ballet – as in the book – as though Armand Duval remembers and retells the sad tale. He had also made a felicitous choice in the music for his ballet: Chopin. Chopin, as many choreographers have discovered, is superbly danceable and in the case of *Lady of the Camellias* proved totally apposite to the spirit of the story. Neumeier succeeded in exploiting the drama of the *demi-monde* scenes of the early nineteenth century: the elegant and extravagant gowns, the coquetry of the kept women, the perfumed manners and toilette, not to mention Marguerite Gautier's soulful transcendence and the pathos of her death. Marcia Haydée's Marguerite Gautier, together with her portrayal of Blanche DuBois in another of Neumeier's literary ballets, *A Streetcar Named Desire*, revealed her consummate talent as the dancer/actress of her generation. Apart, possibly, from her Tatiana in *Onegin*, she had never been shown to better advantage than in this ballet. Jürgen Rose's costumes and decor opulently abetted the early nineteenth-century atmosphere.

Neumeier's *Lady of the Camellias* is made up of many *pas de deux* – including three main ones, one in each act, for the principal roles. Nevertheless, the ballet not only caters for the main protagonists; a large corps de ballet within each of the three acts has ample opportunity for challenging choreography. Here, Ray was of immense help. As he and Neumeier both lodged in the Schlossgarten Hotel, they inevitably got together before the rehearsals to plan the action of the day, either to count out the music or to try out steps. And Ray, an expert in *pas de deux* work, invented many of the steps for the group dances with Neumeier: the Blue Ball, the Red Ball, the Golden Ball and the second act country scene. They often got all tangled up while experimenting with the steps, either in the corridor or in their rooms – or wherever there was sufficient space – not quite knowing who was the boy and who was the girl. The ballet premiered in November 1978 and has subsequently been mounted on most of the main established classical ballet companies.

Ray: 'I was very happy and somewhat surprised at the extent of my welcome back to Stuttgart – especially from Marcia. There didn't seem to be any bad memories about my departure. In fact I had a great time and it was most fulfilling working there again. At the premiere Marcia sent me a thank you card. This is what she wrote: "Dear Ray, This production would not have been possible without you being here. Thank you for your marvellous work and for helping John and all of us. I hope you come back soon. All my love and once again thank you, Marcia."'

Neumeier and Ray were back in Vienna in 1983 for another commissioned ballet evening: *Daphnis and Chloe* and *Firebird*. Neumeier had already choreographed both these ballets in Frankfurt but decided to do *Firebird* anew. What distinguished the occasion was the fact that Lorin Maazel, then music director of the Vienna State Opera, opted to conduct the ballets. Part of the ambitious planning was for Nathalia Makarova and Anthony Dowell of the Royal Ballet to dance the leads in *Firebird*. However, Makarova was unable to participate and Lynn Charles from the Hamburg Ballet danced the bird; Dowell, however, was present while soloists for *Daphnis* came from the house company. Ray: 'What was incredible about the production was the idea of using one set to unite both ballets in some way. In *Daphnis and Chloe* a copy of the Apollo statue from the western pediment of the temple of Zeus at Olympia – now in the museum there – dominated the set. In this ballet a group of young students on an educational trip visit Lesbos to inspect the ancient site and the statuary. In *Firebird*, which follows, the idea of a dystopian world is suggested by using the same location, though in a state of dereliction. The Apollo statue is no longer erect; it lies on its side and seems to have been vandalised. Katschai, an evil despot in command of a robotic army of monsters, rules. The designer of both ballets was Jürgen Rose.

Tennessee Williams' play *A Streetcar Named Desire* was yet another classic of world literature that John Neumeier transposed into ballet. Again this was a vehicle for Marcia Haydée (Blanche DuBois). Interestingly, Neumeier tackled a subject with which Ray had already been involved twice. He had danced in Ballet Theatre's version by Valerie Bettis in 1955 and later took the male lead, Stanley Kowalski, in Kurt Jacob's choreography for German Television, the *Sudwestfunk* (Perhaps someday this TV ballet will be released on DVD. Then we might have a glimpse of Ray in a role that must have suited him superbly). Ray: 'Of course the fact that I had been in two *Streetcar* ballets intrigued John. He wanted to know all about them. *Streetcar*, I think, is really one of John's most successful story ballets; I was most impressed by it. A pity it is not performed that often.'

Ray: 'What was different to the play was the first act, which John had invented, deriving it from revelations Blanche makes during the main action. We are presented with her past: her wedding, the discovery that the man she is marrying is homosexual and his suicide. This act explains the traumatic cause of her neurotic state.' Musically, the division of the ballet into two disparate parts, the first to an orchestral version of Prokoviev's *Vision fugitives* and the second to Alfred Schnittke's cacophonous and aleatory First Symphony provided the drama with a shock factor.'

Freelancing for Neumeier as his assistant proved to be a regular and satisfying activity. Ray was not bound to the daily grind of ballet-mastering with one company all year round. There was only one task and that was the ballet in hand. Also he and John got on very well; there was a mutual respect for the crafting of ballets and Ray was almost always good-humoured, enthusiastic and respected by the dancers of the companies he worked with.

20

Freelancing 2: On his own

At Frankfurt's *Städtische Bühnen* it was usual at that time – the early 1970s – for dancers to participate in the opera house's repertory of operas and operettas. It was the duty of the ballet director/ choreographer or some designated person to create these dance interludes. When John Neumeier opted out of several of these 'chore' choreographies, Ray was all too happy to step in for him. In this way he could continue to hone his hand at dance making. His first choreographies for the Frankfurt opera house included dances in Johann Strauss' operetta *Der Zigeunerbaron* and Tchaikovsky's *Eugene Onegin*.

Choreographing dances or arranging movements for the *mise en scène* of operas inevitably brought about important contacts that were to sustain Ray when he had cut himself off from fixed employment. One of the most important of these dated from the very beginning of his Hamburg term, when he arranged dance for Götz Friedrich's production of *Le Nozze di Figaro* (1973) and the seldom-performed Massenet opera *Don Quichotte*. Götz Friedrich had served under Walter Felsenstein at Berlin's Komische Oper and established himself

Das Lied von der Erde: Ray, Marcia Haydée

Maximo Barra

Frankfurt Ballet Company; John Neumeier and Ray on left
Maximo as Benvolio in *Romeo and Juliet*
Maximo, Marianne Kruuse in *Baiser de la Fée*
Maximo, Marianne Kruuse in *Daphnis and Chloe*

John Neumeier

© Holger Badekow

Ray, John Neumeier
Ilse Wiedmann, John Neumeier, Ray
Illusions – like Swan Lake rehearsal with Max Midinet, Ray, Persephone Samaropoulou

Ray, Victor Hughes, John Neumeier, Truman Finney
Alexandra Danilova, John Neumeier, Ray
Ray, ballet master in Hamburg
Ray trying on the coronation robe, stage rehearsal
Illusions – like Swan Lake

House in Cala Morell, Minorca: Oripando
Maximo, Ray and the Buzzard Ulysses

Maximo and Ray sailing
Unity Grantham and her daughter Rosa

Ballet Nacional de España/Clásico
Ray's first ballet for the Spanish company: *Poema Divino*

Ballet del Teatro Lirico Nacional (Spain)
top row: *Nocturno*
Second and third row: *Hoja de álbum*

© Holger Badekow

Ray rehearsing Maya Plisetskaya
Presentation to Queen Sofia of Spain
Giselle Roberge, Ray's ballet: *Cain*

Deutsche Oper Berlin
Götz Friedrich (Intendant), Ray
The Snow Queen
Yannick Boquin, Raffaella Renzi, Tomas Karlborg, Lisa-Maree Cullum,
Alexandre de la Caffinière, Alexej Dubinin

Bavarian State Ballet (Ballet director Konstanze Vernon / Ivan Liska)
Don Quixote: Peter Jolesch, Tomasz Kajdanski
Raymonda: Amilcar Moret Gonzalez, Lisa-Maree Cullum
Swan Lake: Natalja Trokaj, Kirill Melnikov
The Team: Trudie Campbell-Tandy, Cherie Trevaskis, Ray, Thomas Mayr

Konstanze Vernon and Ray
Raymonda, première curtain call:
Lise-Maree Cullum, Klaus Hellenstein, Kirill Melnikov, Ray

Badisches Staatstheater Karlsruhe (Ballet director: Birgit Keil)
Carmen Act 2: Ensemble – Stage Design Klaus Hellenstein
Carmen Act 1: Carmen and Don José: Anaïs Chalendard, Flavio Salamanka

Teaching in Athens: Deni Tsekoura, Ray, Rosa Sicart
Friends: Sid Ellen, Andria Hall / Gudrun Sutherland
House in Marbella

as one of East Germany's most brilliant opera directors. He became something of a DDR cultural emissary, one of the few trusted to guest in the West. Nonetheless, in 1972, the year he directed *Tannhäuser* at the Bayreuth Festival, he did not return home. August Everding immediately snapped him up for the position of principal producer (*Oberspielleiter*) of the Hamburg State Opera. Friedrich took on the post in the same year Neumeier and Ray transferred to Hamburg and August Everding became intendant. From 1981 until his death in 2000 Friedrich served as *General Intendant* of the Deutsche Oper.

Friedrich and Ray, both born in the same year, 1930, immediately got on well. Their friendship later developed in Berlin when Friedrich, in urgent need of a ballet director, asked Ray to step into the breach at very short notice. Ray: ' I always called him "Prof" and he called me Ray. In my opinion his productions were generally full of sexual implication – and he couldn't get enough of the red light milieu! While we were busy on *Nozze di Figaro* he wanted to know if the Spanish aristocracy was still concerned with things like inspecting the sheets for traces of blood after the first matrimonial night to check if the marriage had been consummated. I suppose he needed this information for *Nozze de Figaro.* But I had no clue what the Spaniards thought important about such matters. Anyway, I am an American!'

Unlike many opera directors, Friedrich was not averse to dance in his productions. Perhaps his second marriage to a dancer accounts for this tolerance. The Massenet opera *Don Quichotte*, which was their next collaboration, must have provided both Friedrich and Ray with great amusement as they could indulge in satirising bourgeois taste. This production of *Don Quichotte* was more or less a return to the one Friedrich had originally directed for the Komische Oper in Berlin in 1971. It was set in some unnamed city in the year of the opera's premiere, 1910. For his *mise en scène*, Friedrich, abetted by Ray, set about integrating chorus and dancers – a fashionable practice in opera production at that time. The most extended piece Ray choreographed, entitled '*Ballets Russes*', was a parody of the sort of ballet Diaghilev's company presented in the early decades of the twentieth century.

Probably at Friedrich's instigation, Ray was encouraged to do a drag-queen number, 'El Flemenca', danced by Max Midinet.

Ray's next assignment in Hamburg was Donizetti's *opera buffa Viva La Mamma*. The production proved to be an unexpected box-office and audience success during the 1975–76 season. This opera, Donizetti's twenty-fifth, had recently been rediscovered amongst a disordered mass of music scores and given a new lease of life in a Kassel production. The Hamburg production, directed by Nikolaus Sulzberger, followed soon after. The Mamma of the title is sung by a bass or alternatively by a baritone. Two dancers, la Primaballerina and il Primoballerino, and a ballet master, are involved in this parody of stage conventions of opera productions of the 1830s. Ray explained that he was inspired by Antony Tudor's *Gala Performance* which, though he had not danced in it, he knew from his ABT days. In *Gala Performance* Tudor satirises three ballerinas, Russian, Italian and French, who try to outdo each other in a performance. Ray's version featured a ballerina whose feathered headgear always gets in the way. Victoria Pulkkinen and Richard Gibbs danced these roles. During Ray's Hamburg days they were his and Maximo's closest friends.

August Everding, during his term as intendant of the Hamburg State Opera, also requested Ray for his 1976 production of *Parsifal* (costumes and decor: Ernst Fuchs). According to Giselle Roberge, new to the Hamburg Ballet and cast as a flower maiden in the second act of *Parsifal* – her first opera duty – Ray made the scene in Klingsor's enchanted garden into as much fun for the dancers as possible. Often this scene can be a rather vapid affair – dancers clad in diaphanous apparel attempting to entice Parsifal to perdition – and not something choreographers go out of their way to do.

Everding went on to have Ray collaborate with him on two other opera productions. The first was the baroque opera *Il Saint'Alessio* by Stefano Landi at the Salzburg Festival in 1977. This opera, dating from 1632, is about the life of the fifth-century Saint Alexis; the first ever opera to be written on a historical subject describing the saint's inner life and attempting a psychological characterisation that was new to opera.[70] Just how successfully Everding achieved this was a debatable point. According to Ray: 'There was hardly any dance, only poses, although I did create a successful, even if somewhat anachronistic, thigh-slapping version of a Bavarian *Schuhplattler* dance, which was said to have a rather Spanish influence (I wonder why?). The noted opera director Jean-Pierre Ponnelle who did the costumes for the production and was himself directing *Don Giovanni* in the Kleines Festspielhaus nearby complimented me on my contribution. "You've certainly done a better job than Everding." I was quite bucked by this. I knew Ponnelle from Stuttgart when I danced in a Carl Orff triple bill for which he had designed the costumes. Ponnelle enjoyed a meteoric career, becoming one of the most successful opera designers and directors of the 1960s, 70s into the 80s.' A further collaboration with Everding in November 1984, in Munich, was *Johanna auf dem Scheiterhaufen* (m. Honegger). Neither of these Everding productions had proper dance but they were performed at prominent festivals or in important opera houses.

Verdi's opera *Aida* often became Ray's calling card throughout these years. In all, he must have been involved in at least three productions with his own choreography. If there's one opera where dance is practically indispensible, *Aida* must top the list. Ray's first encounter with *Aida*, other than dancing in it as his debut in Stuttgart, was as Neumeier's assistant at the Salzburg Festival in 1979. Neumeier had been engaged to do the choreography for the Herbert von Karajan production starring José Carreras and Mirella Freni. Ray: 'At the general rehearsal von Karajan showed his imperious dictatorial side. We were on the stage of the *Grosses Festspielhaus* rehearsing the Triumphant March. An enormous pyramid with dozens of extras clustered around its summit was dominant in this scene. The chorus was on the lower level while the extras, representing the captured Ethiopian warriors, were all at the top, on display as spoils of war. As the scene continued they started to hang over the barriers, smitten by the heat of the lights that bore down on them. Fortunately they

---

70   English entry on Landi in Wikipedia.

had safety belts securing them to this structure. Many had fainted [according to Neumeier, only one]. Von Karajan ignored the situation. He relentlessly continued to conduct the orchestra taking no note of these unfortunates. No one dared call his attention to what was happening on stage. He was not to be interrupted.'

Ray: 'The dancers who took part in the Salzburg Festival's opera productions came mostly from the Vienna State Opera Ballet. The Festival gave them the chance to appear at one of the most famous music festivals in the world where there was probably enough free time to enjoy a holiday and make some money at the same time. The dancers had a reputation for being difficult, especially with choreographers or choreography they didn't like, but I got on famously with them. For one thing, I knew most of them from the *Joseph's Legend* production back in 1977. I had also made friends with one of the union leaders, Gerhard Dirtl, and his wife. They were great fun and we laughed a lot. Anyway being "in" with the union was definitely a good thing. I myself had been a dancers' union representative back in my Stuttgart dancing days and had suffered John Cranko's wrath when I took a stand for my colleagues. This was during a stage rehearsal of Kenneth MacMillan's *Danses Concertantes*, which had just been thrown together. The poor dancers, myself included, just didn't know which wings to use for entries and exits. I brought the rehearsal to a stop requesting that someone responsible come up on stage and put us in the picture. Cranko was furious at the tone of my request – yes, I was at that moment frustrated and angry.'

One of the most prestigious *Aida* productions for which Ray did the choreography was Götz Friedrich's for the Deutsche Oper in 1982. This West Berlin production boasted a cast led by Luciano Pavarotti as Radames, Julia Varady as Aida and Dietrich Fischer-Dieskau as Amonasro. Ray said that Julia Varady, Fischer-Dieskau's wife, was very solicitous about him. Perhaps he should not have been singing such a strenuous role at that stage of his career. Ray knew Varady from Frankfurt when they were both engaged there. In *Aida*, for the big celebratory dance ensemble that follows the Triumphant March,

Friedrich requested that four dancers – purportedly generals of the victorious Egyptian forces – replace the solo couple that usually is highlighted in that number. It turned out to be a successful innovation and Ray so liked this idea that he used it in subsequent productions. At the Kennedy Center in Washington he enlarged on this model with dancers from the Washington National Ballet and later did a similar version for the Chicago Lyric Opera. Ray: 'When I did *Aida* in Chicago, Maria Tallchief and her sister Marjorie, both one-time celebrated ballerinas, were present at the rehearsals. They had ties to the ballet company there, Maria having established the Chicago City Ballet. Watching the rehearsal, Maria said to me, "My, you *have* done a very Russian version!" It must have been because I had the men do lots of *double tours*, split jumps and other showy bravura steps.'

21

Minorcan days

Maximo, though happy to have his dancing years behind him, was soon drawn back into the sphere of ballet. It was inevitable that this should happen as it was common knowledge that he had had a successful career with important ballet companies in Germany. It all started when he was asked by a gym teacher in Ciutadella to help train a talented young pupil. The teacher wanted her to look more graceful, in fact, more balletic. Maximo duly set about this task and, it seems, was successful. Then, when the brother of this teacher opened a fitness studio at the beginning of the aerobic craze, he asked Maximo to teach there. Of course what Maximo taught wasn't quite authentic aerobic or even ballet, but a jazz-like version of his own concoction. Those who frequented the gym were just normal people; what they wanted was a serious workout, and if it was combined with interesting dance movement, so much the better. Word spread and Maximo's aerobic classes became very popular. It must have been the choreographic element of his classes that then led to his teaching ballet. For it soon occurred to the mothers of many young girls on the island that there was someone, on hand, who could teach their darling daughters ballet – in all probability without the prospect of them continuing on to a professional level. And so Maximo began to give proper ballet classes. Apart from introducing his young pupils to the rudiments of ballet, he taught them the value of discipline. Ballet is a perfect medium for doing this; it is structured and requires concentration. When attending class Maximo's students had to have their hair in a kempt state, usually tied back into a bun. They were not allowed to be late and there had to be silence during the lessons. In the end it was the parents who benefitted from Maximo's strictness. Their offspring acquired a modicum of discipline, something often lacking in modern families. Ray: 'The school grew, and when there were enough pupils and a certain standard had been reached, we arranged a performance to show off what had been achieved. This is where I entered the picture: I did the choreography. I did so many ballets for children; it became all the rage. We put them on in the cinema of Ciutadella's big square. I choreographed *Peter and the Wolf*, Mozart's *Eine kleine Nachtmusik*, Britten's *The Young Person's Guide to the Orchestra* – even Gounod's *Walpurgisnacht*. As we became more ambitious, what we needed for the productions were boys. So we persuaded the brother of one of the girls to participate. We showed him how to partner. At first he was not required to do any steps, just accompany and support the girl. Very soon we roped in all his friends into our productions and in this way ended up with a little ballet company. Some of Maxi's ex-pupils did in fact become professional dancers. Other than ballet, Maxi taught English. He was especially proud of one of his pupils, Pedro. I had overheard one or two lessons but once, on my return from working in Germany, I was surprised to discover that he spoke English with hardly any accent at all. Maxi modestly said that there was a faint trace of an accent, but I couldn't detect it. In all, he was very busy and it was an exceptionally fulfilling time for him.'

Ray: 'It took about nine years before work could be started on our dream house and then one year for the building of it. Obviously we wanted a house that suited our needs and reflected our tastes. We had initially spoken to Stuttgart friends who, though not architects, knew something about building construction. They came up with a design influenced by the German Bauhaus aesthetic, rather Teutonic, box-like and simple. On showing the plans to the Cala Morell property developers from whom we had bought the land they just laughed. It was out of the question to build anything as un-Spanish as that and they suggested we use their architect, a Catalan, Señor Rey. We accepted the recommendation. In fact the finished house, with typical Spanish features, though somewhat resembling a ski ramp, was quite wonderful. We named it "Oripando" – a gypsy word meaning the sun, derived from the two words which form it: gold and tambourine. Unfortunately we made the wrong decision about the heating. At that time under-floor heating was the rage. It was advanced and modern; just right for our house, we thought. But we had not reckoned with the Minorcan climate. It was just too humid; we were so near the sea. When we used the heating the floor tiles bulged and bubbled. It was a disaster and had cost us a fortune! Luckily there was a huge fireplace in the main living room; you could walk right in to it. That fireplace became the sole source of heating for the entire house. During our first winters we virtually camped with our German shepherd dog, Lucky, on mattresses on the floor of the living room in front of the fire. Later we moved into one of the guest bedrooms on the ground floor, the one Maximo's mother used to occupy when she visited. There we set ourselves up with an electric blanket! Our proper bedroom was situated on the first floor, reached by a sort of spiral staircase. Under the staircase we had the library and from there one could access the two guest bedrooms.

'The acute cold and storms of the Minorcan winters were something we had not anticipated, but having bought the land and built our house we just had to grit out teeth and wrap up at night in the winter. It was amazing that from about the 15th of August each year – the middle of summer! – the storms started. Apparently they come from way north, from the Rhône valley. Otherwise the humidity was the bane of our existence. Humidity led to mildew; it was everywhere. It destroyed most of our books and LPs. One could not get rid of it. Even now when I open a book that comes from our Minorcan days, there is a smell of mildew. I got quite neurotic about it and to cover it up rather overdid the eau de toilette – I doused myself in Knize Ten. Ever since my Ballet Theatre days I have used the same perfume, which I order from Vienna. It was very popular in the 1920s.

'Minorca was a most wonderful time in our lives. We were very happy there. For the first ten years we came to the island in summer staying in the holiday flats we had bought. Permanent residence started after the house had been built and that had been delayed because there was no road to our property. In the meantime I had made enough money to pay for the building of the house, so there was no mortgage to be arranged. When we finally moved in, it was a dream come true: we had our own castle, beautifully located, in a Spanish environment right next to the sea. Away from the coast the island was dry, rather arid, with little vegetation, though not far from our property there was a forest of pines. In fact, we later invested in buying property there because of the trees: it became a popular place to live in. The sea at Cala Morell was crystal clear, beautifully translucent. When we first arrived the sea was full of clams that were easy to fish out, but by the end of our stay, I don't think many were left.

'Maximo had always dreamt of having his own yacht. We took a small step in that direction when we bought an inflatable rubber boat – a sort of extra-large dinghy, coloured orange and blue. It had an outboard motor, a Johnson and Johnson if I remember correctly. It could take about five or six people and was great for cruising about the northern part of the island. One of our favourite spots for swimming was a small beach not far from Cala Morell itself, a jewel of a place, privately owned, where you felt you were transported to the South Seas.

'Maxi's mother moved in with us when the house was finished, taking over one of the guest rooms, but after a time I had a falling-out with her. She seemed intent on controlling our lives and had started spying on us. I told Maxi she had to go! Of course, when Maximo's family visited, the house was crammed. And they came every summer. Apart from his mother there was his brother Manolo, Manolo's wife and four children, and Maxi's sister Julia. Sometimes Manolo was accompanied by various sisters-in-law. One of them, Manina, fell in love with Maximo. They had got close through the time she spent helping him with mathematics, which he needed for his navigation licence. Maximo wasn't content to sail the coves of Minorca. He wanted to be out in the Mediterranean. So when we got a bigger boat, a proper sailing yacht, he needed this licence. He had started studying navigation with a harbour captain at Ciutadella and went several times to Valencia for more lessons and the exams. Manina's obvious puppy-dog attention to Maximo provoked a most delicate situation as it seemed no one suspected we were a gay couple. They thought we were the best of friends. Some time later the penny dropped but there was never any big discussion about sexual orientation. We sensed that Manolo's wife disapproved of us. When Manolo introduced me to people I didn't know, he would say jokingly, "This is my American brother." On the other hand Manolo was quite discreet about the situation, knowing full well the nature of our relationship. Apparently when his daughter Estefania, then aged eighteen, asked him why Maxi and I were always together, he replied, "It's none of your business; has nothing to do with you." Estefania told us this not long ago.

'Cala Morell rapidly expanded with each summer season. In the beginning the population was made up of holidaymakers who only came in the summer. When we moved into our house we were the only permanent residents – staying the whole year. This was probably more true of Maximo than me as I was often in foreign places working on various projects. Those nights, when I gazed up at the stars and took in the beauty of the night, ours was the only house with lights on. I suppose, in a way, as theatre folk, and dancers at that, we were celebrities. As more and more people came to Cala Morell, we got to know most of the inhabitants of the village. Most were from the mainland, from Catalonia, though we also made friends with a French and an Italian couple. All our shopping was done in Ciutadella; only later a grocery shop opened in Cala Morell, but the choice there was not that great and anyway it was much too expensive.

'One of the most surprising acquaintances we made in Cala Morell was with an Englishwoman called Unity Grantham. She must have heard that we had been dancers for she targeted us one day, when we were out walking, by offering us a lift. The man accompanying her in the car was much younger and, apparent to all, her lover. We suspected a gigolo. That did not seem to be a problem. She told us she was born in Zululand, Southern Africa, and came from a well-off family. It was when the family returned to the UK that she took up a dancing career. I nearly fell over backwards on being told that she had been with the Ballets Russes de Monte Carlo. Those days seemed so far away, but considering her age – by this time she was rather elderly – it must have been true. Talking of her time with the Ballets Russes, Unity said that she had never danced on *pointe*. Rather, judging by photos, the company showcased her in exotic and sexy roles where she appeared barefoot or in soft shoes. We knew all the names of the famous dancers she mentioned – the celebrities she had toured with! She was a most colourful personality and was vastly entertaining. We loved hearing those wonderful tales from her time as a dancer. Never was there a more open and free-spirited woman. She was probably all too happy to have found people with a similar background. Often, after lunch, she would walk up to our house to continue the gossip. And she followed my career with great interest and pleasure. Later, when I was director of the Ballet Nacional and we toured Palma de Mallorca, we would look her up or she would come to performances. She introduced us to two of her English lady friends there; one was called Vivienne and the other Tits! I could hardly suppress my laughter and astonishment at the latter's name. After Unity's death her daughter Rosa edited and published her mother's autobiography (*Beginning Early, Starting Late*). Unity was not really a permanent inhabitant of Minorca; she lived on Mallorca and came to our island in the summer to get away from the ever-increasing holiday crowds on the largest of the Balearic Islands. We formed a very close friendship with Rosa and we are still in contact. Rosa married a *Menorquin* called Emilio – a sweet man. When I set off on my travels he often used to drive me to the airport. Rosa worked at the information office of Ventura. This was an important place for telephoning, as no one in Cala Morell had private telephones. One had to visit the office to make calls or, in fact, to receive them.

'In addition to our German shepherd dog, Lucky, we acquired an unusual house pet. For a short while a buzzard joined our family. The bird was brought to us by one of the builders who had worked on our house. His family had had it since it was a chick and, now fully grown, it had become something of a problem. A largish bird with a light rust-like colouring and a little white around the neck, it had a rounded red tail – hence its name, red-tailed buzzard. It was not really a suitable house pet; it had to be fed daily and it messed up the previous owner's yard with its excrement. The poor thing had never been allowed to fly freely or learnt how to hunt for itself, but spent every day tied to its perch by a leather cord. We were considered suitable future owners and the bird, which Maxi christened Ulysses, was left in his care. I was away at the time so Maxi took on a parental role as he was the one to feed it, and I'm sure it enjoyed the sort of food he got from Maxi more than its previous diet. But about two days after Ulysses had been deposited with us, he gained his freedom. Not that we deliberately released him; it was quite by chance. Maximo was working in the garden, with Ulysses squatting on his perch. As the bird spread out his wings to stretch himself, a gust of wind thrust him upwards. The air current carried higher and higher until the worn leather cord that held him broke. All of a sudden he discovered he was free to fly anywhere. He circled about a bit and then disappeared. We thought that was the end of the story. But two days later, he was there again, flew a few circles and came down to be fed.'

Maximo: 'I think he adopted us. He seemed to like the house and the food and accepted me as his nurturer. Shortly after his return, while I was working in the garden again, he flew down and ruffled the back of my T-shirt with his claws – not in any way aggressively or dangerously, but just to distract me from my work. I had taken off my gardening gloves and before I knew it, he whisked away one of them as if he was going to hide it. He wanted to play. It was the most unusual behaviour for a bird of prey. We got to know each other and he was happy to have me as a playmate.'

After a while, Ulysses accepted Ray, too, because he also fed him; the bird was quite tame with people he knew. Ray: 'When Ulysses was with us his perch was on our roof and he was always free to come and go as he pleased. He took to waking us up early in the morning because he wanted to be fed, or else he thought we should be up and about, ready to play with him. He would give a squawk or two, which was the sign. As an early riser, I didn't mind.

'Ulysses also liked to go out for walks with us; well, he flew and we and our dog Lucky strolled to the forest. Ulysses soon cottoned on to the game we played with the dog. It was the usual game of throwing a stick for it to be retrieved. As we headed for the forest one day Maxi hurled the stick with considerable force. It was meant for Lucky but Ulysses, with a speed that only raptors can generate when on the hunt, zoomed down from behind the dog, brushing the dog's ears with his breast feathers. Ulysses was a real tease because Lucky, intent on where the stick would land, didn't know where the attack was coming from. Before the stick was anywhere near the ground, or Lucky in its vicinity, Ulysses had it in his beak. He circled off triumphantly. This delightful and unlikely form of cohabitation between a domestic dog and a bird of prey unfortunately didn't last long. One morning Ulysses didn't appear and we didn't see him again. Friends suggested that maybe, and hopefully, he had found a mate. More ominous was another conjecture: that a farmer had done away with him. We lamented his disappearance.

'Eventually, after some twenty years on Minorca, we decided to move. The decision was not exactly a painful one. The realisation that we could have a more comfortable lifestyle and milder winters came to us one December while visiting Maximo's family on mainland Spain. His mother, brother and sister all lived in Marbella where they had settled after Manolo made it his home. Manolo had become a very successful ophthalmic optician and the proprietor of a chain of optical dispensaries on the Costa del Sol. That December in Marbella, in mid-winter, we were astounded by the climate. It was so mild. Undoubtedly, for this very reason, this part of coastal Spain attracts pensioners – many from the UK and Germany – who want to get away from the cold and the depressing winters in their home countries. The mild climate on this part of the coast is due to the geological formation of the landscape: a mountain range encloses and shields Marbella from inclement winters. Maxi remarked: "If this is what it is like here in winter, maybe we're doing something wrong." There and then we decided that we would move. We had had enough of mildew and of the awful winters on Minorca. The El Mirador suburb of Marbella, where Maximo's family had settled, also appealed to us. That area is not near the sea, nor was it at that time much developed. Soon we singled out a property owned by an elderly Dutch woman that was up for sale, and managed to acquire it. We have lived in this house ever since although we have altered it a lot. We did not sell our Minorcan house immediately. For several years we had a holiday agency rent it out and, in this way, it brought in some capital. We also had a swimming pool built to enhance its value. But then it was time to close the book on that chapter of our lives and we sold it. Ever since we moved into our present house in Spain we have been very happy here. It is secluded and gives us a wonderful private sphere. One can see nothing of the property from the street and only one neighbour has a view of a part of the garden and pool. It has acquired our patina.'

22

The Iberian Mainland: Ballet Nacional de España/Clásico

Ray: 'Just before we left Minorca for good, we ran into a dancer from our Stuttgart days, Hilde Koch, who was on holiday with her Spanish boyfriend Antonio. Delighted to renew contact after almost twenty years, Maxi and I invited them to lunch. It was great seeing her again, and we spent a delightful afternoon catching up on news. Much wine flowed as we reminisced about our Stuttgart days. At about 10:00pm we suddenly realised how late it was and improvised a spaghetti supper into which Hilde generously piled tons of garlic! And as it was so late we arranged for them to sleep over. Hilde's boyfriend was a guitarist and during all the ballet talk he revealed that he was a friend of María de Ávila's daughter Lola. Now María de Ávila was the director of the Ballet Nacional de España/Clásico and it occurred to our new guitarist friend that he could get in touch with her through her daughter. He suggested I might do something for the Madrid company, perhaps choreograph a ballet. In addition to directing the national company, de Ávila also ran an excellent ballet school in Saragossa. Many of her graduates, mainly female, were accomplished dancers and had embarked on international careers. Trinidad Sevilliana, later a Royal

Ballet ballerina, was one of her pupils. Since María de Ávila was not a choreographer, she was keen to acquire new ballets for her company; perhaps an original work from me would have more appeal than something that was already known.'

Contact was established between de Ávila and Ray via the holiday rental office in Cala Morell. This was the only means of reaching Ray and Maximo by phone on Minorca. They had no landline. De Ávila duly invited Ray to choreograph a new ballet for her company, the Ballet Nacional de España/Clásico (the term *clásico* was used to distinguish this company from the national flamenco company, which she also directed). The creation of Ray's ballet coincided with the move to Marbella in 1985. Ray: 'As the alterations and renovations to our new house would take some time, we thought we might just as well rent an apartment in Madrid while I worked on the ballet. The ballet I devised for the Ballet Nacional was set on Aleksandr Scriabin's Third Symphony, called *Poema Divino*. I kept the music's title. In order to make the ballet less abstract, I introduced themes and moods suggested by the music and gave the three movements of the work the following titles: "Conflict", "Desire" and "The Game". Scriabin's Third Symphony is not exactly dance music; it's rather long, and proved quite a challenge. The conductor of the orchestra had drawn my attention to this piece; I don't think I would have attempted it without his forceful persuasion. Though helpful in the choice of music, he became something of a hindrance while I was working on the last movement. There was no doubt that he could analyse the music according to the themes and the structure, but when he insisted that I was not doing the music justice by choreographing on the dominant main theme instead of the subsidiary one which underlay the music in question, I had to point out that I was the one choreographing. The choice was mine. The premiere was scheduled to take place in Bilbao in the Basque Country in the north. I had arrived there a few days earlier. When Maximo joined me in Bilbao there was still time to kill before rehearsals began and we went to have a coffee in a nearby bar. We were conversing in English, as we usually did, and a man at a nearby table overheard us. He was curious about what we were doing in Bilbao. Were we tourists? No, we explained, we lived in Spain and we were here for the performances of the Ballet Nacional de España. Hearing the word *nacional*, our interrogator became apoplectic. How dare one use the word *nacional* as it did not really include the Basque Country? Without realising it we had stirred up a veritable hornets' nest at a time when the Basque separatist movement was at its most radical and virulent. We didn't care to discuss the semantics of the matter and Maxi and I beat a hasty retreat.

'As I now had entrée to the Ballet Nacional and the hope of other creations, I was feeling rather expansive and thought we should have a first-night party. Right opposite the theatre I checked out a bar which seemed suitable and made inquiries there. The owner was quite delighted to host the celebration and promised us Spanish champagne – Cava – and canapés. After the performance, which went very well and was quite a success, we waited at the restaurant for the dancers to turn up. I noticed, to my alarm, that the party was swelling to a larger gathering than I had anticipated. Naturally the orchestra, as participants of the event, came out in full body; I hadn't reckoned with them. Well, the bar owner, pleased with such a multitude on his premises, was quite happy to open more and more bottles of Cava. As the party developed into a rollicking event I grew worried about the cost of it all. In the end, though, I didn't have to pay more than the price fixed, which was very fair of the owner. A few months later, the Ballet Nacional presented *Poema Divino* in Palma de Mallorca and we were invited to attend. When I saw the dancers rehearsing, I was most upset by the shortness of the women's skirts, which were much briefer than they had been at the Bilbao premiere. I told María de Ávila this whereupon she questioned her assistant, "Are you responsible for this?" When he replied that, yes, he had ordered the skirts to be cut that way, she impetuously told him, "You're fired." The long and short of this episode, together with the success of my ballet, was that she offered me his contract. I think she needed someone who could run the company in a professional way as well as my being an experienced ballet master. I readily accepted the offer as it would give me a chance to choreograph, and this was my primary interest. And my joining the Ballet Nacional also drew Maximo back into the heart of ballet; he became my assistant and ballet master.'

However, María de Ávila's tenure as director of the Ballet Nacional de España/Clásico was clouded by a lack of leadership skills. Amongst the dancers there was an undercurrent of disaffection. According to Ray, she just would not respect the dancers as adults and treated them as if they were all children from her school. On top of which she favoured her own pupils in the casting of ballets. This grated terribly and provoked an insolence at times verging on outright rebellion. Where and when the dancers could find a way of humiliating her, or showing her up disadvantageously, they did so. Once at the end of a performance a banner was let down from the flies; on it was written, 'María de Ávila – traitor of ballet'. Ray had not been aware of this before he joined the company; once engaged as her deputy, he increasingly had to calm troubled waters. Things came to a head during the last performance of a tour to Germany. On this tour the Ballet Nacional presented a triple bill in various German cities: Balanchine's *Serenade*, the *Don Quixote pas de deux*, and Beethoven's *Sinfonía Pastorale* by a Jugoslav choreographer Milko Sparemblek, which was enthusiastically applauded. Often during the last performance of an extended tour dancers indulge in silly little in-jokes, sometimes incomprehensible to the public, like men dancing an entrance choreographed for the women or dancers wearing incongruous costumes. During this performance, which was given in Bonn, the joke was driven a notch too high. The first ballet was *Serenade*, which ends with the *Elegy*, a sort of apotheosis in which a female dancer is carried aloft as if she ascends to some sort of balletic heaven. In this performance, instead of the cortège of female dancers who *bourrée* as they accompany the transfigured person, male dancers in full travesty, i.e. in full make-up, costume and *pointe* shoes, danced this entrance. Ray, outraged by this tasteless incident, rushed backstage to berate the culprits. He warned them, in no uncertain terms – they had never experienced his wrath in full fury – that if they were going to continue with those tasteless antics – and they did have more planned – he would bring down the curtain on the performance and then there would be all hell to pay. Back home the Minister of Culture called a meeting of the direction and the dancers involved. At this meeting, de Ávila was adamant that the culprits should be fired; Ray's opinion was that it was a grave offence but dismissal was too strong a measure. The dancers, nevertheless, were summarily dismissed and though de Ávila was not directly responsible for the scandalous incident on the German tour, she must have felt threatened. The prevailing atmosphere in the company under her direction came to light and, feeling vulnerable and exposed, she announced her resignation. At this most unexpected turn of events the minister in charge turned to Ray and said, 'This is rather short notice, but do you think you can take over the direction of the company?' De Ávila had expected that Ray, in a gesture of sympathetic solidarity, would join her by resigning too. But he had no intention of doing so, and instead, somewhat nonplussed, though elated, he accepted the invitation.

Ray: 'This period, when I started to choreograph for the Ballet Nacional, was a very creative and fruitful time of my life. At last I had the opportunity of working with an ensemble of very gifted dancers and having the full resources of a proper theatre. One cannot create ballets in a vacuum; one needs dancers, a space to rehearse and a theatre for the performances. I got off to a good start with *Poema Divino* in 1985. This naturally led to another choreography: one of my most successful *pas de deux*. Even if, in ballet terminology, it is a *pas de deux*, I preferred to call it a ballet for two people. I wanted to avoid the expectation of a sort of bravura piece. *Nocturno* (1986) to music by Dvorák, was about a girl in a transitory state. She is on her way to eternity. What was wonderful and added tremendously to the piece was the lighting created by Federico Gerlache, a Dutchman and the company's lighting designer. The ballet is full of lifts and was never better danced than by the original cast: Elena Figerova and Santiago de la Quintana. However, I must say that after Santiago left the company, the next cast to dance it, Eva López-Crevillén and Hans Tino, were equally wonderful.

'After de Ávila's resignation, and now directly responsible for the repertory, I had to consider doing a work that would involve the whole company. I decided on *The Nutcracker* – my first full-length ballet. The task was made a little easier by including some of the traditional choreography of the second act like the *grand pas de deux* and the variations. These I knew from Beriozoff's version, which I had danced in Stuttgart. I basically stuck to the main action of the original libretto: it's a Christmas celebration; there is a Christmas tree but, inspired a little by *Graduation Ball*, I had all the girls as students of a particular school and the boys, cadets from a military academy. The young Clara, in her dream, is taken on a voyage through the Kingdom of Snow to the Kingdom of Flowers. As I didn't have any small children to portray the rodents in the usual battle between the tin soldiers and the mice, I made these dancers more witch-like and fantastic. My *Nutcracker* proved to be a big success and there were many requests for more performances, but because of the sets, it was impossible to tour.'

'My next ballet, *La Espera* (*Waiting*), was a short one using a small group of dancers. The mood of the ballet is about waiting; waiting for something to happen. The composer, Miguel Angel Roig-Francolí, was a dear man whom we all adored. Listening to a selection of his compositions that had been recorded for home use, I was struck by one that used a lot of percussion. It made me think of the buzzing of insects. I told him that it interested me – not that I wished to do a ballet about termites. He said that if I wished to use it for choreography he would check it over, even perhaps revise it.

'Of all my ballets during the Madrid period, the one I am most proud of is *Hoja de Álbum* (*A Page from an Album*). It contains pure dance, an interpretation in movement of Felix Mendelssohn's *Song without Words* for solo piano. Obviously, at that time, the most influential ballet of this type was Jerome Robbins' *Dances at a Gathering*, but I would say that I was perhaps more influenced by Jiri Kilian of NDT.

This meant that, although I used a neoclassical style, I incorporated a more modern idiom, investigating possibilities I had never imagined could be part of my movement vocabulary. My ballet opens with a section using all the girls, followed by a series of *pas de deux*, *pas de trois* and *pas de quatre*. The Madrid dancers apparently loved it and it enjoyed great success with the public. Federico Gerlache once again did wonderful lighting. In my opinion he was a world-class lighting designer – so much better than some from the States whom we were often obliged to accept as part and parcel of a ballet deal. I was so lucky to have him light at least two of my ballets.

'*Alborada* (*Dawn*), a short ballet to music by Maurice Ravel, which I had choreographed in Munich for the Bavarian State Ballet in 1982, enjoyed even greater success in Spain than in Germany. It was also selected for performances at the Festival of Venice.

'My last ballet for the Madrid company, *Caín*, was nothing like Kenneth MacMillan's Berlin *Cain and Abel*. Instead I developed the biblical narrative in a very abstract way as if it were the archetype of mankind's first homicide. There was a large corps de ballet representing Eden, and five soloists: Adam, Eve, the Serpent, Cain and Abel. This was the first time I commissioned music for a ballet of mine. I asked the composer Rafael Reina, whom I had met in Madrid and who had studied at the Julliard School of Music in New York, to do it. He was delighted and produced quite an avant-garde composition. I think this was the most modern score I've ever used. The first performance in Cordoba was a wonderful success; it was quite an event for that city: a world premiere!'

23

Maya Plisetskaya and the Ballet del Teatro Lírico Nacional

'For almost two years Maxi and I enjoyed directing the Madrid Company. We were in charge of the general running of it, the organisation of rehearsals, the tours etc. and especially the artistic side. I think the company was never better then with the artists we had assembled and the wonderful and varied repertory we presented. Apart from my ballets, we performed Balanchine's *Serenade*, *Symphony in C*, *Concerto Barocco*, *Agon*, Tudor's *Lilac Garden*, Tetley's *Voluntaries*, and *Swan Lake: Second Act*. We also invited many guests: several established ballerinas such as Carla Fracci, Eva Evdokimova, and Lynn Charles. At a certain point the Ballet Nacional de España/ Clásico was renamed: it became the Ballet del Teatro Lírico Nacional. Then all this came to an end. One morning in the spring of 1987 as we entered our office to start work, a dancer came up to us waving a newspaper. "Have you read about Maya Plisetskaya?" "What about her?" "Well, she's going to take over the company." This was a shock, and yes, the news item stated that the famous ex-Bolshoi ballerina was going to become artistic director of the company. We rushed to the Ministry of Culture to find out all the details and if, in fact, the report was true. Somewhat apologetically the minister confirmed the news item: Plisetskaya would become the artistic director – the emphasis was on artistic – but I would remain in charge of running the company, I would be the managing director or, in Spanish, the *director estable*. The truth of the matter is that when Maya eventually appeared in person to take over the artistic direction of the company, she did practically nothing. In fact, this suited us as she left the running of the company to Maxi and me. And she was pleased with the way we did it. So our fears about being relegated to serving some exalted Bolshoi diva were unfounded. What she wanted to do was perform, to extend as long as she could her ballerina existence. And we served this wish whenever possible. As far as new roles were concerned we realised that these had to be tailor-made for her. She was in her early sixties, definitely past her best years. Her favourite and much-performed solo at that stage of her career was the *Dying Swan* which she offered in several versions. Sometimes she had to encore the short ballet four times and each time she did it, she did it differently. The way she performed her reverence – that too was a little performance – just drew more and more applause. Mostly it lasted longer than the solo. When she asked me – and she often did – which of the encores I liked best, I replied that the third one was definitely the superior version. During the first I thought she was warming up, by the second she was more in control of her body while the third time allowed her to project it both technically and artistically. The fourth time round, she was just too tired.

'Maya got a very good deal from the Spanish government: a suite in Madrid's Palace Hotel and a car and chauffeur to take her about. On tour she never went with the company in the bus, always in her own car, sitting in front next to the chauffeur. Maximo rapidly became her darling as he was so good at organising her private touring schedule – an extra-curricular activity. As he was polyglot in at least four languages he was most useful for international contracts; she didn't need an agent or secretary, Maximo did it all for her. And he didn't mind being taken advantage of at all. Maya had made herself into an adorable waif who needed the help of well-intentioned and sympathetic co-workers. And we were prepared to go along with it. Once she told Maxi, "You must know: I am like a dog. I don't really understand exactly what is going on, all the conversations – in English or Spanish – but I do understand the underlying sense.'"

Maya Plisetskaya was not able to take up her position as artistic director immediately; she had too many commitments. Before resigning from the Bolshoi she had eminently served Russia as a so-called cultural emissary with her appearances as a guest artist all over the world. Garnering the plaudits of an adoring public, she earned the title of 'the ballerina who did not defect'; who did not want to, or need to – in contrast to the three Kirov stars Nureyev, Barishnikov and Makarova, who sought fame and fortune in the West. Maya was especially popular for her flamboyant style, never afraid to bring ardour and vehemence to the stage. Ray: 'Before she arrived in Madrid we had unfortunately exposed ourselves to a heavy dose of Russian intrigue and exploitation. We had heard of a critically well-received ballet programme danced by the Stuttgart Ballet consisting of *Chopiniana, Seasons,* a very Russian-styled classical *pas de quatre* for four men, and the *Third Act of Raymonda.* We went to Stuttgart to see a performance and were suitably impressed. Responsible for this "Russian ballet evening" were Maya's brother Azari Plisetzki and the ballet teacher Valentina Savina. We thought this programme might be a good addition to our Madrid repertory and we so we invited Plisetzki and Savina to mount it in Spain. Plisetzki and Savina came and stayed. By becoming teachers of the ballet school they managed to get entrée to the company as well. In this way they assumed a position of deputising for Maya before she came. But when she arrived she was not pleased: "What are they doing here?" She felt that they were threatening her position.

Ray: 'Maya's one attempt at introducing a ballet that did not feature herself was when she decided to have the Russian version of *La Fille mal gardèe* (*Vain Precautions*) mounted on the Ballet Nacional.

Unfortunately the person responsible for the production, a teacher from the Bolshoi ballet school, was totally incompetent. She had no idea of the big group scenes. As there was a definite scheduled date for the premiere, Maxi and I threw in our lot by inventing, as well as we could, the missing scenes. Of course our knowledge of the ballet was based on Frederick Ashton's 1960 version and probably did not tally at all with the Russian one. It was an amazing patchwork affair. Another problem that arose was that, initially, one could not get the musical scores for the orchestra. Maya fortunately had the good sense to get her husband, the composer Rodion Shchedrin, to arrange that. In the end, the ballet, in spite of the vagaries of the version and the hodgepodge mounting of it, had an enthusiastic reception.'

In 1988, Maya Plisetskaya commissioned José Granero, an Argentine choreographer, to create *Maria Estuardo* (*Mary Stuart*) for her and the Madrid company. Granero was better known as a flamenco choreographer but, at Maya's suggestion, he agreed to create a neoclassical piece based on the tragic Scots queen. For this role Maya forwent her *pointe* shoes: she danced in soft, laced sandals. One of the ballet's four male protagonists – perhaps Lord Darnly, Mary Stuart's second husband – was cast with a corps de ballet dancer from the company and prepared for the role. When Maya saw him she refused to dance with him; she objected to his smell and he had to be replaced by someone else. In performance *Maria Estuardo* earned only mild success, as the libretto was too convoluted and the Spanish public was not that conversant with the historical circumstances enacted in the ballet. Nor was the ballet helped by the ending: a ball of wool thrown at Mary's feet. Throughout the performance four shadowy female figures – a chorus of four Marys or ladies-in-waiting, perhaps even the fates – busy themselves with the winding of this symbolic stage property. It came to represent Mary Stuart's decapitated head and rolling about the stage it could just as well have been a football. Maya, in this sort of choreography, was easily confused. She was seldom on that side of the stage where she should have been, and her partners had to rush to her to continue the choreography.

'One incident that showed up the diva-esque side to her personality and how she rated her own artistic worth was when she was contracted to appear in Puccini's early opera *Le Villi* in the open-air festival of Peralada in Catalonia with Montserrat Caballé and José Carerras.' Caballé, the Spanish prima donna, then at the height of her career and popularity, was to sing the soprano lead in *Le Villi*, Puccini's first opera. A short and seldom-performed opera with an inadequate libretto, *Le Villi* shares certain similarities with *Giselle*. In the second part the heroine Anna, who has died, returns with a troupe of wilis to wreak vengeance upon her faithless lover. He is forced to join them, dancing himself to death. The opera, styled a 'ballo-opera', is not exactly a viable theatre piece, and for this reason it was decided to produce it in a special way: the singers would sing their roles from a podium while dancers performed the dance sequences with Plisetskaya doubling for Caballé. Moreover, Plisetskaya was not only going to dance in it, she would be choreographing it. In Russia she had made something of a name for herself as a choreographer with her ballets, *Anna Karenina*, *The Seagull* and *The Lady with the Lap Dog*. In these ballets she danced the leading roles and, however successful she was at that, the general opinion was that her choreographic talents were very limited.

Ray: 'Maya baulked at the task of doing the choreography for the opera *Le Villi*: "You do the choreography," she told me, "and I will pay you for it." Of course she would still dance the lead in the ballet. I realised that in order to show her off advantageously I would have to restrict, drastically, the steps she would do on her own and have her carried about whenever possible. In this way I got a corps of men to lift her most of the time and she hardly ever touched the ground. In any case it suited the theme as she represented a spirit. I was given no credit for the choreography – ostensibly it was Maya's – but what ultimately astounded me was the reason for her not paying me. Somehow or other she found out how much Montserrat Caballé was being paid for her appearance in the opera. As a world-class opera diva, Caballé naturally commanded royal imbursement. The discrepancy between their fees, Caballé's and Maya's, was just too much for Maya to bear and, for that reason, she told me that she couldn't afford to pay me. The minister of culture was no more helpful. He warned me that if I made a scandal I would be out!'

In her biography, Plisetskaya claims 'the work' (in *Le Villi*) as her own, though she does not specifically say choreography.[71] She relates how José Manuel Garrido, the deputy minister of culture, came to Moscow to offer her the position of artistic director of the Spanish ballet company. Even if *perestroika* was already in its second year, her contract had to be negotiated through Gosconcert, the Soviet performing agency notorious for paying a pittance to the artists on their books. In the light of what she was earning through this agency, it is perhaps understandable that she felt she was never suitably remunerated.

Ray: 'It would seem that I have a lot of negative things to say about Maya Plisetskaya. However, I will say that she was a wonderful and unique artist and someone I really got to like. She was, apart from the ballerina persona, a real person and one I respected. Even if I had not seen her at the height of her powers, I could appreciate, from filmed extracts and her manner on stage, evidence of just what made her one of the greatest Russian ballerinas of the twentieth century. My experience of her came when she was over sixty and when she felt she had to make the most of her waning powers. Also possibly she had the need to make up for the deprivation she had suffered during Soviet times: the harassment on account of her artistic instincts and especially of her being Jewish and, for a long time, not being recognised as the prima ballerina *assoluta* she felt she was.

'As Plisetskaya's term as artistic director neared its end, after some two and a half years, Maxi and I felt that we didn't want to continue running the company. We had had enough of touring – the company went all over Spain, even to remote little towns. There had also been international tours to Italy, Japan, Israel and Taiwan. Enough was

---

71   Maya Plisetskaya, *I, Maya Plisetskaya*, Yale University Press, New Haven & London 2001, p. 350.

enough; we just felt like going sailing; thus our thoughts about who might replace Plisetskaya – and us. At the time there was a Spanish dancer/choreographer, Nacho Duato, who was much talked about. He had become a successful house choreographer of Nederlands Dans Teater under Jiri Kilian's directorship. In fact he was very influenced by Kilian's style and the NDT approach to dance, which has a classical basis but veers extensively into modern directions – naturally without the use of *pointe* shoes. Having heard that Duato was thinking of leaving NDT, my feeling was that he could be ideal for the Ballet del Teatro Lírico, even if he did not choreograph anything remotely like our repertory. And he was Spanish! I reckoned his ballets would admirably complement what we were performing. Therefore I went to the Ministry of Culture and told them of my proposal. Duato was duly approached and he accepted. When he arrived to take over, the first ballet he set on the company was something he had done before (*Danza*). He gave it a new name, *Sinfonía India*, the musical title of the piece by the Mexican composer Carlos Chavez. I thought the ballet was excellent; I really liked it. At the beginning he was especially friendly and said to me, "We'll make a good team, you can do your neoclassical ones and I will do my thing." But this was not to be; Maxi and I had already made up our minds to leave and Duato was slowly becoming less and less sympathetic.

'Before Maxi and I left the company in 1990, Duato and I shared a ballet programme at the Italica Summer Festival in Southern Spain – about ten kilometres from Seville. Italica had once been a thriving Roman town but because the river had naturally diverted, it became an abandoned site of picturesque ruins. We performed in the Roman amphitheatre, which is still in good condition and is used for the summer festival. The programme consisted of Duato's *Sinfonia India* and a solo he had choreographed. My ballet *Caín* concluded the programme. After the performance there was no formal goodbye speech of thanks, but as a farewell present Duato gave us a large ceramic vase, which we still have. Maximo then had the job of getting it to our house in Marbella as I was contracted to go immediately to

Greece where I was to teach at the State School of Dance. After we left, the company changed drastically. We heard that Duato felt we were too friendly with the dancers; he seemed to think that a certain distance was imperative. This was not our style. He modelled the Spanish company on that of NDT where he had been a dancer and choreographer, reducing the amount of dancers from sixty-five to about thirty, a size, in fact, that suited his works. The pity of it all was that a large, thriving and national classical ballet company capable of performing a variety of styles and genres was no longer. It had become something like a copy of NDT, serving only one choreographer.'

24

Greece (1): Athens, State School of Dance

It was through Persephone Samaropoulou, a dancer Ray knew from his Frankfurt and Hamburg days, when she had been a first soloist under John Neumeier, that he was introduced to another corner of the world where classical ballet is danced: Greece. Although Persephone, an Egyptian-born Greek, had long since left Greece, she remained good friends with Victoria (Vicky) Marangopoulou, a teacher of the State School of Dance in Athens. Victoria taught classical ballet there, a dance subject of somewhat secondary importance since the main focus of instruction was on modern, emphasising Graham technique. Deni Efthymiou Tsekoura, too, was a teacher there, giving lessons in a version of Laban technique developed by Sigurd Leeder with whom she had studied in Switzerland. After teaching at the State School for some thirteen years, the bizarre appointment of the Prime Minister Andreas Papandreou's daughter, Sofia, to head it brought an end to her teaching there. Along with many others, Vicky Marangopoulou and Deni Tsekoura were fired. Deni Tsekoura reacted to her dismissal pragmatically: 'OK, now I think it's time to make some money,' and duly became a stockbroker during the so-called economic boom. Not three years later, the newly appointed Minister of Culture approached Deni offering her the post of director of the State School. Surprised, though prepared to take on this responsibility, she told the Minister she would accept the offer under three conditions: 1. The school should be allowed to invite prominent teachers from outside Greece. 2. Essential equipment such as a fax machine and tape recorders should be provided 3. There should be no interference in school appointments i.e. no nepotism. This was all agreed upon, but presumably the then Minister of Culture did not last long; Deni Tsekoura explained that in her nine-year tenure as director of the school there had been ten ministers of culture. How all this intrigue touches upon Ray's story is that when Deni Tsekoura took over as director of the State School of Dance in 1990, she decided that classical ballet, as part of the curriculum, needed a fresh impetus. The mainstay of the State School (Kratiki) was contemporary dance, but interestingly enough Deni Tsekoura, though championing it, felt that ballet had been drastically neglected. She was convinced that the rigorous and logically pure structure of classical ballet, properly taught, would be an invigorating and reinforcing element in all the types of dance taught at the school.

Deni Tsekoura: 'I knew the school needed to reinforce its ballet sector and I was looking for someone in Europe who would come down south and guide our teachers and students.' Upon taking over the directorship, Deni Tsekoura reinstated Vicky Marangopoulou as a teacher and told her of her plans. This naturally led Vicky to ask her friend Persephone if she could suggest a suitable candidate as guest teacher. Persephone had enjoyed a successful career in Germany as a soloist with several important companies and choreographers (John Cranko, Papa Beriozoff and John Neumeier) and was therefore in a good position to know about such matters. She recommended Ray, whereupon Deni Tsekoura wrote to him inviting him to teach at the school. In Madrid Ray was on the verge of relinquishing his duties with the Spanish company. He suggested they meet to discuss matters. Deni Tsekoura vividly remembers their first encounter in the café of the St George Lycabettus Hotel, Athens: 'I tried to explain the situation; what he would have to deal with at the State School, and how we urgently needed professional guidance. He told me of his recent tribulations with Maya Plisetskaya as artistic director of the Spanish company. We exchanged thoughts on dance in general and ballet in particular. It was a most exhilarating meeting. It didn't take me long to realise that I had the big Lotto in front of me and that there was no way I would lose this man for our school.'

Ray: 'I was not too keen to be away from Maximo for any length of time, so I said that I could come for certain periods. In any case after directing the Madrid company and coping with Maya Plisetskaya I was in need of a change or rest. The idea was that I should teach the senior class at the school as well as coaching students in small choreographies or variations. This time my pedagogic talents were requested. It was a tempting offer as I would not be in charge of the school nor be required to choreograph anything substantial. I had had my fill of that with the Madrid company. Other people were in charge of the organisation and I could stipulate when I would be available. So, hardly having dusted my hands of the Spanish company in Italica, I flew directly to Athens to start what would become another very satisfying and stimulating part of my ballet career.

'In discussion with Deni I said that I could not also cope with the lower classes or the very young students. I had almost always dealt with professional dancers and that was the sphere where I functioned well. I had no diploma in dance pedagogy and in fact it wasn't really my scene, though I could coach single young dancers or a small group. A person I knew who did have a diploma, one based on the Vaganova system, was Rosa Sicart, a friend of mine from my time in Frankfurt and Hamburg. She was a lovely dancer, a most musical one, and since she was Spanish it was quite natural that we should hit it off. We have remained friends ever since I left Hamburg. Though Rosa's father was Catalan she had been brought up in the Castilian part of Spain where she had also been a student of Mariá de Ávila's in Saragossa. When I approached Rosa she was immediately eager to be part of the venture. As it turned out it was an optimal choice. Not only was she an excellent teacher but she was wonderful with children. It was a great solution and we made a great team. Another plus was that she was more readily available than me and, in the end, probably spent more time than I did in Greece at the State School.'

Deni Tsekoura freely admits that the main problem facing anyone trying to teach ballet in a Greek institution is discipline. Ballet is a long and disciplined process and above all requires dedication: 'I think what Ray achieved on this level, which was astounding, was through being an example. He was fair, critical and superbly generous towards the students. Of course the fact that he had had such a remarkable career and worked with many famous choreographers gave him a firm but friendly authority when he taught or took rehearsals. And on top of it all there was his boundless enthusiasm and love of ballet. Teachers from the institution came to watch Ray and Rosa's classes and the school started to show signs of innovation and improvement. Ray's supreme gift to the State School was the taste and experience he had acquired throughout his great career. He immediately put his finger on the weak point of the school's strategy: the fact that we were instructing young dancers for a theatrical profession and we weren't instilling in them any feeling for the stage. There was one end-of-the-year performance and that was that. He exhorted us to give the students as many opportunities to dance before an audience as possible. He said, "The stage teaches." And gradually we managed to do that and eventually we performed all over Greece. The school's first performance under Ray's guidance and supervision was a huge success. He knew how to make people look great on stage according to their possibilities. We got the best reviews, having the critics writing about a "Spring of Dance in Athens".'

Deni Tsekoura: 'Ray also believed that the students had to practise and rehearse by themselves; they had to, of their own love of dance, wish to improve. And one can only do this by repeating and repeating the exercises or variations. He said that the ballet studio should become a sort of desirable second home and that students should be able to use this space whenever necessary, even outside school hours. For this reason I had a second key made – probably a contravention of the rules – and it was freely available to those who wished to practise on their own. The encouragement Ray gave to the students about self-improvement or even trying out choreography brought about a change of attitude. He was so pleased once, when passing by the studio rather late at night, to realise that some of the students were practising on their own. We also profited enormously from Ray's theatrical expertise: he gave us a lesson in tasteful presentation, everything from setting up the stage, the lighting and proper stage decorum right down to the costumes the dancers wore.'

Later, as ballet director of the Deutsche Oper Berlin, Ray was able to reciprocate the hospitality he had received from Deni Tsekoura and the State School. He invited a group of six female students with their teacher, Eva Kapazoglou, to give a lecture demonstration on Graham technique in the Deutsche Oper. Ray had been so impressed by Eva Kapazoglou's teaching methods that he wanted the German public to see what was being achieved in other dance centres. Deni Tsekoura acted as presenter.

Ray formed a special relationship with Deni Tsekoura beyond that of being a respected guest. She was the person with whom he spent most of his time outside school hours. She became a dear friend. Acting as his tour guide on many excursions to historical sites around Athens, she regaled him with tales from ancient Greek history. And in the nature of typical Greek hospitality, he was insistently invited to her place for meals. There he got to know Deni's mother and her mother's three sisters. These ladies would reserve a certain day of the week for a get-together, which started with afternoon tea. Taken there by Deni on several occasions, Ray was quite amazed at the attention the three sisters had given to their toilette and dress. They were dressed and made up to the nines. When he first encountered the tea ritual he couldn't resist saying, 'Oh my God! It's *Les Girls*.' Tea would be accompanied by babel-like chatter and there would be an attempt to involve Ray in the conversation, but unfortunately they spoke very little English. When they moved on to playing cards and things got a little more argumentative, this was the cue for Ray and Deni to leave. Deni, who speaks excellent English and several other languages, wrapped up her thoughts and her feelings for Ray in this way: 'Whoever meets this man, has flowers.'

25

Family Matters

It was inevitable that with time Ray's ties to the States weakened. His career had shaped itself in Europe so remarkably well that Europe became his permanent home. Ray: 'I really liked living here; first in Germany and then certainly in Spain. It had got to the point, too, where my artistic tastes had definitely become europeanised. And my activities left me with less and less time for my own family who seemed to be on the other side of the planet – actually in California. Maximo's family, though, was easily accessible. Having left Malilla, the Spanish enclave in Morocco, they had settled in Barcelona and then moved to Marbella. We didn't have to make much effort to see them; they were relatively close by and visited us regularly when we lived on Minorca. As for my family, my mother was always the most important member of it and I kept up contact with her on the telephone or through my sister. About the time of my engagement with Ballet Theatre she separated from my father. She couldn't tolerate his lifestyle once he stopped going out to sea. With too much time on his hands he took to smoking and gambling. Poker was his game and he ran a table at a bar in the neighbourhood. This was all too much for my mother and she ended the relationship decisively with a divorce. The last time I saw my father was when I returned to San

Francisco after serving in the army in Japan. I made the trip to Eureka by bus accompanied by a fellow dancer of mixed race. His name was Robert Curtis and I had invited him to come along as he would've been alone over Easter. My mother had no hang-ups about his colour. Robert went on to have a very successful career as a teacher, mainly in Italy. As it was Easter time a small family get-together celebrating my safe return was planned. And since it was obvious that, because of his gambling activities, my father wouldn't be present at the meal, I went to see him in the bar where he had his poker table. It was the afternoon, so we were not disturbed. He was wonderful. I spoke to him about my taking up ballet and my plans for the future. He had no problem with my wanting to become a dancer and said, "If that's what you want to do with your life, then you must go for it." He told me that, unfortunately, he was not able to help me financially. After this short encounter I didn't see him again. As a heavy smoker he developed emphysema. I must have been working for Kenneth MacMillan in Berlin at the time of his death at the age of sixty-nine.[72] My sister wrote to tell me about it. I had not been aware of the seriousness of his condition. I was sorry that he had not played a bigger part in my life or been more present. I really loved him. I don't think his status as an American citizen was ever cleared up. Even if he managed to acquire a social security card, he remained an illegal immigrant all his life.

'I adored my mother too. She was very close to my sister Josephine, and after she had separated from my father, considered moving in with her. But finding her son-in-law, Josephine's husband, so unsympathetic, she decided not to. When my sister divorced, my mother did, in fact, move in for a while, but then decided that Josephine should live her own life. Josephine remarried and my mother moved into a small bungalow and was happy there. I wasn't able to see her for quite some time. It was only when she suffered a stroke that I made the long journey back to the States to see her. This happened while I was on tour with the Spanish company in Israel. My sister managed to track me down by contacting the

---

72   Ray's father was born in 1900 and died in 1969.

administration in Madrid who then got hold of me. They told me about my mother's condition and that I should go immediately. This was more easily said than done. I had entered Israel on the Ballet Nacional's collective visa and was thus required to quit the country with them. The Israelis were reluctant to make any exception. They were very particular about who entered their country, how, and on what sort of visa. Eventually with the help of the Spanish consulate I was allowed to leave. I found my mother in a hospital in Hayward, California. Apparently my sister had discovered her incapacitated in her bungalow – heaven knows how long she had lain there. As a result of the stroke she could hardly speak and was semi-paralysed. In fact she never got out of bed again though she did recover the ability to talk, if somewhat haltingly. I had not seen her for some time so my first sight of her was a shock. In my memory she was a beautiful, petite woman, but now she seemed to have got even smaller. It was a relief that she recognised me; she was so happy to see me. I remember her as a very affectionate parent and also one to encourage my independence. She had not gone beyond sixth grade at school, was mostly occupied at home though she did occasionally work in a peanut factory. The foreman there was mad for her; he wanted to marry her and was prepared to pay for the divorce. But she would have nothing of it. She taught me how to bake... well, there was one special cake I often made, an orange blossom cake. She used to say, "Ray, you make the dessert; we need a cake." And then I would get the ingredients out and do my thing. She also taught me to iron. This was useful because my outfit for cheerleading was white and it had to be absolutely presentable. She had also met Erik [Bruhn] at the beginning of our friendship – we were on tour in San Francisco. She liked him though I don't think she realised there was something going on between us. Often she would ask, "Ray, when are you going to get married, settle down, have children?" I avoided the real answer by responding that, as a dancer, I was always on the road, often on unemployment because of lay-off periods; my profession was not exactly conducive to married life.

'Also present at the hospital on that first visit was my brother Manuel, his wife and son. There was no love lost between my mother and her daughter-in-law and I presume this was the reason Manuel had almost nothing to do with my mother after her stroke – neither financially nor having much contact. Later, when my mother's condition had improved, I presented her with a small gift. I had brought her a bottle of perfume, Chanel No. 5, which I knew she liked. My sister took charge of the bottle saying that we could not leave it in the hospital. It would disappear before our next visit. She said, "I will bring it with me on each visit. Then, when a family member is present, we can be sure that she has the use of it." I stayed on in California for as long as I could, but the Ballet Nacional was scheduled to tour Japan and I had to rejoin them. When it was time I flew directly from San Francisco to Tokyo. From then on my sister took over complete responsibility for my mother's well-being – and I was very fortunate that she did so. Josephine found a good care home for her in Hayward where she was doing voluntary work as a receptionist. Engaging in charity work at that establishment paid off: my mother was allocated a single room. It was there that she stayed until her death in 2000. By that time she had turned 93. Josephine arranged for her to be buried in the same grave as my father.

'My mother's stroke and my return to California to see her inevitably brought about a sort of family reunion. We had not seen each other for umpteen years, and although I had always had news or been in contact with my sister and mother on the telephone, I had not seen or spoken to my brother since the early 1950s. In fact the only news I had of Manuel was through my sister. My brother was older than me by one and a half years, and as kids we did not get on that well. After high school we went our respective ways. I thought his wife, an Italian, was just terrible, pretending to be oh-so-devout. Their son, disavowing the Spanish side of his parentage, claimed to be Italian. He developed into a nasty piece of work. In retirement Manuel unfortunately contracted Parkinson's disease, which with time got progressively worse. He was financially very well off though, profiting from a pension scheme which paid out handsomely. When he got really bad his son took charge and tried to cut off contact between us. Manuel, though, managed to find out my telephone number in Spain and would secretly call me. What with his health in the state it was in and the bad atmosphere between him, his wife and son, he would pour out his heart to me. He told me that my nephew was trying to drive a wedge between us; he had revealed that I was gay. This was something Manuel had not been remotely aware of when we were young. In fact, he didn't give two hoots about my homosexuality. It was my business. He told me he admired me for having been adventurous enough to leave the States, for returning to the country of our parents and for having had so successful a career. He would cry on these occasions. I was happy that, even at this late stage of our lives, and if only on the telephone, we finally developed some sort of sibling bonding.'

Postscript

Victor Hughes: 'In July of 1989 while I was assisting John Neumeier in Tokyo with his first creation for the Tokyo Ballet, Ray and my paths crossed unexpectedly. It was another of those amazing coincidences; heaven knows why we should meet again in the Far East of all places. It had been many years since we had last seen each other: I think it must have been when he returned to mount *Lady of the Camellias* on the Hamburg company. Afterwards the ballet grapevine kept one in the picture and I knew that, at that time, he was choreographing for and directing the Spanish company. Naturally John and Ray came into contact – two foreign ballet celebrities in such an exotic clime could surely not be unaware of who was in town – and a reunion was arranged. We were to meet in a Japanese restaurant. The restaurant chosen, a traditional one in Shinjuku, was not at all chichi. Shoeless, we sat on *tatamis* on the floor. Much sake flowed. In fact, I was particularly partial to rice wine, especially the warm sort. Ray, totally at ease in the Japanese milieu on account of his military service during the Korean war, naturally became the host. He did the ordering and made sure we were all well supplied with food and drink. The Japanese sake cups are notoriously deceptive for keeping tabs on how much one has drunk. Generally one does not replenish them oneself, so it's hard to know just how much one has drunk. The evening was most delightful as we reminisced about bygone times and what we were currently up to. Ray proved a diligent host; my little cup was never empty. After a most convivial evening with old friends – a heart-warming *Wiedersehen* – John and I got up to leave. We were both in the same hotel. As I stood up I knew immediately that I had drunk too much sake. John, realising what the situation was, came to my rescue. Taking my arm he manouevred me out of the restaurant and into a taxi. On reaching our hotel I was guided to the lift and into my hotel room. Somewhat mortified I fell onto my bed and before passing out thanked my lucky stars that I had not disgraced myself by bringing up the evening's imbibition.'

26

Return to Berlin: Ballet Director (1994-1996)

Ray: 'In August of 1993 Maxi and I went on a wonderful sailing trip. From Marbella we went up the Spanish coast to Barcelona, then via Ibiza to Mallorca and on to Minorca. We sailed in our yacht, the Alfard, the largest of the three sailing boats we had possessed over the years. It was a real state-of-the-art beauty made by the Belliure company, large enough to sleep six persons. The weather was just great and as I was not a born sailor, it was just as well. Maxi excelled in any activity that involved the sea and he was in his element navigating while I, on his orders, managed the sails. I was in good hands. Our voyage was a nostalgic one as we were returning to Cala Morell, in the north of Minorca where we had built our dream house and set up home for some ten years. There was no need to rush so we made our way at leisure, sailing by day and sleeping over in our yacht at some port for the night. On arrival in Cala Morell our previous neighbours and friends gave us a wonderful welcome and we were very touched by the warmth of it. After much celebrating we retired to our yacht anchored in the cove for the night. Sometime in the middle of the night I thought I heard a spooky whoo-ing sound of the wind. I got up to check, but on deck in the dark there didn't seem to be any sign of a storm. Back in my bunk I was woken again by the same sound and got up once more. Viewing the sky I had the feeling that there was definitely something building up and woke Maximo. "You'd better check this out." Maximo, more in the know about such things as weather hazards, immediately said we'd better make a run for it otherwise the approaching storm would drive us on to the beach – Cala Morell did not have a proper harbour and we were anchored in an exposed position. So we hoisted sail, weighed anchor and beat all hell out of the small cove. Luckily the wind had changed and we were more or less pushed around to the western side of the island towards Ciutadella. This suited us fine but when we arrived there we couldn't believe our eyes: the harbour was crammed full of boats and sailing vessels. All had sought shelter from the strong wind; there was not one anchorage available. So we decided to try our luck further down the coast. There we were faced with the same situation. By now the wind was so strong that Maxi decided to down sails and use the motor. We went back the way we had come, in the hope of finding shelter in one of the many coves close to Ciutadella. We found just the thing near the opening to the harbour and were tying up to a rock beside a very posh holiday house when its owner emerged with angry cries that we were invading private property. He ordered us out in no uncertain terms. This was at 3:00am. So we moved our yacht some ten to twelve metres further away and luckily there we were able to stay. By now it was 4:00; I was so exhausted I nearly fainted. Maxi, a born seaman, was not perturbed – or he didn't show it – and calmly went about adjusting plans and managing the situation. Finally, relieved to be out of harm's way, we were able to go to sleep. The next morning we got up late, breakfasted sometime past noon and emerged on deck to survey the situation. We saw that we were close to another property where there were people about and a man called out, in tones of some surprise, "What are you two doing there?" He had recognised us; he was the brother of an acquaintance of ours in Cala Morell. "Why don't you join us? We'll be roasting lamb later today." So, hardly recovered from our night's adventure and the previous day's eating and drinking, we picked up another hospitable invitation. But this was not the end of the saga of our return to Minorca. We had barely finished eating a most delicious meal with our friends when the wind came up again. Unbelievable! Our yacht was being driven sideways towards rocks. We downed our knives and forks and rushed to it. Actually this time the situation was not that serious; all we had to do was re-anchor, positioning our yacht to face another direction.

'On our return to Marbella we had hardly walked in through the front door when the telephone rang. The voice at the other end of the line was German and one I recognised. It was Prof Götz Friedrich's secretary. She put me through to the Intendant of the Deutsche Oper Berlin. After a warm, if perfunctory, greeting, Prof Friedrich got to the heart of the matter. He explained that he needed my help and soon. His ballet director, Peter Schaufuss, had resigned.

'Schaufuss was a Danish dancer/ballet director of international acclaim who had recently made a name for himself with his production of Bournonville's *La Sylphide* and as director of London Festival Ballet. Under his aegis he brought about an upgrade of this company and its status. It was renamed the English National Ballet in 1989. Schaufuss was leaving Berlin to take over the Royal Danish Ballet, a company with which he had strong ties. Prof Friedrich continued: would I help him out and run the company from January 1994? I was very touched and flattered that he'd thought of me. When I worked with him on choreography for his opera productions we had got along extremely well and I felt at ease in his company. I said that I would have to think about it and, in any case, would have to discuss the matter with Maximo. After going into the pros and cons of an offer that would separate Maxi and myself for some time, we agreed that I should accept it, but under certain conditions. Maxi would remain in Spain while I took over the running of the German company. But we were not going to be separated for any great length of time; I had a clause in the contract allowing me the right to spend extended weekends of four days in Spain once a month – flights paid for. It was the best contract I'd ever negotiated!

'Returning to Berlin was a bit weird. It awoke so many memories of my time with Kenneth [MacMillan] and that awkward period when we, Kenneth, Lynn and myself were all in the same flat. But almost twenty-five years later and returning to where I had my first ballet master job, I enjoyed the situation: I was my own boss. Friedrich's request for me to replace Peter Schaufuss was meant to be provisional – for a period of six months. In the end I stayed two and a half years!' According to Maria Helena Buckley, a dancer with the Berlin company during Ray's interim period, she said that it was the company that petitioned Götz Friedrich to extend Ray's initial six-month directorship. The dancers were so happy that they wanted him to be permanently engaged. Maria said, 'He was the best director I ever had in Berlin – and I was there for at least eighteen years!'

Ray: 'It was a fulfilling time and it led to a new burst of creativity on my part and to my first original full-length ballet. Schaufuss had practically walked out on Friedrich and, as I heard, left a bad atmosphere in the company. I soon realised that I would have to have a supportive and reliable deputy for my long weekends away. Andria Hall, previously a dancer in the UK and now engaged by the Berlin company as ballet mistress, caught my interest. With London's Festival Ballet under Beryl Grey's and her successor Peter Schaufuss's directorship, Andria had risen from the corps de ballet to become an acclaimed ballerina. She danced all the big classical roles: Giselle, Nikia in Makarova's *La Bayadère*, Aurora in *The Sleeping Beauty*, Juliet in Nureyev's *Romeo and Juliet*, and was particularly successful as Odette/Odile in *Swan Lake*. Making the transition from dancer to ballet mistress, she had followed Schaufuss to Berlin in 1991. As it turned out, Andy, as I got to call her, was an excellent choice as my deputy, and she developed into a fantastic ballet mistress and coach – especially for the girls. She became a dear, dear friend; like a member of the family. I felt as though I had known her all my life. She and her husband, Sid Ellen, who at that time was lighting designer at Theater des Westerns – a theatre specialising in musicals in West Berlin in the 90s – are probably my best friends. Sid did very innovative lighting for a production of Kurt Weill's *Street Scene* at the Theater des Westerns. For this production he devised a single lighting cue: a cue that extends over the course of the whole piece. As the action takes place in one day, the lighting went from morning to night. It went without saying that he would light my *Snow Queen* ballet. Sid returned to the UK to work for Festival Ballet as their lighting designer and is now retired. During that period, as director of the Berlin Ballet, Andria and Sid took such good care of me. I used to dine with them nearly every evening. I'd bring the wine: bottles of the Spanish bubbly, Cava! Now we telephone regularly or they come and visit. For many years, some twenty-three or twenty-four, they have come annually to see us in Marbella. Andy is very busy; she travels a lot, is a much sought after teacher and coach and works part time as ballet mistress for the Stuttgart Ballet. My Berlin team, headed by Andria, was largely female, though Klaus Beelitz, and for a short period David Nixon who had been a first soloist of the company, acted as ballet masters. Apart from Andria there was the excellent and wonderfully competent Ursula Held, my administrative secretary. She knew exactly how to deal with the bureaucratic side of running the company. I don't think I could have managed without her. Later Felicitas Binder took over from her. Completing the team were the choreologist Marzena Sobanska, dramaturge Franzis Hengst, and Charlotte Butler. Charlotte was in charge of rehearsal schedules – the very tricky business of making optimal use of the time and the studios available. She had a brilliant mind for this.'

The Berlin company in 1994 had an interesting repertory, though some of Schaufuss's productions were not successful and not kept in the repertory. But for Ray's first half season the planning had more or less been arranged. Ray: 'The next full season, 1994–95, I decided to do a new ballet of my own for the company – the only one I took over from my time in Madrid was *Notturno*, but it did not have the success it enjoyed in Spain. At that time there was much talk of the impending fiftieth anniversary of the end of the Second World War. It was to be celebrated the following year. That and the presence of battle scars – especially in the eastern part of the divided city – drew me to a theme that reflected on what it felt like to return to a place redolent of a terrible occurrence, of remorse.' The programme for this ballet contained Ray's explanatory note: 'In a time of war there is no place for tragedy; man is merely foredoomed to utter futility – something I had experienced myself [having served in the Korean war]. Celebrating the end of the war of some 50 years ago, memories surface. Instead of pointing an accusing finger, I let myself be led by the elegiac tones of Rachmaninoff's music [which I had chosen for my ballet] in imagining scenes, a mood and situations of the past. It was a return to a place where memory and perhaps hope for the future exists.'

Ray: 'What triggered my imagination was a film I'd seen. It was a black and white WW2 Hollywood film called *The Young Lions* starring Marlon Brando and Montgomery Clift. Brando – looking wonderfully chic in his uniform and dyed blond hair – plays a Nazi who, at the film's conclusion, at his death, realises just how horribly delusional the Third Reich had been. I had also read the book by Irwin Shaw on which the film is based; it was much stronger. But I didn't, in any way, want to copy that story except for the mood, and my ballet was to a large extent abstract. I called it *Wiederkehr (Return) – A Place Remembered* (1995). It was about the return of a soldier after the conflict to a place where some terrible traumatic event had taken place: a young man is killed by a group of soldiers. In a flashback we witness this; we witness events before his death, scenes with his girlfriend and with his older brother; then the mourning of the parents. Remorsefully overcome by the futility of what he had instigated, the soldier, danced by Can Arslan, tears off his uniform trying to purge himself of his shame.'

Stefano Giannetti, who danced the victim, remembers Ray's time in Berlin and the opportunities he was offered. 'I was so happy to have been chosen for a part in his first ballet in Berlin. He [Ray] was wonderful; how I love that man! I had great things to dance; a lot more than with Schaufuss who had originally engaged me. It was the best time of my dancing career.'

Ray's biggest success in Berlin was *The Snow Queen*, his first complete full-length ballet with his own choreography, which premiered in November 1995. *Swan Lake,* also full-length, which predated *The Snow Queen*, had retained large portions of traditional choreography e.g. Lev Ivanov's white act of the swans, and had an extant libretto. Ray: 'Götz Friedrich suggested I do a full-length ballet – one that would originate from the Deutsche Oper and not something that had been brought in to the repertory – and especially one that would attract a wide audience. This meant children as well as adults. In German my ballet was called a "*Tanzmärchen für kleine und große Leute*" (A Fairy Tale in dance for the big and the small). So naturally my thoughts turned to fairy tales and I had a look at those by Hans Christian Andersen. I chose *The Snow Queen*. As this tale, in seven short episodes, is somewhat complex, I set about streamlining and simplifying it for my libretto. Fortunately, I had help from the dramaturge Franzis Hengst in deciding which parts were suitable for transposition into dance and which were not. There were things like the abduction of Kay by the Snow Queen in her sledge that were not at all viable. As for the music, I was most fortunate in having Michael Heise, the conductor, to advise me. It was he who suggested an arrangement of various Alexandr Glazunov compositions, saying that it was a pity this composer's music is seldom performed. According to Michael Heise, Glazunov's large *oeuvre* contains much orchestral music, apart from the ballets, of excellent quality waiting to be rediscovered. The only Glazunov ballet that is still performed with some regularity is *Raymonda*, and, as destiny would have it, I was to choreograph my own version later in Munich.'

The Berlin company was a large one and therefore the demands of the many roles and situations contained in Andersen's tale were easily met. The libretto, as Ray and Franzis Hengst devised it, required three ballerinas, which was also a good thing. This provided for fair casting according to the individual qualities of each female soloist. The rather complex story also gave Ray the opportunity to differentiate the separate worlds that make up the tale. Ray: 'First there is the world of ice and snow ruled by the Snow Queen (Christine Camillo). Here I used the rather strict vocabulary of classical ballet typical of Petipa: a neoclassicism that suited the abstract frigidity of that world. For the children, Gerda (Lisa Cullum) and Kay (Alexandre de la Caffinière), the central protagonists of the story, their choreography was reminiscent of Bournonville – a fleetingly light and perhaps old-fashioned style. The Rose, danced by Raffaella Renzi who was superb in this part, was actually an ensemble piece. In Andersen's fairy tale the two rose bushes that grow separately in pots beside each child's house, come together to form a single bush – representing Gerda and Kay's burgeoning love. I tried to give this section the aura of French romantic ballet. It contained a demanding *pas de trois* for Raffaella Renzi (the Rose), Thomas Karlborg and Victor Alvarez, while Victor's solo was a real show-stopper. Victor was Spanish, brought up in Denmark where he learnt Bournonville technique. According to Peter Schaufuss, perhaps not one to be over-enthusiastic about other male Bournonville dancers, Victor was the best James (in *La Sylphide*) he had seen. The solo I created for him was not, in fact, Bournonvillesque but exploited his wonderful classical technique. Added to which he was a very attractive man. Victor went on to join the Royal Ballet where he did very well.

'The episode that stole the show, as far as the children's audience was concerned, was the scene in which the robbers seize the golden coach and capture Gerda. It contained a lot of grotesque carryings-on with the robbers' daughter (Marguerite Donlon) and her fiancé (Stefano Gianetti), who were special favourites. It must have been their hilarious, droll way of dancing these parts that took the kids' fancy. The tale, and my ballet, is about Gerda's search for her dear companion Kay who has been abducted by the Snow Queen. Not only that, but his heart has become frozen by a splinter from a magic mirror embedded in it. He is no longer a loveable child: he has become a bad boy. In the

Andersen story, Gerda's tears of joy on finding Kay melt the ice that had congealed his heart. For my staging I had a lighting effect to indicate that the splinter had dissolved. At the end the children are reunited and they dance a *pas de deux* which ends with a kiss. I felt the children had grown up a little by this time and thus their kiss. Then for the finale I reintroduced all the dancers involved in a Petipa-styled *ballabile*. For the curtain I arranged a typical pyramid tableau: those in front knelt; those behind were in a lunge and then a row of dancers standing. In the last row, girls sat in a shoulder lift on their partner's shoulders. The ballet premiered in November 1995 and was a great success; it had many performances especially for children. After the premiere Prof Friedrich, concerned about its length, advised me to shorten it. He remarked that children's attention span is relatively short and I set about pruning the ballet. The cuts I made did it a great service.'

In Berlin Ray was reunited with Gert Reinholm with whom he had shared good and bad times when both worked under Kenneth MacMillan at the Deutsche Oper in the late 1960s. Reinholm's dancing career went back to the post-war years: for many years he had been central to the Berlin ballet scene as Tatiana Gsovsky's leading male star and later, when his dancing career ended, as her right-hand man. Before MacMillan's arrival he had been the Deutsche Oper's ballet director but was content to take an administrative back-seat post when MacMillan took over. All the while he was extremely supportive of the troubled Scots choreographer. Reinstated as director of the West German company from 1972 to 1990, Reinholm was responsible for sustaining its high profile with an eclectic repertory of ballets that explored many artistic directions. Ray: 'Gert was a wonderful and supportive friend. Though he had retired in 1990, he continued to come in to his office in the opera house. He was something of a permanent feature, vitally interested and involved in what was happening. Even if he was getting on – he was quite a bit older than me – he still looked very handsome. As ever, while watching rehearsals with his sunglasses on, he couldn't help himself from falling asleep. Did he think, because of the sunglasses, we wouldn't notice?

'When I left at the end of the 1995–96 season, the Berlin company gave me a heart-warming farewell party. I had enjoyed a wonderful time as director and it seemed the company thought so too. But it was time to move on and Maxi was keen to have me with him; after all we were both now retired. At the party I was happy and touched that Prof Friedrich was present. He gave a speech, praising me no end. He made me cry. I would almost say that our relationship was that of friends. I always felt I could just pop into his office and talk to him about anything and everything.'

27

Going East: Istanbul, Leyla and Majnun

Ray was also able to investigate the ballet scene in a part of the world even further east than Athens; he was invited to choreograph a ballet for a Turkish company in Istanbul. During Ray's tenure as Berlin's director, he had choreographed a ballet called *Wiederkehr – A Place Remembered* in which he had cast the lead with a Turkish dancer. It was through this dancer, Can Arslan, the son of the Istanbul Devlet Opera ve Balesi company's director, that the invitation came about. Can's father, Oskan Arslan, had previously been a soloist with London's Festival Ballet. Andria Hall, Ray's deputy in Berlin, knew him well when she was a ballerina of that company. Andria told Ray that Oskan Arslan had the most beautiful legs and feet of the whole company and was a very accomplished dancer. He spoke broken English, so all the negotiations were conducted through his wife Sonja. Ray: 'They were wonderful, they treated us so hospitably, typical of people from the Middle East. We were really spoiled by them. Eventually we settled on a subject for the ballet that Sonja suggested: "Why don't you try the story of *Layla and Majnun*; it's just like *Romeo and Juliet*?" I had felt that as I would be choreographing for a Turkish audience, then somehow the theme should be something they were familiar with. The story of *Layla and Majnun*, as it was described to me, and as I got to know it better from a translation I read, seemed perfectly suitable. It is, to this day, an immensely popular love story, known throughout the whole Middle East in a version by the twelfth-century Persian poet Nizami Gangavi. *Layla and Majnun* also shares similarities with *Romeo and Juliet*. It is a story of star-crossed lovers of two feuding families and one might wonder if Shakespeare had been aware of the poem. Unlike Shakespeare's characters the lovers do not consummate their passion. Thus it is a story of "virgin love" perhaps typical of high-flown oriental sentiment. I had assumed that Can Arslan, the lead of my Berlin ballet *Wiederkehr*, would dance Majnun. I told Oskan Arslan, "Your son's going to be the star." In Berlin I enthusiastically started to work with him and completed quite a bit. But Can Arslan as Majnun was not to be. As he was the son of the director of the company and was not even a member of it; the company said that it was out of the question for him to dance one of the leads. I thought the objection on grounds of nepotism was, for this part of the world, a little exaggerated. When my first choice for Majnun's role was rejected, I had intimated, rather unwisely, that there was not one member of the male ensemble up to Can Arslan's standard or capabilities. Upon which the company went on strike! There was no way around it; if I was going to do the ballet, I had to give in to the company's selection. As it turned out, the dancer who was forced upon us – "You have to use this boy, he is just out of military" – could hardly remember a step. In class, *glissade assemblé* was a memory problem. I think he was somewhat handicapped in this respect. During all the rehearsals and even throughout the premiere, the ballet master, a Russian who spoke fluent Turkish, prompted him all the way. The situation in the company was rather strange: the girls were wonderfully gung-ho, keen to do whatever was asked of them. They attended class and were most conscientious, while with the men it was another story. Few of them did class and they had to be hauled out of the canteen for rehearsals. Most had an extra job. Perhaps this was justifiable in view of the fact that they were earning a pittance. One of the soloists was a very popular singer appearing most nights at a nightclub. The company was large; I would say there were, at that time, about 120 dancers. And they were engaged for life! No wonder many of them didn't care about doing class or show any interest in what was happening artistically. Maybe things have changed by now, but with Recep Erdogan around, I even wonder if ballet companies still exist in Turkey. In the end, I just accepted the circumstances and made the best of it. They were paying rather well; Maxi and I needed the money, and we knew it wasn't going to be forever.

'My choice for Layla fell on a rather inexperienced corps de ballet girl with no great technique, but she was very pretty and just right for my version of this love story. Unexpectedly, the female corps de ballet's choreography turned out to be the most successful and interesting part of the whole ballet; they represented the desert, the sand. In the story, after Majnun is prevented from being united with his dearly beloved Layla – her family having arranged a marriage to someone rather like Paris in Shakespeare's play – he disappears into the desert. Here it seems he spends the rest of his life in a state of madness, inconsolably writing poems to his beloved. The desert is thus an important part of the story and I invented a dance vocabulary to suggest the shifting sands and desolate ambience to which Majnun has banished himself. The girls were really great dancing it. They were so happy to be challenged by a different and interesting dance style. Some of them were good on *pointe*, and for these dancers I invented a so-called "friends of Layla" group that danced in a neoclassical style. Undeniably there were several good male dancers and where I could, I used them prominently but on the whole, the men were pretty awful. I cast the role of Layla's father with an excellent dancer who had come from the Ankara company. On the day of the general rehearsal he tore a calf muscle! At such short notice it was impossible to replace him but, thank goodness, he declared himself game to try and dance his role. On that day we went through the ballet, arranging the choreography so that he could avoid steps on his injured leg. A lot of the time, he just walked, or limped!

'Having decided on the theme, I needed to find music that encapsulated the spirit of an ancient Persian love story. My choice fell on Sergei Balasanian, a Russian composer of the Soviet era who had also been a Professor of Composition at the Moscow Conservatorium. In many of his works he adapted folkloric material from Afghanistan, India and Indonesia. The music suited the ballet beautifully. There was, however, an *allegro* movement that I asked the conductor to play as if it were an *andante*. He agreed and we went ahead with it at that tempo. Quite unexpectedly the composer's wife turned up at the premiere – perhaps she was widowed at that time – and though, in general, pleased with what she heard, she said that we had to do that movement at the correct tempo. But this would have ruined the dramatic expressivity of the scene. We promised to correct it in the following performances. But we never did and I presume she never found out.

'We were in Istanbul, off and on, for a period of under three months, during which time Andria Hall acted as my deputy in Berlin. She used to call me nearly every day about problems or decisions that had to be taken in my absence. I considered myself lucky in having chosen her for that duty; she enjoyed my full trust and was immensely loyal and competent. In spite of the difficulties Maxi and I faced with the Turkish company, we really enjoyed ourselves – Istanbul was such an exciting city. We visited all the sites, the Hagia Sophia Mosque, the Topkapi palace and just soaked up the atmosphere. We adored the food; it was quite delicious. The hotel we stayed in belonged to a Japanese group and was thus well run. The staff were amazed at the length of our stay; we were always turning up for breakfast. We didn't have time to explore Turkey further than Istanbul, but as the ballet was a new creation and a difficult one at that, we were happy to just get on with the task at hand and enjoy the wonderful oriental ambience. Other than our concerns for my ballet, there was an occurrence – an ever-recurring seasonal one for that part of the world – that stays in my mind. We were in the last stages of rehearsing the ballet with all involved in the big ballet studio on the top floor of the building.

Seated against the wall that had large windows behind us, we looked directly at the dancers and the mirrors behind them. All of a sudden everything came to a halt. After a brief hush, cries of wonder went up. The dancers' attention was drawn to something that was happening outside, in the sky. They rushed towards us, almost as if some sort of military charge was taking place and streamed through the glass doors that led to the terrace. What they wanted to see was happening in the sky. It was just teaming with flocks of storks. The birds, true harbingers of spring, were returning from their African migration. I couldn't believe that there were so many and marvelled at the beauty of the formations in which they flew.

'The premiere was a success, there was a lot of cheering and in the end I had coped rather well with the company. We received many thank you cards, some of which were quite funny. Several, especially from the girls, apart from thanking me wholeheartedly for my work with them, added a footnote: "If you are ever in need of a dancer for your German company, I would be readily available."'

28

The Munich Connection: The Bavarian State Ballet

Ray: 'I was invited to choreograph *Don Quixote* in 1991 for the Bavarian State Ballet, but this was by no means the beginning of my association with that company. I had danced in the Prinzregententheater with the Cuban ballerina Dulce Anaya who, having transferred from Stuttgart to Munich, requested me as her partner. We did the *Nutcracker grand pas de deux*. This led to the offer of a permanent engagement with Munich which, in the event, and happily, I declined. But there had been another unusual invitation to dance in Munich: Arthur Mitchell asked me to deputise for him: to dance a solo intended for him in a newly choreographed ballet. Arthur was one of the first black American dancers to have made a name for himself in classical ballet. Later he probably achieved even greater fame as co-founder of the Dance Theatre of Harlem. At that time he was a soloist with the New York City Ballet and much talked about for a *pas de deux* in Balanchine's *Agon* – black man, white woman. Though abstract, the *pas de deux* seemed erotically charged. It was quite a shocking event in the late fifties! I saw him dance it with Diana Adams; it had been created on them. I was most impressed.

'I first got to know Arthur when I was with Ballet Theatre. I didn't know him very well, but we knew each other as colleagues from different companies: he was with New York City Ballet; I was with the other classical company. When we were in town we had our rehearsal studios close to City Center where NYCB was then performing – this was long before Lincoln Center was built. NYCB was the resident company of City Center and the dancers would hang out at a coffee shop nearby where we all went for a coffee or a snack. Later I got to know Arthur better when he was invited to dance with us in Stuttgart. He guested as Mercutio in Cranko's *Romeo and Juliet*. As I danced Romeo we naturally got to know each other in a comradely way.'

In those days, Mitchell, on account of his colour, was something of a rarity and certainly, for Europeans, had an exotic appeal. Heinz Rosen, Munich's ballet director, invited him to dance in the ballet he was choreographing for the reopening of the National Theatre. The ballet, called *Dance Panels in Seven Movements*, was to music by Aaron Copland, who himself conducted.

Ray: 'I got this call from Arthur who was in Munich rehearsing *Dance Panels*. He was desperate. He said that he just couldn't dance the solo; would I please help him out and dance it? It was an unusual request, but the event – the first ballet evening (3rd December 1963) in the newly reopened opera house – was of some importance and I thought, *Why not?* All I had to do was learn the solo, come on stage when required and that would be that. He would dance the rest. I can't, for the life of me, remember what the solo was like, but it must have been awkward for Arthur who was a Balanchine dancer. So I appeared in this ballet and was amused when the critics confused me with Arthur. I was labelled "the black Ray Barra". Were they colour-blind?' Ray took over the full role after the first performance and danced the whole first series.[73]

---

73 The other guest for this creation was Liane Daydé, an ex-Paris Opéra *étoile* and ballerina with Grand Ballet du Marquis de Cuevas. I am indebted to Wolfgang Oberender for tracking down all the information relating to Ray unexpectedly stepping in for Arthur Mitchell in Heinz Rosen's ballet.

Much later, in 1973, Ray was sent by John Neumeier to mount *The Nutcracker* in Munich. There he was pleased to find that the standard of the company had improved considerably. Heading it were the principals, Konstanze Vernon and Heinz Bosl. Vernon, a Berlin-born dancer who had studied with Tatiana Gsovsky, was Munich's reigning ballerina, while Bosl was considered one of Germany's best male dancers. He achieved wider acclaim partnering Margot Fonteyn on tours, but tragically succumbed to leukaemia in 1975. He was only twenty-eight. In remembrance of his great talent and their partnership, Konstanze Vernon, on becoming director of the Ballet Academy in Munich, together with her husband Fred Hoffman, created the Heinz-Bosl-Stiftung (Trust) in his memory. Since *The Nutcracker* premiere in Frankfurt, Ray had already mounted it on the Royal Winnipeg Ballet (1972) with Violette Verdy as the ballerina and Marina Eglevsky as her younger sister, Marie. Ray said that it was in Winnipeg that Neumeier expanded on his original ideas about the ballet, though it would reach its final shape in Munich. Much loved and universally appreciated as a ballet for children, *The Nutcracker* can be a rather sugared affair. In his version Neumeier eliminated all the Hoffmanesque elements – the fight between the toy soldiers and the mice – and amplified the ballet into a celebration of, and homage to, the Petipa era in Russia. In this way Drosselmeier, a *maître de ballet* – a sort of fictionalised Petipa and less sinister figure than E T A Hoffman's – becomes the ballet's leading protagonist. He introduces the young Marie to the world and magic of ballet. Luise, Marie's sister and ballerina, is imbued with the aura of Anna Pavlova. In Munich, a new and important scene between Drosselmeier and the ballerina was created: the so-called *barre pas de deux*. Here Drosselmeier gives the ballerina a private lesson that starts with exercises at the *barre*. It is a scene which, to all ballet history buffs, clearly has the connotation of Pavlova being taught by Enrico Cecchetti in her own St Petersburg apartment. Konstanze Vernon was especially proud of being the first to dance this *pas de deux*; it had been choreographed on her and Max Midinet. In Munich, Marina Eglevsky, daughter of the famous Russian-

American dancer André Eglevsky, who had already danced Marie in Canada, and Max Midinet, the original Drosselmeier, were guests. The production was opulently mounted on Munich's vast stage in the decor and costumes of Jürgen Rose. Indeed the whole presentation was an affirmation of John Neumeier's flair for a Gesamtkunstwerk. There was an admirable coalescence of all the elements that made up the ballet: Tchaikovsky's superb score, a dramatically fascinating libretto that offered roles of a depth and variety not generally found in such a ballet, and choreography that rendered a visualisation of this homage to Russian classical ballet – not to mention the decor and costumes.

Ray: 'I got on well with the company and especially with Connie (Konstanze) – we became good friends later. Heinz Bosl, as Günther, was excellent; he was given a new and difficult variation in the first scene and in the second act he finished his variation brilliantly with three double *saut de basques suivis* after the *manège*! This was technically quite something in those days; I can still see him doing it. *The Nutcracker* was a feather in all our caps.' This version, Neumeier/ Rose, was subsequently mounted on the Ballet of the Hamburg State Opera, the Paris Opera Ballet, and the Dresden Ballet.

Something like a decade later Ray was back in Munich, invited by Edmund Gleede, ballet director successor to Lynn Seymour, to choreograph a short ballet. In all, four ballets to music by Maurice Ravel were scheduled and Ray's piece was up against established warhorses such as Balanchine's *La Valse* and Béjart's *Bolero*. Ray: 'I called my ballet *Alborada* (*Dawn*), purposefully omitting the rest of the title, *del Gracioso*, as my theme was certainly not gracious. It was about a rape: a symbolic one. I had recently been reading a history of Spain and had become fascinated by the period when Napoleon invaded the Iberian peninsula. This ballet represented, in a coded way, the rape of Spain. It was basically a *pas de deux*, but I extended it into something like a *pas de quatre* by having two male dancers send up or exaggerate the main action. I played on the idea that Louise Lester, who danced the female role, represented a hapless Spain, while Dinko

Bogdanic, her tormentor (France or Napoleon), was abetted by two malicious youths. There was also the conceit of voyeurism indicated by a projection at the back of the stage: a detail from a Goya painting depicting a woman sitting on a balcony and gazing out at whatever is happening in front of her. I think my ballet held its own against the three others and I was quite proud of it.'

It was during the creation of *Alborada* that Ray became firm friends with the company's choreologist/ballet mistress, the Australian Cherie Trevaskis. She fully notated Ray's ballet *Alborada* in Benesh and would continue to do so with each new one he created in Munich. Cherie Trevaskis: 'I met Ray for the first time when he came to Munich to mount John Neumeier's *The Legend of Joseph*. At that time I was dancer and choreologist, responsible for the corps de ballet. Ray also liked giving company training, for which he quite endeared himself to the dancers; he was wonderfully entertaining, absolutely competent and humane. So full of humour, lightness; in one word, he was a delight – it was just like group therapy. We loved him for it. The way he corrected was always positive, it was never destructive or trying to put down the dancers and, as those in the ballet world know, this is no matter of course.' It is interesting that Cherie has such positive things to say about Ray and his humane manner in the ballet studio, for she herself enjoyed a similar reputation as ballet mistress and was unreservedly loved and admired. Ray's second ballet for the Munich company, to three piano pieces by Sergei Rachmaninov, was called *Wandlungsmomente*. It premiered in the Cuvilliés Theatre on 1st March 1984, and, in Ray's assessment, is rightly forgotten.

Ray: 'A few years later as I made my way as a choreographer and ballet director, I was approached by Konstanze Vernon to choreograph *Don Quixote* in Munich. By his time Connie was director of the company – now called the Bayerisches Staatsballett/Bavarian State Ballet. Thanks to her persuasive skills she had acquired financial and artistic autonomy for the ballet company, even if it remained under the Opera House's administration. Since Neumeier's *Nutcracker* in Munich, I hadn't really had any contact with her, but she must have heard about my choreographic activities as I got a desperate phone call from her. She needed someone urgently to mount a production of *Don Quixote*. The intended choreographer and designer had walked out on her. She wanted a version of *Don Quixote* based on the Russian Petipa/Gorski one, but I was at liberty to give it my imprint. This was an offer not to be sneezed at. The company was large and in good shape and the Munich State Opera had plenty of funds. The problem with *Don Quixote*, notwithstanding its popularity, is the title role. Having an old man as the central character of a classical ballet is not really a viable undertaking. In order to bypass it, most versions follow Petipa in highlighting the Kitri and Basilio episode and retain some of the original choreography but remain close to the libretto. In the case of *Don Quixote* so many have had a finger in the ballet pie that it is difficult to know exactly what an original version could be. The Kitri/Basilio episode is but one of many in Cervantes' picaresque novel. It is about a vibrant young couple in love and initially thwarted in their wish to marry. I decided to stick to the main structure of the original libretto but thought that Dulcinea, the Don's idealised vision of womanhood, should be a danced role and that she should not just walk through the ballet at pertinent moments. For this reason, I decided to give her choreography. For each of her three main appearances I used the same piece of music; it was as if I gave her a leitmotiv. I thought this would underline the errant knight's *idée fixe*, making Dulcinea's appearances more interesting and, importantly, enabling her to dance with Don Quixote. In my version I had her first appearing in the prologue as an emanation of Don Quixote's reading – the bookshelves part to reveal her – and they dance an extended and quite complicated *pas de deux*. I am still rather pleased with this choreography. Peter Jolesch who danced Don Quixote was a wonderful artist. At the time he had, in fact, retired from dancing and was working in the administration. Apart from characterising the deluded knight in a very creative way, he had three very demanding *pas de deux* to cope with. He was an excellent partner. For the minuet in the first scene, after Don Quixote's entrance in Seville, I had the

Don dance with Dulcinea who surreptitiously replaces Kitri. The Don had effusively greeted Kitri mistaking her for his unattainable ideal and as they are about to start the minuet, Kitri disappears while the whole stage freezes. Only the Don and Dulcinea dance this minuet, which I choreographed anew.

'The Dream, which supposedly happens in Dulcinea's enchanted garden and follows the battle with the windmill, is itself a mini ballet rather in the manner of Petipa's Vision scene of his *Sleeping Beauty*. This involves a sort of Dryad Queen, two soloists and a corps of forest spirits. One of the soloists is generally Kitri, deputising for Dulcinea. In keeping with my decision to make Dulcinea a dancing role, it was natural that she, and not Kitri, dance this role. Amor, who appears in this section and whose presence is generally incomprehensible, functions as a master of ceremonies. She – a female dancer – presides over the dream, presenting it as Don Quixote's reverie. Another big addition I made was in the second act after the Tavern scene. Here I developed Dulcinea's third 'leitmotiv' appearance into a *pas de trois*, with her, the Don and Sancho Panza. This became, choreographically and dramatically, an unexpected high point of the ballet. In her previous two appearances, Sancho was always asleep i.e. unable to see the Don's vision. Now, awake, he both sees and participates. For the finale, as in most productions, I retained Dulcinea's last appearance but as the curtain closes, she walks across the forestage as if to join Don Quixote and Sancho Panza who are seated at the side and have been watching the wedding celebrations.

'Another important change I made was to upgrade Sancho Panza's role. In many productions he is a somewhat ineffectual foil to the Don with choreography consisting of buffoonish pantomime. I changed this thereby giving him, in his big scene in the first act, a properly danced variation or *pas d'action*. In the event, the polish dancer Tomasz Kajdanski, who danced Sancho Panza in balloon-like trousers, stole the show. When the ballet was performed in the State Theatre, New York, he received the most applause! It was no wonder he garnered the plaudits; in all his scenes he was wonderful and was so inspirational in the creation of his character. I was not too happy about the sets where the designer had set up many canvas shades to give the idea of sunny Spain. To me it all looked like a lot of sails in some nowhere land. But, on the other hand, the costumes of Silvia Strahammer were excellent. She was a wonderful costume designer as well as being indispensible to the National Theatre's wardrobe department. I got to know her better with each visit to Munich. She was married to a pilot, a handsome man whom I found very attractive. They lived outside Munich and once I was invited to her home over the weekend. I can still remember the guest's bedroom. In it there was a gigantic ficus tree which dominated the room. I had the feeling of being in *The Little Shop of Horrors*. Also on the enormous side were two Great Danes. Oh my God, I was terrified of them!

'I was surprised and delighted that my *Don Quixote*, a regular crowd-pleaser, was one of the ballets taken by the Bavarian State Ballet on their tour to New York in 1993. This was an occasion I couldn't miss as the performances were in the State Theatre, Lincoln Center, home to the New York City Ballet. Friends and ex-colleagues from ABT whom I had not seen for years came to the performance. And I had so much praise; it was quite overwhelming. I couldn't believe the rapturous reception the ballet had.

'My second ballet for the Munich company, *Swan Lake*, had a somewhat shaky genesis. Connie asked me to choreograph it without telling me the reason she had chosen me. I went to Munich in November of 1993 to sort out details about the production and to sign the contract. Coincidentally, John Neumeier was also present at the National Theatre. He was supervising the mounting of his *A Midsummer Night's Dream*, scheduled for December of that year. Naturally, as former colleagues and friends, we got together for a lunch date at the Hotel Vier Jahreszeiten where he was staying. "Well, what are you doing in Munich?" he asked. With some pride, I responded, "I've just signed my contract to do *Swan Lake* with the Munich company." There was a moment of hesitation then he responded, "What do you mean? I'm doing *Swan Lake*." When it dawned upon them that Konstanze Vernon was negotiating with both of them about the same ballet, they couldn't contain their amusement. It was just like a Hollywood comedy from the thirties. According to Ray there was a problem with Jürgen Rose and the National Theatre. The administration of the opera was unwilling to have him do anything in that house for the present. It was an incredible scenario as he was their star designer. Should Neumeier's *Swan Lake* (*Illusionen – wie Schwanensee*), which had premiered in Hamburg in 1976, find its way on to Munich's stage, it could not be produced without Jürgen Rose's sets and costumes. He was indispensable to the production. It seems that Connie knew that it would be impossible to have that version for Munich and went about finding a substitute choreographer. Busy with her plan B, she had been tardy in getting to Neumeier and explaining the situation. In the event Ray went ahead and did the production.[74]

Ray: 'On Connie's suggestion I decided to retain most of the traditional choreography (Ivanov's white act) and whatever was considered more or less authentic Petipa in my version of *Swan Lake*. As Connie explained, it would be easier for guest dancers to adjust to the production as there would be less new choreography for them to learn. Having thought back to all the many productions I had danced in and seen, I decided to make Siegfried the main protagonist. The fairy tale of the bewitched princess who is transformed into a swan would thus be the chimaera of a neurotic and disturbed young man. Unfortunately I did not get on with the designer of the costumes and the sets. I felt he did not understand that ballet needs space to dance in. He practically ruined the third act by having an architectural diagonal divide up the stage. There was absolutely no space for a *manège* and I had to make a scene in order for this obstruction to be moved back a few metres. In my scenario there was only one fiancée whom the Queen mother is forcing upon Siegfried. The dilemma the Prince faces is being forced into a marriage he finds abhorrent. For the Black Swan *pas de deux* of the third act, I emptied the stage except

---

74 John Neumeier's *Swan Lake: Illusions – like Swan Lake* did finally reach the stage of the National Theatre in Munich. Ivan Liska acquired the performing rights for Munich; it premiered in 2011.

for Siegfried, Odile and von Rothbart. All the guests and courtiers exit as if they had been called to table in another room. Through the doors at the back of the stage, when they were opened, one could see a banquet in full swing. But, in fact, there was a reason for emptying the stage: as the ballet was in two parts with one interval, the girls had to leave the stage in order to change into their costumes for their next appearance as swans. In this scene, originally the fourth act, I choreographed an extended and desperate *pas de deux* between the Swan Queen and Siegfried. He is unable to save her, or his vision of her, and she remains under the spell of von Rothbart. Siegfried expires as if a victim of his own delirium. The set disappears, revealing the courtiers slowly advancing forward him. The Queen mother takes her son in her arms and cradles him as the curtain closes.'

Ray's third full-length ballet for the Munich company turned out to be another Russian ballet of the nineteenth century. This was *Raymonda*, Petipa's final grand ballet; the last of his *oeuvre* that is still performed today. It is not often mounted in the West possibly on account of a rather inconsequential libretto, though it does boast a beautiful score by Alexander Glazunov. The Munich company had already a series of grand classical ballets; the recent success of *La Bayadère* made *Raymonda* seem a logical successor. Ray: 'By this time Ivan Liska had succeeded Connie in Munich. I knew him from my time as ballet master in Hamburg. He had been a principal there and I was happy to renew contact and to have been invited by him to do *Raymonda*. Fortunately he agreed with me about the project: that we should retain its old-fashioned nineteenth-century structure but improve on dramatic aspects we felt lacking. *Raymonda* is generally considered a ballet glorifying the female dancer. This ballet, as performed in Russia today, is full of formulaic elements not particularly beneficial to the libretto's drama. I had to consider carefully how to cope with a story which, at first glance, seems to be a black and white affair about a young woman having to choose between two men. With my background, having worked with Cranko, MacMillan and Neumeier, all of whom excelled in dramatic narrative works, I thought the ballet needed to be brought, where possible, closer to the realm of a danced drama. I wanted to make the dramatic situations more logical. There was no question about keeping as much of Petipa's choreography that seemed authentic, but there were large parts not notated or obviously from the Soviet period. Therefore a lot of new choreography was necessary. Typical of ballets from this period where the ballerina is dominant, her male counterparts have very little of substance to offer, be it choreography or characterisation. I therefore tried to make flesh-and-blood characters out of the main three characters. Firstly there is Raymonda, on the verge of marrying someone deemed perfectly suitable and attractive, but wavering in her commitment to the union. She has plenty of authentic choreography; in fact she has seven solos. My intention was to differentiate each of these solos so that they reveal her emotional state. I did not want them to be just one difficult turn after another. They should illuminate her inner thoughts and feelings. The most famous solo, during the Wedding in the last act, is sometimes done as if it were a *pas de caractère*. There is certainly a Hungarian folkloric flavour to this solo, due to the music, but I wanted her to imbue it with an aristocratic grace and aplomb – a coming to terms with her destiny.'

Raymonda's intended spouse, Jean de Brienne, is an attractive, forthright and chivalrous knight; however, he is, in her eyes, disappointingly lukewarm in his attentions to her. He is on the verge of going off on a crusade to the Holy Land, so naturally he is a little distracted. It was necessary to underline this seeming lack of interest in order to contrast him with someone who is demonstratively taken by Raymonda's charms. In this case the Saracen leader Abderakhman presents a potent oriental sensuousness and an ineluctable fascination. Raymonda cannot help herself from being drawn to him. The only trouble about Abderakhman, as it was originally conceived, is that his is not a dancing role. In the St Petersburg premiere (1898) it was mimed by Pavel Gerdt. Ray's decision, as he had done with several of the roles in *Don Quixote*, was to have him dance. Therefore the solos and *pas de deux* with Raymonda were new. Another walking or mimed part in the original *Raymonda* was that of the White Lady, a sort of good fairy, intent on guiding Raymonda's love interests. This too became a dancing role. Ray enlarged the White Lady's role into the spirit of chivalrous love, typical for this historical period. She is present in the early scene as a statue that comes to dancing life.

Ray: 'In all, there was a lot of new choreography to be done as most of the *pas de deux* for the principals had to be choreographed anew. Also, I was not satisfied with most of the corps de ballet's choreography – which I was able to study on DVDs of productions by the Maryinsky and Bolshoi companies. In the spirit of Petipa I re-choreographed much of it, either shortening or adapting it as I went along. One big hit with the public was the dance of the children in the Hungarian act. This dance seems to have got lost after the premiere production and I think I was the first to reintroduce it.

'I was very fortunate in having, as a music consultant, the company pianist Maria Babanina, who was invaluable with her suggestions and insight into the Russian ballets of the late nineteenth century. She had access to the Theatre Museum in St Petersburg where her sister worked. Maria Babanina suggested the musical piece which I used as a solo for Jean de Brienne in the Hungarian Act. It was a polonaise from another ballet, *Scènes de Ballet*, perhaps unusual for a male variation. But it turned out to be most successful. I seem to have become something of a Glazunov specialist having created two ballets with his music. The music is very beautiful, has great romantic lushness and is also perfectly suitable for dance. Perhaps I should try the *Four Seasons* (another Petipa creation, from 1900) as my next ballet? My cast for *Raymonda* was also exceptional and brought me, if I might boast a little, to a high level of inspiration. Firstly, I was thrilled to have Lisa-Maree Cullum as the ballerina. I knew her from Berlin when she had portrayed Gerda in my *Snow Queen*. During her Berlin engagement she made rapid progress becoming a first soloist. Among the solo parts that she danced there, she was a very moving Tatiana in Cranko's *Onegin*. Now, in Munich, she was at the height of her powers – both technical and interpretive. Perhaps she became something like a muse for me in this ballet. Though born in New Zealand, she made her career in Germany. A dancer with wonderful line and refined technique, she was superb in *Raymonda*, bringing the house down with her solo in the *Grand pas hongrois* of the Wedding scene. I also had great fun with Kirill Melnikov as Jean de Brienne with whom I choreographed the polonaise solo in the last act. And the Cuban Amilcar Moret Gonzalez brought a sinuous and erotically charged persona to Abderakhman. The high point of the dream sequence in the first act was his *pas de deux* with Raymonda. With every appearance he dominated the scene; one could hardly take one's eyes off him. Then, last but not least, I thought Klaus Hellenstein's designs for *Raymonda* were just wonderful. I first met Klaus when he did the costumes and set for John Neumeier's *Joseph's Legend* in Munich. I thought that production was the best, as far as the decor and costumes of that ballet go, of all I had been involved in. For several years he was production director of the Münchener Kammerspiele, a prestigious theatre in Munich, before going freelance. At the National Theatre, now that I had the opportunity to choose a designer of my own choice, I followed my instinct and gave him the commission. This would be the first of our collaboration – in all he would design three of my ballets. Klaus, with whom I developed a friendship outside the theatre, is a very versatile artist, designing a full palette of opera, theatre and ballet productions. Of my three Munich ballets, *Raymonda* was, in my opinion, and all round, the most successful and beautiful. Klaus made my *Raymonda* look sensational.' The Bavarian State Ballet took on tour two of Ray's Munich ballets: *Don Quixote* to New York and Venice, and *Raymonda* to Canada and China.

29

Greece (2): The Snow Queen Revivals

Finally, in 2004, having busied himself over the past decade with trying to breathe life into three nineteenth-century classical ballets, Ray was given the opportunity of returning to his own choreographic creations. He was invited by the Greek National Ballet to mount his Berlin *Snow Queen* on that company. It seems that Ray's Greek connection was alive and well, though this time it was not Persephone Samaropoulou who had set the ball rolling, but a friend and ex-colleague of hers, Yannis Metsis. Metsis was a person of some influence in the Greek ballet scene having enjoyed a successful career abroad. For seven years he had been engaged as a principal dancer with Ballet Rambert when that company still performed a classical repertory. Homesick, he returned to Athens to set up his own ballet school and private company. Having frequently visited Persephone while she was dancing in Germany, Yannis must have got to know Ray from that time. He had surely been aware of Ray's connection with Deni Tsekoura and the Greek State School of Dance. It was then Yannis who recommended Ray as a possible choreographer for the Greek company. Christiana Stefanou, at the time ballet mistress with the said company, enthusiastically endorsed this recommendation. She knew Ray well, having danced as a soloist in two of his Munich ballets: *Don*

Quixote and *Swan Lake*. The choice of a ballet for the Greek company fell on *The Snow Queen*, Ray's 1995 Berlin production. Feeling that it needed a new designer, Ray approached Klaus Hellenstein with whom he had collaborated in Munich on *Raymonda*.

Ray: 'Unfortunately I was not very happy about my *Snow Queen* in Athens. For one thing I had to rearrange steps and use many of the senior dancers who did not really interest me. There were even some, mainly male, dancers who refused the parts they had been cast in. They showed a visible disinterest in appearing as robbers or the like. A young girl who appeared as a devil at the beginning of the ballet – a small role – got the best review; she was excellent, otherwise I thought the principals were good though not inspirational.

'Incredibly, my *The Snow Queen* was revived in 2010. This was indubitably due to the partisanship of Christiana Stefanou who had now become director of the company.' Interviewed, she enthused: 'I have been a big fan of Ray's ever since I worked with him in Munich. I think he is an amazing storyteller. There are so few choreographers who can tell a story with choreography, and he has this talent. That's why, on getting the job, I immediately thought about reviving his *Snow Queen*. It was the first ballet I scheduled.' Again there were problems: the company had lost or destroyed the costumes and sets of the original production and it was decided to do a new version albeit on a low budget. Ray: 'The designer chosen was Greek, Tota Pritsa, and I thought she did a great job. She was a wonderful woman; when there was a problem, and there were many, she just set about fixing it herself. For instance she went out and bought, with her own money, fabrics needed for the costumes. I don't know if they reimbursed her. Talking about money, it took them three years to pay me for *The Snow Queen* and *Canto General*. Of course now one knows why: there had been that terrible economic crisis.

'The second time round my *Snow Queen* was much improved. It was better danced as the company had got used to me. After *Canto General*, which I did in 2005, they were now familiar with the sort of expressive movements I asked of them and not just classroom steps.

And in fact, I thought the sets and costumes did better justice to the fairy-tale elements of the ballet than in 2004. For instance, when the curtains part at the beginning of the ballet, what one sees is a giant book, in the manner of some Disney films, filling the stage. The book opens to reveal the title of the story, divides itself in half whereby each segment, manoeuvred to the sides, forms the wings. And by then the ballet had gotten under way.'

30

Greece (3): Mikis Theodorakis & Pablo Neruda, Canto General

In 2005, the year following *The Snow Queen* in Athens, Ray was asked to choreograph Mikis Theodorakis's *Canto General*. Apparently, whatever misgivings he had had about his first ballet for Athens, the Greek National Ballet felt it could entrust him (a non-Greek) with this rather prestigious, semi-political undertaking. This project was a much more interesting one than the revival of his *Snow Queen*, and though braced by having to tackle something totally new, what Ray was faced with was indeed a mega-challenge. *Canto General*, based on a selection of poems from Pablo Neruda's famous work, was to be performed in Athens's Herod Atticus theatre with live orchestra, singers and dancers, in the presence of the composer himself; it was the year and month of Theodorakis's eightieth birthday (born July 1925). Ray: 'It was an event of such importance that I could hardly refuse. I had, in fact, met the composer many years before when he came to Stuttgart for the revival of his *Antigone* ballet and I danced Antigone's lover Haemon. When I met him again to discuss *Canto General*, I mentioned this, but of course, after such a long time,

I was the only one to remember the occasion. On acquiring Pablo Neruda's *magnum opus* and getting down to reading it, I realised I had let myself in for a truly daunting project. It's all very well choosing a novel or even a poem like *Eugene Onegin* in order to adapt it into a ballet, because the original work's narrative can help in forming a structure for a ballet. Neruda's *Canto* is such a vast, fragmented, all-encompassing poetic omnibus on themes relating to the myths and history of South America, that I hardly knew where to begin.'

Canto General was published in 1950 in Mexico at the time when Neruda was in exile. He was not only a distinguished poet but had been a prominent member of the Chilean Communist party. In 1947 Neruda helped forge a coalition with González Videla's Radical party that, should they win the elections, had agreed to broad and drastic political reform. On taking power Videla reneged on his promises and started a virulent anti-communist campaign, whereupon Neruda, in an open letter, accused Videla of a betrayal of his campaign promises. In a counter-charge Neruda was arraigned for contempt (insulting the president) and a warrant for his arrest was issued. He went into hiding and in 1949 escaped on horseback over the Andes into Argentina. From about the time of his rupture with Videla, Neruda decided to extend his projected *Canto general de Chile* by including themes from the whole of the South American continent – and not just Chile. It thus became the collection we now know as the *Canto General*. This was at the height of the Cold War when communist affiliations in the West were regarded with the greatest of suspicion and the McCarthy era witch-hunt hysteria was underway. The USA was determined to rid itself and its South American neighbours of any communist contamination and they went about it with great subterfuge through the CIA.

Mikis Theodorakis is generally considered the greatest Greek composer of the twentieth century, a hero of the people who had been active in left-wing politics and at one time a prominent member of the Greek Communist party. He had met with both Neruda and Salvador Allende shortly before their deaths and had promised Neruda that he would set the *Canto* to music (or parts of it). Theodorakis was only able to complete his *Canto* after the poet's death in 1973,[75] having worked on the composition from 1971 until 1983.

Ray: 'What with poems dealing with the complex political agenda of historical figures and events in Latin American countries, interwoven with Neruda's own destiny, I hardly knew where to start. Having taken on *Canto General* as a ballet, it was imperative to make a choice of musical pieces that would suit a theatrical presentation. Together with Mikis Theodorakis we decided on a selection from the thirteen parts of the oratorium and ordered them so that there would be some sort of combining or interweaving thread – if not a feeling of chronology – in the ballet. I suggested that we start with Neruda's death; the universal mourning of the South American peoples for the loss of a great poetic voice that had spoken to, and for them. For the opening we used the *Neruda requiem aeternum* section. Here with little choreographic movement, mainly walking, three figures emerged from the mourning mass: his wife, a male dancer representing death and a sort of Mother Earth figure.'

Neruda's *Canto* is often a cry of wrathful outrage at the exploitation and suppression of the peoples of the South American continent throughout the centuries. Yet, at the same time, it is also a celebration of the nature and indigenous beauty of the land. In the section, *Los Libertados*, a tree is the metaphorical emblem. The poem enumerates how countless millions of corpses nourish it; how the tears and the blood of innumerable martyrs feed it; nevertheless the tree can bear fruit and bread and is to be protected and revered. Ray: 'Choreographing this section I would have preferred to have tried out a more modern approach – perhaps something in the manner of my *Caín* ballet, where a large corps de ballet represents Eden. Obviously one cannot literally represent the Garden of Eden with ballet steps; rather one seeks an equivalent, a parallel mood, which in my case took me in the direction of contemporary dance. Now the Greek company

---

75 This historical and political information derives from Roberto González Echevarria's introduction to Pablo Neruda's *Canto General* translated by Jack Schmitt, University of California Press, Berkley and Los Angeles, 1991, pp. 9–11.

had several excellent dancers, but most had been trained mainly on a classical ballet syllabus. There had been no exposure to modern dance. Many of the male dancers were from Albania where they had profited from Russian tuition, and good as they were, they rather looked down on modern dance. So the majority of the company was very reluctant to investigate any movement outside of *en de hors*. Rolling, crawling, twisting or contracting were quite out of the question. And they were most adamant! I was therefore helplessly restricted to a classical vocabulary! I noticed one senior member of the company, a woman who occasionally did class but had a most attentive aura. Observing her dedication I decided she should also participate and I gave her a small cameo role in this section. She represented the spirit of the tree and danced with two male dancers in a *pas de trois*.

'The tree itself was a quite beautiful and a most inventive piece of scenery. It was the only scenery we had in the whole ballet. During *Los Libertados* it seemed as if two trees slowly and mysteriously materialised, emerging from wings on either side of the stage. They were gently manoeuvred to centre stage where they formed a single unit: a tall dominating plant which remained there for the rest of the ballet. The second part contains a section symbolising the rebirth of the spirit of liberation. Here, after what seemed like the utter devastation of the land, all the principals of the ballet resurrect themselves and the tree miraculously grows leaves. How this was managed I don't know, but presumably there were stagehands inside the tree who executed this effect. It was quite wonderful and touching.

'My other problem with *Canto General* was that many of the themes expressed by Neruda cried out for male dancers. The perpetrators of exploitation, suppression, rape and mayhem, as well as rebels, freedom fighters, insurrectionists etc., are all generally male. And I didn't have enough of them. There were lots of female dancers, with the result that for this "macho" work, I just had to make the best of things with the women. For the section *Algun Bestias*, which describes the manifold array of exotic creatures and the untamed nature of the continent, I was reduced to a mainly female contingent. How was I to render the lines "the puma bolts through the foliage like a raging fire, while in him burn the jungle's alcoholic eyes"? Another almost impossible section was the *United Fruit Company* where the poem, in succinct forty-two lines, tells of the exploitation by this North American company. The United Fruit Company was infamous for treating the South American continent as if it were made up of colonies waiting to have their produce and natural resources plundered. Here I had five or six men in business suits harassing a group of workers. This led to a symbolic rape.

'I managed to get better choreographic results in the second part of *Canto* as I had at my disposal a Greek dancer of great artistic instincts and a striking stage presence. His name was Agapios Agapiadis and he was from Crete. When I started to choreograph he had just got back from doing his military service. At first he was a little out of practice, but rapidly got back into shape. Now here was someone who could lead the fight for freedom. In a way he became the spirit of Neruda and I used him whenever possible. What was great about Agapios was his attitude. Nothing was a problem; he understood immediately what I was trying to do and he had most helpful suggestions. It was a relief to be able to work with someone who totally backed me up. He and another dancer from Albania who was good at *pas de deux* were the stars of the ballet.

'The second part of *Canto* started with *Amor America (1400)*. This was, in fact, the first poem of *Canto General* and in it I tried to express the love for the land. In *Vegetaciones*, which followed, things really got under way with the appearance of three representative freedom fighters, Lauturo (Mapuche, a native Indian), Emiliano Zapata (Mexican) and Sandino (Nicaraguan). However they remained generalised figures participating in the battle for freedom which involved everyone. Freedom was to be the linking theme of *Canto* and at the conclusion of the work, I had all the dancers rush toward the audience and with the culminating crescendo of the music scream out "Liberta!"

'At the end, the audience, brought to such a pitch of excitement and so aroused, exploded into an answering volley of cheers. They were beside themselves with excitement; they screamed and applauded wildly. Sitting behind me was a man who had being involved in the administration of the production. He leant over to comment, "Oh, you've done a wonderful job! But it is rather like women's emancipation." This was his reaction to all the women involved in this turbulent section. I retorted, "Yes, give me some more boys and then I can do the job properly!" The performances were very successful, and in spite of my difficulties, there was great jubilation on all sides. The singers were especially lauded, although I thought that they had seen better days. But I understand they were the same ones – Maria Farantouri and Petros Pandis – who had sung at the premiere and were much loved. For the bows, Theodorakis hauled me on stage as if to make up for my name not being on the programme. There had been a mistake – a gross one I would say! Those responsible had forgotten to credit me with the choreography and production. But at this stage there was no way of correcting it. I was invited to the party after the performance and was very touched when Agapios's family gave me a thank-you present. It was an old-fashioned pocket watch. They were so proud and happy that their son had been given such prominence in this eventful ballet. All in all, in spite of the success that *Canto General* enjoyed – and I was rather surprised about that – the experience for me was disappointing. I was just not given the chance to explore the sort of choreography that would have done justice to this practically impossible undertaking.'

31

Late autumn: fulfilment, Carmen

However difficult Pablo Neruda's poems had been as a basis for balletic movement, and however great the effort needed to get the dancers to participate in the creation of something new and special, the *Canto General* ballet in Athens had, at least, been a work of Ray's own imagination. It had not been a warming-up of old fare from the past as the three Petipa ballets had been. Ray was keen to pursue his inclination, which was towards choreography with a strong narrative bent and less of the poetic and ambiguous. Ray: 'In fact, for some time, I had been mulling over two story ballets based on Spanish historical personages and strikingly dramatic events which I had read about since settling permanently in Marbella. I tried to interest the Munich company in these projects, but the answer was, "No, it's all too remote. No one knows anything at all about these characters and happenings."

'Eventually I decided to get in touch with Birgit Keil, an ex-Stuttgart ballerina, successor to Marcia Haydée, who was now ballet director of the Badisches Staatstheater, Karlsruhe, in the South of Germany. Birgit must have heard about my Munich ballets – or even seen them – and of the recent success of my *Raymonda*. "Well," I remarked, "what about me doing something for your company?" The outcome of this remark was that she did invite me. At first I suggested my historical Spanish ideas to her but she, like Munich, was not interested. Then I proposed *Carmen*, a project which had almost come about in Athens. This was to have been a follow-up ballet to my *Snow Queen* and Maximo and I had drawn up a libretto based on Mérimée's novella. Preparations had reached an advanced stage; the composer, Kostis Kritsotakis, had even completed a considerable amount of the score. However, everything ground to a halt when the main partner of the scheme, the Festival of Athens – the annual Summer Festival – pulled out of the deal. The Festival's new director – for whatever reason, one never knows in that part of the world – refused to present any ballets of the Greek National Company during the festival. This was a considerable setback for the company as it meant that venues and box-office returns were no longer available. I, too, was most disappointed. And so *Carmen* was put aside.'

However Birgit Keil showed an interest as she was on the lookout for original choreography for her young company and a *Carmen* ballet intrigued her. Ray knew Birgit from way back when she was still a student of the ballet school affiliated to the Stuttgart company. As an eleven-year-old, her first appearance in a ballet had been in Beriozoff's *Sleeping Beauty* in 1955, several years before Ray joined the company. When John Cranko took over as director of the Stuttgart Ballet, she joined the company and was soon being groomed as a soloist. In 1962, in a new Cranko creation, *Scènes de Ballet*, she and Ray danced the leading roles. The adagio movement of the ballet was her first exposure to intricate *pas de deux* work, as opposed to supported pirouettes. As she mentions in her biography,[76] she was very thankful to have the star of the company as her partner. There were, for her, unusual features to this *pas de deux*: off-balance promenades and a 'hand drill' promenade in which Ray manipulated her while she was bent over in extreme *penché*, holding on to her standing foot. The following year, 1963, Kenneth MacMillan cast her as the youngest of five sisters in his *Las Hermanas*. This was a further challenge to the

---

76 Wiebke Hüster, *Birgit Keil, Ballerina*, Henschel Verlag, Leipzig 2014, p. 28

very young dancer; a chance to develop interpretive skills. In this role Birgit had to throw caution to the wind and hurl herself with erotic and passionate abandon into the arms of the man, Ray, intended for the eldest sister. Ray: 'I enjoyed dancing with her; she was new to it all, delightfully fresh, perhaps naïve, which suited the role.' Another ballet in which they appeared together was Cranko's *Firebird*. When it was revived in Stuttgart, Ray reassumed his old role and Birgit was cast as the Tsarevna.

Perhaps the most successful *Carmen* ballet to date is Roland Petit's from 1949, which was a sensation at the time for its sexy and *outré* bedroom *pas de deux*. Cranko, too, had choreographed *Carmen* two years before his death and, although successful at the premiere, it has not survived as a repertory piece. Ray: 'In one section of Cranko's ballet, instead of music, he made use of *palmas*, the clapping of hands as in flamenco, which I thought a terrible mistake. If one is going to go flamenco, and Antonio Gades did a wonderful version of it, then one has to study it properly or even know how to dance that sort of thing. I decided my *Carmen* would be no *espagnolade* and that Andalusian clichés were to be avoided. A close reading of Prosper Mérimée's novella convinced me that it should be the basis of my ballet, rather than Bizet's opera. And, as in the novella, I decided to have a dancer function as the narrator of the tale.' In Ray's version the narrator is a journalist/photographer who befriends José and reports on the tragic developments. When the ballet starts the journalist is in his studio examining photos. As he gazes fixedly at one in particular, the orchestra strikes up the fate motif from Bizet's opera *Carmen* and the stage action zooms to the end of the story. We witness the execution of José by a firing squad, distanced behind a gauze drop. The fatal shooting echoes the musical climax and José falls dead to the floor. There is a blackout. The action returns to the journalist who now, facing the audience, speaks a short monologue announcing that the story he has to tell is about 'the will to be free, requited honour and fatal, obsessive love' – in fact, all ingredients of the Carmen story.

Ray: 'I had to find a way of suggesting the narrative aspect of the ballet. I did so in this way: my narrator dances many small solos throughout, some with the aid of small accessories, which all prefigure various episodes of the Carmen story. In the first act I introduce Carmen as she appears in the novella: she is instigated by her pimp El Tuerto to steal from an unsuspecting punter and snitches his pocket watch. Therefore, in the narrator's first solo, before the theft is perpetrated, he dances with the watch in his hand. And similarly later, he unfolds a kerchief to reveal the flower Carmen will toss at José's feet. When José, charged with guarding Carmen after the fight outside the cigarette factory, through ineptitude, lets her escape, he himself ends up arrested. Prior to this, the narrator's solo is danced as if his hands are bound together. These intermezzi, compositions of Kostis Kritsotakis, cleverly complement the Bizet arrangements, and are heard only in scenes involving the narrator. Otherwise all the music is derived from Georges Bizet's *oeuvre*, orchestrated and adapted by Kritsotakis. Most of it is from *Carmen* but Kritsotakis also chose pieces from other compositions such as *Les Pêcheurs de Perles* and *Djamileh*.'

Ray introduced another figure, perhaps reminiscent of ballets of his youth, into his *Carmen*. This is the figure of Death. Costumed as if he were part of the architectural setting, he has the air of being invisible when he appears. The figure of death is superbly serviceable in one important scene: the reading of cards when Carmen draws the card of death. In the ensuing *pas de deux* with the figure of Death there is a therefore a visualisation of the fatal prediction she believes in – a physical confrontation with death. Death is omnipresent in Mérimée's story: José kills at least three people before doing away with Carmen. Ray, too, presents José as he essentially is: a flawed character, driven to great violence, capable of killing.

Narrative ballet, while never being as explicit as the spoken theatre, has one great advantage over it. It is easy to leave the realistic level and, as it were, reflect or meditate, as in a reverie or dream, on the dramatic situation. A stream of unrelated characters, the juxtaposition of situations, without logic, can be evoked. This type of 'dream sequence' is often used in musicals. Ray indulged in just such an extended scene towards the end of the first act when José lies in his prison cell as punishment for letting Carmen escape. Nearly all the characters of the story except for the torero make an appearance here.

Ray: 'The Badisches Staatsballet dancers were excellent and all my principals could hardly have been bettered. Anaïs Chalendard, a French dancer, was a sexy, vibrant spitfire, a Carmen intent on living her life freely and to the limit. She danced with a sensual and nonchalant eroticism. José, beautifully danced by the Brazilian Flavio Salamanka, gave a seemingly much softer characterisation than one expects for this role. His obsessive passion for Carmen, driving him to kill for love, was all the more interesting because of this discrepancy. Impressive, too, Arman Aslizadyan as the journalist, who invested his role as the knowledgeable outsider with intense concentration. Above all, I was very happy with Klaus Hellenstein's contribution. As I've said, I had loved his set and costumes for *Raymonda* in Munich. With *Carmen*, I thought our collaboration reached a new artistic height. It had an aesthetic that avoided Andalusian kitsch while allowing for great dramatic clarity. The architectural setting and costumes date our Carmen more or less to the 1930s, and thus give it a Spanish ambience at the time of Franco.

'*Carmen* had a very positive critical reception from the press, from important newspapers like *Die Welt* and the *Frankfurter Allgemeine Zeitung* and I was very pleased, but there were one or two dissenting voices. I suppose this was because I had opted for Bizet's music – that was my choice. Bizet's opera, an archetypal tale of a *passion maudite*, is undoubtedly one of the masterpieces of lyric theatre, and for that reason I doubt if the novella, per se, still attracts that much attention. Perhaps *Carmen* and Bizet exist in a symbiosis that cannot be undone. I suppose I gave in to the lure of Bizet's music and wanted to have my cake and eat it. Kostis Kritsotakis re-orchestrated and arranged certain sections of the opera according to his taste without necessarily following the musical sequence as it is in Bizet's score.

He did, though, have a chance to compose his own music and these parts are the short intermezzi danced by the journalist. Then he also extended the musical palette by using music from compositions other than *Carmen*. The most daring choice was to end the first act with the famous duet 'Au fond du temple saint' from *Les Pêcheurs de Perles*. This I used for the love *pas de deux* between Carmen and José – in the opera an omitted event. Maybe I should have given the ballet another name, perhaps *Carmen, a tale of passion told by a Frenchman*, or *by an American ballet master?*'

Ray's *Carmen* was choreographed in 2007. He was then seventy-seven years old – an age at which such an undertaking could challenge even a younger choreographer. However, it is surely his best full-length ballet. The theme of a 'fateful erotic passion' in a Spanish setting, however daring it might be considered for a man his age, certainly helped him mine out new depths of creativity. In a way, Ray's *Carmen* is the summation of a long career. With this late autumnal creation, all the experiences of a lifetime coalesced into a work that embodied his own artistic taste and temperament. Apart from the very accomplished choreography for the corps de ballet, one can sense in the flowing and individual *pas de deux* – probably his trump card – that he had worked with several master choreographers whose contribution to narrative ballet lay exactly in this field. But, of course, what counts is what one does with influences.

32

Winding down

Ray: 'Coincidental to my *Carmen* in Karlsruhe was a revival of Cranko's *Carmen* in Stuttgart. I didn't have time to go and see the ballet myself; anyway I was not so impressed by it when it was first done – I had seen rehearsals. Two Stuttgart acquaintances, ballet fans, a mother and her daughter, whom I knew from the time I danced there, came to the premiere of *Carmen* in Karlsruhe. Actually it was a nice gesture and I was pleased that there were ballet fans who were interested enough to make the trip to see my latest efforts. The mother and daughter were big Cranko enthusiasts and they had enjoyed the Stuttgart revival of *Carmen* enormously. But they were extremely dismissive of my ballet – and in no uncertain terms. They said that my *Carmen* was one of the worst ballets they had ever seen! This, just immediately after the premiere! Well, a verdict like this from people one expects to be supportive really dampened my first-night euphoria. I told myself, I should get over it. But what these two fans had said must have stuck in my gullet. When Maxi and I got back to Marbella, I was naturally quite exhausted. I suppose, at my age, the stress of a full-length ballet, and such an emotional one at that, was much more than I had reckoned with. All of a sudden, I fainted. I was immediately taken to hospital where they put me through numerous tests. It seems I had had a minor stroke, but luckily was not in any way seriously disabled by it. Discharged from hospital after one or two days I could not help but think that the stroke had been provoked by what those two fans, by what the mother and daughter had said about my *Carmen*. Some time later, after further tests, it was discovered that my heartbeat was arrhythmical and rather low at night. A pacemaker was implanted.'

It was not as if Ray had lost interest in choreographing ballets any more. No, it was rather the natural process of getting older, a weakening of one's natural vigour as well as the advice of his doctor not to travel unnecessarily, that curtailed his activities. Coaching Kenneth MacMillan's *Las Hermanas* for three different companies in 2011/12, (the Royal Ballet Covent Garden, the Stuttgart Ballet and the Bavarian State Ballet), probably brought down the final curtain on these activities. This ballet, which had been created in Stuttgart in 1963 with Ray in the male lead, an unsympathetic Lothario, was all of a sudden up for revival and Lady MacMillan – who on MacMillan's death inherited the performing rights – had asked Ray to look in and check the productions. In Stuttgart and Munich, Georgette Tsinguirides assisted the revivals, teaching the choreography of the mother and the five sisters while Ray concentrated on the two *pas de deux* and the dramatic presentation. Georgette Tsinguirides was Stuttgart's first choreologist – at the time something of a *rara avis* – and a loyal keeper of the Cranko flame. Apart from most of Cranko's *oeuvre*, she had also notated several of the ballets MacMillan created in Stuttgart. Portraying the mother, Marcia Haydée returned to the stage of her early triumphs. Almost fifty years previously she had danced the elder sister in the premiere and now it seemed that everything had come full circle. In the same role Trixie Cordua appeared with the Bavarian State Ballet. Ray: 'It was a bit weird for me to be working with these now-mature dancers – my former partner and, in Trixie's case, a former colleague, but hopefully they benefitted from my watchful eye.'

Though Ray is no longer in a position to be active as a coach or choreographer, he has not cut himself off completely from the world of ballet. Occasionally he is asked to help out at a ballet school in

Marbella. He definitely doesn't want to be giving class any more, but feels that what he has to offer will be helpful to young students. He likes to coach them on basic technical requirements, correcting placement, *port de bras* and coordination. Other than this, there is the Internet: a useful tool for keeping up with what's happening out there. Here Ray is fortunate that a former colleague and friend, Gudi Sutherland, supplies him with links to the ballet scene in Germany and possibly the whole of Europe. Ray: 'I'm so lucky that Gudi does this for me. Without the links I would really be out on a limb. Ballet is my ruling passion and I don't know what I would be doing without such news.'

Ray's friendship with Gudi (originally Gudrun Lechner) goes way back to his Stuttgart dancing days. As a ten-year-old she started ballet with the school affiliated to the company, then directed by Papa Beriozoff. Ballet lessons were given in one of the opera house's studios, which was also used by the company. By having entry to the opera house she was able to observe the company's dancers at close quarters. Otherwise the artists' loge in the theatre was a place from which one could watch performances free of charge, though it afforded a restricted view of the stage. In an email of 30th June 2018 to Ray, Gudi describes her first contact with him. 'In Nicholas Beriozoff's new production of *The Nutcracker*, the Prince (Ray) was supposed to float three metres above the stage in a nutshell. I was beside myself with joy at being chosen to be his double. For my first appearance on the stage of the big house, wearing a black curly wig in order to look like you [Ray], I was doubling for my heartthrob. On top of it all I was paid to do this, even earning extra "danger" money. It was a pity that when I joined the company as a professional dancer we shared the same stage for only a couple of years – until your Achilles tendon tore. [Your stopping dancing] was a great blow to the company as our Romeo and Onegin were practically irreplaceable. In the meantime sixty years have passed and my former idol has become my friend. I am proud that I can call you my friend.'[77]

---

77 Email from Gudi Sutherland to Ray Barra on 30th June 2018 (my translation).

Ray's friendship with Gudi developed from the time he danced Romeo in Cranko's *Romeo and Juliet*. At the beginning of the ballet, having greeted Rosalinde, Ray would wait in the wings for his next appearance. There he would chat with Gudi and her friend Gaby who were waiting for their cue to enter. The friendship deepened even further when Gudi married David Sutherland, a dancer in the company. He and Maximo became great friends; Maximo was best man at the wedding.

For their 2017/18 season the Bavarian State Ballet revived two of Ray's ballets: *Don Quixote* and *Raymonda*. This was somewhat unexpected as the company's directorship had now passed from Ivan Liska to Igor Zelensky, and one assumed that, if he was going to present any Russian classical ballets, then they would be in versions he was familiar with. Zelensky had been a principal dancer with St Petersburg's Maryinsky Theatre and the Royal Ballet before becoming artistic director of the Stanislavsky Theatre Ballet in Moscow. In 2016 he was invited to direct the Bavarian State Ballet. Presumably the revival of these two ballets was caused by a lack of funds due to overspending in his first season. As the National Theatre was in possession of the sets and costumes of *Don Quixote* and *Raymonda* and they were still in good condition, there was no reason not to revive them. The fact that they belonged to a repertory that the direction was familiar with (Russian) must also have played a part in their choice. Ballet masters who had been there at the time of their creation would rehearse them. Hopefully, despite the company's increasingly Russian profile due to an influx of dancers from Russia and East European countries, they would be mounted as Ray had conceived them. Unfortunately, Ray was not able to attend any of the rehearsals or performances as his doctor had advised him not to travel. By all accounts the revivals were successful.

For the creator of dance pieces, the most saddening aspect of this theatrical form is that it is so ephemeral. The ballets only exist in performance. Afterwards there is but the memory of what one has seen, which with time will inevitably become more and more dim.

Today we are fortunate that many performances are recorded and shown in the cinema with direct streaming – or indeed, transferred to DVDs. This is a fairly recent development. Presumably Ray will be able to view these revivals in the comfort of his home.

33

Epilogue: November 2018

When I first flew to Marbella to visit Ray and Maximo I had not seen them for a considerable length of time. I chiefly wanted to re-establish proper contact, but, at the same time, I was curious to see how they were living and what it was like in that part of Spain. We had maintained telephone contact, but this was nothing like my seeing them in their home setting. We were all getting on and I thought it was high time for a reunion. In November 2016, on my first visit, I realised immediately what the allure of this part of Spain was: there were the attractions of beautiful countryside and mountains, a coastal region that had not been spoilt by real estate excesses and a mild climate in the winter months. On that November day the sun was shining brightly as if it were summer. I was much impressed, too, by the beauty of their house in Spanish-Moroccan style and by its location. The reunion was, I think, a happy and joyful one for all of us. Of course, talk revolved around our shared experiences, about working for John Neumeier in Frankfurt and Hamburg and what we had been doing since that time. This naturally extended to gossip about people we knew, dance personalities and the current situation of ballet in Germany. Ray is someone who relishes this sort of talk, finding it riveting especially if it concerns his sphere of interest, ballet.

Judging by the number of phone calls I have had with him and the gossipy chit-chat we have exchanged, I imagine a world without the telephone would be a miserable place for him.

Even during my first visit I began to notice that Maximo wearied of all this chatter. He let Ray and me do all the talking. Ray explained that Maximo was not really interested; he had closed the door on that chapter of his life and just wanted to get on with the present. But Ray was delighted to have a gossiping partner who knew and responded to all the names he dredged up: dancers from ABT days, the famous choreographers he had worked with, the trials and tribulations he had experienced in Berlin, then his working for Maya Plisetskaya in Madrid, etc. I think, too, I was a good sounding board for all those names he had had contact with, many of them now relegated to history. There was a good reason for this. When I took early retirement from the Hamburg Ballet I was asked to teach Dance History at the John Neumeier Ballet School. The idea interested me and I readily agreed to do it. But realising that I would have to immerse myself properly in the subject in order to teach it, I began a crash course in ballet history. This goes a long way to explaining how I was able to keep up with Ray's name-dropping.

On my first visit I noticed that Maximo, who by this time had put on weight and was practically bald – this affliction had been the bane of his dancing days – was much concerned about his physical condition. Each morning after breakfast he would diligently mount his stationary gym bike and pedal away for half an hour. And then he would find a place to continue something like *jambe à la barre* – stretching exercises he knew from ballet. To top it all, depending on the temperature of the swimming pool, he sometimes took a dip. But all this exertion tired him tremendously and it was a struggle for him to keep up the routine. On my second visit, when it was decided that I would try my hand at writing Ray's biography, Maximo told me that he was about to have a serious health check-up. The doctors had discovered that he was anaemic. Just why he was anaemic was not immediately apparent. Bowel cancer was diagnosed and an operation followed. Hardly recovered from that operation, he was told that the cancer had spread to his lungs and liver. Chemotherapy was recommended and, with Maximo responding well to this, one hoped for the best. But though the cancer in his lungs receded, further chemotherapy during the next six to eight months brought no improvement and the doctors said that they could do nothing more. It was a harrowing time for Ray. After the initial operation he had became Maximo's nurse. Ray: 'This is something I do not wish upon anyone. It was just too terrible for words.' When the doctors stopped the chemotherapy treatment, it was obvious what this meant. And Maximo knew and understood that he was going. Though brought up a Catholic, Maximo was extremely critical of the church and thought that what the church had become was a betrayal of its origins. He told Ray that he did not want any religious ceremony after his death. He wished to be cremated – unclothed, just as he came into this world – and that would be that. He told Ray this on numerous occasions. His ashes were to be strewn in the ocean, the element he had loved.

At 6:00am on the morning of 9th August 2018, Maximo died. Ray, who was lying in the adjacent bed, woke up at 5:00am and, as ever, looked concernedly toward Maximo. He noticed that he was breathing strangely. It was an ominous indication that the end was near. Ray took Maximo in his arms. Ray: 'He murmured, "I'm so tired, let's sleep," and closed his eyes. With that, I sensed his life ebbing away. He died in my arms.'

For Ray, Maximo's death at the age of seventy-seven was a terrible and unexpected blow. According to the age difference, just under twelve years, one could have assumed that Maximo would be the one to look after Ray as they got older. But it was not to be. Ray's own family, in the meantime, has shrunk to a few nephews who live in America with whom he has no contact. The only people whom Ray could call family are Maximo's nephew, Ivan, and the three nieces, Estefania, Elena and Patricia, who all live in Marbella not far from his house. They are all especially solicitous about his well-being and are there to help when needed. When Ray and Maximo entered into a *parejas de hecho* (civil union) in 2005, one could say he joined the family – on Maximo's side. The *parejas de hecho* is no longer in force, as marriage at the registry office is now available to both same sex or hetero partners. Before this legislation came into force, they had felt that marriage was going a step too far and marriage vows were not necessary for them to stay together. All told, they were together for an amazing fifty-four years. Ray: 'Maximo was the best thing that happened to me.'

Ray's lifeline to the outer world beyond his Marbella enclave is the telephone and I am sure it is in good use daily. He now has three important and loving friends with whom he is in constant contact: Andria Hall and her husband, Sid Ellen, and Gudi Sutherland. But I imagine he has a large network of friends all over Europe who often give him a call. There are also the countless invitations to visit, but he has no wish to travel.

Ray told me that he has got over the worst since Maximo's death. 'I'm okay now, though I do feel terribly lonely. The house is so empty without Maxi. Everybody is trying to help me. I don't need help. I can cope by myself. The other day I had a phone call and the message was "You've got to be strong." That annoys me no end. For Christ's sake, I'm strong. I can walk, go shopping, do things. I think I'm in better shape than most eighty-nine-year-olds.

'One afternoon, a few weeks ago, I was sitting on the sofa watching a film on the television. I thought I heard something fall and as I turned to look my glasses came off. I tried to grab them before they fell on the floor and in doing so, slipped off my seat. Having got up and having put my glasses back on I felt a little funny; after all there was no reason for me to slip off my seat. Then I had a strange feeling as if I was being directed or pulled in a certain direction. I looked all over, but there was no one. Estefania, when I told her this, said immediately, "That was Maximo." She believes in reincarnation and spirits. I don't know, but I would like to think that his presence is still in our house. Sometimes I talk to him.'

Ray Barra: Ballet Creations

Mein junges Leben hat ein End (m. Karl Höller: Sweelinck Variationen für Orchester, Opus 56), Noverre-Gesellschaft, Stuttgart 9th March 1962

Elegie (m. Sergei Rachmaninoff), Noverre-Gesellschaft, Stuttgart 9th July 1964

Rossini Divertissement (m. Gioacchino Rossini, Streichersonate), Noverre-Gesellschaft, Stuttgart and Stuttgart Ballet 8th December 1964

Alborada (*Dawn*) (m. Maurice Ravel: *Alborada del Gracioso* from *Miroirs*), Bavarian State Ballet, Munich, 28th November 1982, Castellón, 28th May 1987

Wandlungsmomente (m. Sergei Rachmaninoff), Bavarian State Ballet, Cuvilliés Theatre, Munich, 1st March 1984

Poema Divino (m. Aleksandr Scriabin), Ballet Nacional de España/Clásico, Bilbao, April 1985

Nocturno (m. Antonin Dvorák), Ballet Nacional de España/Clásico, Madrid, 4th January 1986. Lighting: Federico Gerlache

Cascanueces/The Nutcracker (m. Pyotr Tchaikovsky), Ballet Nacional de España/Clásico, Valladolid, 7th December 1986

La Espera (m. Miguel Angel Roig-Francolí), Ballet del Teatro Lírico Nacional, Madrid, 13th September 1987

Romanza (Felix Mendelssohn), Ballet del Teatro Lírico Nacional, Madrid, 8th October 1987

Hoja de Álbum (*A Page from an Album*) (m. Felix Mendelssohn), Ballet del Teatro Lírico Nacional de España-clasico, Madrid, 19th November 1988

Caín (m. Rafael Reina), Compañia Nacional de Danza, Cordoba, 11th May 1990

Don Quixote (m. Ludwig Minkus), Bavarian State Ballet, Sets: Thomas Peckny, Costumes: Silvia Strahammer, Munich 22nd December 1991

Swan Lake (m. Pyotr Tchaikovsky), Sets and Costumes: John McFarlane, Bavarian State Ballet, Munich 22nd March 1995

Wiederkehr – A Place Remembered (m. Sergei Rachmaninov, 2 Trio élégiaque op. 9), Deutsche Oper Berlin 10th June 1995. Sets: Susanne Ketterer. Costumes: Dietlinde Calsow

Die Schneekönigin (The Snow Queen), Tanzmärchen für kleine und große Leute (m. Alexandr Glazunov), Deutsche Oper, Berlin 25th November 1995. Libretto by Ray Barra and Franzis Hengst based on Hans Christian Andersen's fairy tale. Sets: Susanne Ketterer. Costumes: Dietlinde Calsow. Lighting: Sid Ellen

Layla and Majnun (m. Sergei Balasanian), Devlet Opera ve Balesi, Istanbul, 23rd March 1996

Raymonda (m. Alexandr Glazunov), Sets and Costumes: Klaus Hellenstein. Bavarian State Ballet, Munich, 1st December 2001

Canto General (m. Mikis Theodorakis), Greek National Ballet, Athens, July 2005

Carmen (m. Kostis Kritsotakis), Sets and Costumes: Klaus

Hellenstein. Badisches Staatstheater Karlsruhe, 17th November 2007

Revivals

The Snow Queen – Sets and Costumes: Klaus Hellenstein, Athens 2004

The Snow Queen – Sets and Costumes Tota Pritsa, Athens 2010

Don Quixote – Munich 2017

Raymonda – Munich 2018

Ray Barra: Activities

17th February 2011 Stuttgart: Revival of Kenneth MacMillan's *Las Hermanas* with Marcia Haydée as the mother

30th January 2012 Munich: Revival of Kenneth MacMillan's *Las Hermanas* with Trixie Cordua as the mother, Lucia Lacara, the eldest sister and Cyril Pierre as the Man

17th November 2012 London: Royal Ballet revival of Kenneth MacMillan's *Las Hermanas* with Aline Cojocaru as the elder sister

Every effort has been made to acquire permission for the publication of the photographs in this book. We thank those photographers who have generously given it. In many cases, however, this has not been possible. Justifiable claims may be made to the publisher.

Bibliography

Anderson, Zoë, *The Royal Ballet, 75 Years*, Faber & Faber Ltd, London 2006

Cordua, Beatrice, interviewed by Angela Dauber, *Beatrice Cordua*, Hamburg Ballett Verlag, Hamburg 1987

Fischer, Dagmar Ellen, *Egon Madsen, Ein Tanzleben, Biografie*, Henschel Verlag in der Seemann Henschel GmbH und Co. KG, Leipzig, 2012

Fischer, Dagmar Ellen, *Ivan Liska Tänzer, Die Leichtigkeit des Augenblicks*, Henschel Verlag in der Seemann Henschel GmbH und Co. KG, Leipzig 2015

Gruen, John, *Erik Bruhn, Danseur Noble*, The Viking Press, New York 1979

Gruen John, *The Private World of Ballet*, The Viking Press, New York 1975

Hüster Wiebke, *Birgit Keil, Ballerina, Glück ist, wenn auch die Seele tanzt*, Henschel Verlag in der Seemann Henschel GmbH und Co. KG, Leipzig 2014

Koegler, Horst & Madeline Winkler-Betzendahl, *Ballett in Stuttgart*, Chr. Belser Verlag, Stuttgart 1964

Koegler, Horst, *John Neumeier, Bilder eines Lebens, Pictures from a Life*, John Neumeier Foundation 2010

Meylac, Michael, *Behind the Scenes at the Ballets Russes*, L B Tauris & Co Ltd, London and New York 2018

Neruda, Pablo, *Canto General*. Translated by Jack Schmitt, University of California Press, Berkley and Los Angeles, California 1991

Parry, Jann, *Different Drummer, The Life of Kenneth MacMillan*, Faber & Faber Ltd, London 2009

Percival, John, *Theatre In My Blood, A Biography of John Cranko*, The Herbert Press, London 1983

Plisetskaya, Maya, *I, Maya Plisetskaya*, Yale University Press, New Haven & London 2001

Schäfer, Walter Erich, *Bühne eines Lebens*, Deutsche Verlags-Anstalt GmbH, Stuttgart 1975

Seymour, Lynn with Paul Gardner, *Lynn, the Autobiography of Lynn Seymour*, Granada Publishing Limited, London 1984

Thorpe, Edward, *Kenneth MacMillan, The Man and the Ballets*, Hamish Hamilton, London 1985

Wright, Peter with Paul Arrowsmith, *Wrights & Wrongs, My Life in Dance*, Oberon Books Ltd, London 2016

Zehle, Sibylle, *Jürgen Rose*, Verlag für moderne Kunst, Nürnberg 2014